Government Contracts Made Easier
Second edition

Judy Bradt

Why "EasiER?"
Because "Easy" is fiction.

Government Contracts Made Easier (second edition)

ISBN-13: 978-0-578-62132-6

Cover: Sarah Gertler
Layout assistance: Nat Gertler

For reprint permissions, contact Judy.Bradt@GrowFedBiz.com

Do you know how to win in the federal market? Judy does! This book is comprehensive and full of practical advice and actionable tips. You will get a great return on your efforts by following the process that she provides. Buy it. Read it. Do it.

PATRICK THEAN, BEST-SELLING AUTHOR OF 2 BUSINESS BOOKS, *RHYTHM* AND *PREDICTABLE RESULTS*

Judy provides a practical step-by-step guide to getting started in federal contracting. Government business is not easy or quick, but this book can expedite your entry, help you avoid costly mistakes, and most importantly, win the business!

MARK AMTOWER, GOVCON MARKETING SME AND CONSULTANT

Judy Bradt knows government. This second edition of her acclaimed book *Governments Contracts Made Easier* delivers on its promise to simplify government contracting. Between checklists, short lessons, and real-life examples, her expertise shines through. Judy's gift is taking the complexity of government sales and breaking it down into common-sense steps. This allows anyone to utilize her concepts and measure their progress. If you're new to federal business and trying to sort it out, this is an excellent book and resource. This is also an excellent resource for onboarding new team members. Even seasoned government contractors will gain value from the concepts and resources in this book.

JOSHUA P. FRANK, MANAGING PARTNER, RSM FEDERAL AND #1 BESTSELLING AUTHOR OF *AN INSIDER'S GUIDE TO WINNING GOVERNMENT CONTRACTS*

This insightful guidebook is full of real, actionable, useful exercises – and it's the reference you'll keep close at hand. Use this book to do the essential work to prepare for success in the federal market. Bonus: you'll discover how to see your company's overall strengths, challenges, and opportunities in a new light!

ANNA URMAN, FORMER DIRECTOR, VIRGINIA PROCUREMENT TECHNICAL ASSISTANCE CENTER AND PRESIDENT, TACTICAL INSIGHT

Government Contracts Made Easier is a rare find. It lives up to the promise of making government contracts easier. It will also make the reader more successful. Government selling is both a technical exercise and an art form. Ms. Bradt provides practical techniques covering the art and science of turning federal contracts into a solid contributor for any business. She carefully leads the reader through a success methodology, beginning by helping the seller understand their own value & positioning from the buyer's perspective, how to become relevant and visible, and of course, the rules of engagement. I highly recommend this book to anyone interested in pursuing federal contracts in an effective, elegant and productive way.

DAVID POWELL, CEO, FEDERAL BUSINESS COUNCIL, INC.

Success in the federal marketplace is a journey. Any journey in life requires a roadmap to reach your destination. Judy provides the roadmap for your success. Success comes to those who have a plan and work the plan. Success in federal contracting takes persistence. This is not the lottery! You must do your homework, be knowledgeable, focused, determined, and know how you fit the mission of your potential customer. Follow Judy's roadmap and you will be successful!

SCOTT DENNISTON, EXECUTIVE DIRECTOR EMERITUS,
NATIONAL VETERAN SMALL BUSINESS COALITION

Finally, a book that removes the mystery behind how the federal government buys and what we expect from suppliers! This book is essential for anyone interested in doing business with the government, and for everyone who's serious about growing their federal business. You'll get a clear a path to understand how federal buying works, and what the government buyer needs to make an informed decision. Even better: you'll discover how to give your federal buyer the information they want, help them make their decision, and see you as a trusted partner when they do. This is one of those books you'll read again and again...and learn something new every time you pick it up!

DOTTIE ROMO – FORMER GOVERNMENT CONTRACTING OFFICER

Table of Contents

Chapter One: Strategy   1

Chapter Two: Focus   25

Chapter Three: Process   55

Chapter Four: Competition   111

Chapter Five: Teaming and Subcontracting 133

Chapter Six: Relationships –
The Ten People You Need To Meet 173

Chapter Seven: Sales and Marketing 207

Conclusion 251

Foreword

I'll never forget the day when my phone rang and I heard the enthusiastic sound of a friendly voice saying, "Hello, Eileen! I think it's time we join forces – and become teaming partners – just like we advise our federal contracting clients every day!" It was Judy Bradt, a 30-year veteran of federal contracting and Author of "Government Contracts Made Eas*ier*" and I couldn't have felt more honored by the personal invitation of such a well-known industry expert.

It was 2014 – almost ten years after I originally met Judy at a special workshop helping companies fill out the large pile of paperwork necessary to apply for their GSA Schedule, a contract vehicle any federal agency can use to award a commercial company a contract without posting on the public bid sites. These GSA proposal applications were a bear to fill out, and while some companies still take up to a year to fill out the application, we worked together on a team of four experts, where companies filled out their applications in *three days*. It was so exhausting at these workshops, Judy and I never had a chance to come up for air to even have a one-on-one conversation to discuss the state of "federal contracting" or "teaming" together.

Those were the "Wild West" days of federal contracting where consultants were all finding ways to help companies to do business with the federal government, but the quality levels between legitimate businesses and self-proclaimed "experts" were night and day, and it was tough for federal contractors to decipher who were the good guys – and who were the really, really good guys.

More recently, however, the game has changed, and that is why Judy reached out to me in 2014. I had started my own business two years prior and developed a series of training programs, which Judy quickly added into her service offerings, and we have since worked together with dozens and dozens of companies – training them on the federal sales game, performing deep dives into the contracting data resulting in custom competitive analyses, and building federal sales action plans which lead these contractors to millions of dollars in contracting opportunities

Throughout these programs, Judy and I have discussed, in detail, the best strategies and approaches for these organizations. Every approach has nuanced differences because the contracting data reveals the truth about how the government buys what they sell, and once that intelligence is uncovered, then a federal sales action plan is built and executed.

While there are differences in what agencies to approach, the one critically important common thread in all of our years working in the industry is this: "Does this potential federal contractor have what it takes to create a *trusting relation-*

ship with the person who buys what they sell, and does this company have the perseverance and attention to detail to make sure they embed themselves deeply enough into the agency to know the Project Managers, and then to follow up, follow through, close, and deliver within budget, perfectly, on time and every time?"

If the answer is "Yes," the rest of the process to capture and win federal contracts... is a series of tasks that can be learned and, more importantly, *achieved.*

Judy calls this book "Government Contracts Made Eas*ier*" for a reason. They're NOT easy. This is NOT a business for dabblers. But Judy has a great way of communicating how you can save a lot of time and money avoiding common beginner federal-contractor mistakes and focusing on capturing the *winnable* opportunities. This Second Edition is the update the industry has been highly anticipating, because it incorporates all the latest in technology, databases, social media, and new websites to explore, revealing the secrets of how to capture the real "under-the-radar" opportunities so we never again have to surf the public databases for baldly described projects we can't understand and aren't likely to win. This edition has made government contracting ...*Easier*...for All of Us.

Eileen Kent
Federal Sales Sherpa
President, Custom Keynotes, LLC

Introduction to the Second Edition

"A billion here, a billion there, and pretty soon it adds up to real money."

SEN. EVERETT DIRKSEN, R-IL, SENATE MINORITY LEADER, 1960

Is federal business good business for your business?

Whether you've never won a federal contract, or are looking to grow your federal business, congratulations! You're in the right place.

Businesses of every size that have determination, and passion for excellence, are welcome in the federal contracting arena. Thinking about it? You'll learn a lot. There is fellowship and a lot of personal and professional development on the road. But it's more than a game: it's a life that's going to cost you time and money every day you're in that arena.

Every time I watch Olympic athletes perform, I think of how hard they worked simply to get to the starting line of their events. And any time I hear about someone who's won a federal contract, I think of them the same way. Both kinds of elite performers train for years, study competitors, get the best coaching, compete and lose as well as win, and know the rules of their sport as well as how to get every possible legal advantage for success.

Welcome to the Olympics of business.

So, what brought you to the arena door?

Maybe it's the excitement and potential.

The U.S. federal government is the world's biggest buyer. What's not to like? It's no surprise that you and I get emails about "The Proven Way To Win Government Contracts!" or invitations to "Meet Our Top Agency Decision-Makers." Do consultants keep calling with package deals to take care of your registrations and send bids to you? If you're thinking there's probably more to it than that, and are looking for answers, you're not alone.

Maybe you've heard about money that's set aside for small business.

Three things are absolutely true. First, the federal government has goals to award billions of dollars' worth of contracts to small business. Second, big companies that win federal contracts must set and account for commitments to subcontract to small business. Third, your company might qualify for preferences if it's owned by women, service-disabled veterans, or is considered otherwise disadvantaged by location or socio-economic status. Wondering how to get your "fair share"? Read on!

Maybe you're almost ready for action.

You've done your due diligence. You've spent countless hours at industry days, small business events, seminars and webinars on federal regulations, teaming agreements, protests, Best-in-Class vehicles. You've had it with well-meaning advice about certifications and GSA Schedules and "doing your homework." You want a clear path forward. I'm with you.

Maybe you want to show your company's owners or colleagues the way to tap the potential you see in the federal market – or maybe they've just said to you, *"Get us there."*

The checklists and resources in this book can help you make your case – or get you a head start on success before your next annual performance review.

What does federal business success take? Over the past 31 years, I've learned from a lot of smart people in the course of guiding over 5,000 people to more than $300 million in federal contract wins. What I've found is that the keys to success are aligned with research into what motivates people to high levels of achievement in complex, non-mechanical, creative efforts. It's not money.

Winning a federal contract takes so much effort, relative to winning business from just about any other customer, that it's hard to imagine why owners of any business, large or small, would even want to try. Those who succeed are very much driven by these three things: Autonomy, purpose, and mastery.

I wrote this book to give you more of those three things you'll need to get to the top of your game.

Government Contracts Made Easier *lets you leverage the most powerful asset of all:* your *time.* You're about to get a phenomenal return on your investment of time as you consider whether the federal market is good business for your business, and chart a clear path to a specific buyer.

Most of the marketing e-mails you get about government contracting don't tell you this: federal business isn't right for *every* business. The facts and the data about your niche in the federal market could lead you to decide that this isn't the right customer for your company right now. Whether you decide you're in or you're out, a confident decision is a win. This book will help you make that decision *before* you invest heavily in time and money. But if federal business *is* a good fit, I want your business to thrive.

Running a business is *hard.* Those who don't run a business have no idea what it feels like to say goodbye to the security of a regular paycheck when you get on this rollercoaster of the American dream.

You're here because you want to figure out the federal market for once and all, make a good decision, and move forward or move on. Our time is our most precious resource as we work every day to take care of our employees and our families as well as our clients. You deserve reliable information and proven tools to make those decisions.

Have I made mistakes? Oh, my goodness, yes. All the best guides have cautionary tales, and I have plenty of them. You might not make my mistakes, but you'll make your own. We all do. Be ready to pick up and keep moving.

I do what I do so that you can make a difference in the world. If you want to make that difference, you have to win the work first.

There are a lot of places you can do business that are easier than the federal arena. Many customers make decisions far faster than federal buyers do, and are easier and less expensive to reach. What's so special about this buyer for you?

In the long run, federal business is not just a hard-won paycheck with some weird twists and turns. It's a mission. You're thinking about this market, or stay in it, because you have expertise, products, or services that make a difference for how your federal buyer serves citizens and delivers their missions. In your own way, your work is *transformative.* Something works better, happens better, for your buyer when they choose you.

If only they would give you the chance. Which is why you're here: to figure out how to make that possible.

The least you need to know is this:

- **Federal contract wins don't happen fast.** You don't "apply" for a government contract. You don't just register, fill out forms, and get in line for your contract. It's not a numbers game either: many companies make dozens of proposals and win nothing. What every winner learns, sooner or later, is...

- **The federal government does not have to do business with you.** Yes, federal agencies have goals to award a certain number of dollars for various kinds of small business. Sometimes they fall short, sometimes they meet or exceed their goals. Their files fully document their best efforts to do that, year after year. Realize this: your status as a small business is not a major differentiator. Thousands of other companies have the same certifications that you do. Read on, and discover how to get to know your buyer and begin to engage them: first with your experience and past performance, and then with your ability to show them how well you understand what's important to them.

- **What takes so long isn't so much the "procurement process" as written:** it's the part nobody seems to teach about how to build relationships long *before* the successful proposal is written.

- **Federal contracts aren't for everybody.** Yes, a federal contract can help your company grow. But success takes a fresh injection of time and money, *up* *front, often for a full year or more,* to pursue the business and with no guarantee of a win. Got enough working capital to stay in business long enough win as well as to perform the work...and to get paid for it? If winning federal customers is important enough for you, then you'll find the determination and the resources to go the distance. The last few years have also shown me, over and over, that if it's not, you won't. It's your call.

This book rises from the hearts of my clients: people like **Mike Osredker**. Mike's a tall, friendly, mild-mannered, genial business-development professional with perfectly coiffed white hair, a warm smile, well-fitted suits, and well-shined shoes. He's done a LOT of successful business development in his career, and knows his field – human capital management – very well.

The company he worked for had a strong track record in delivering leadership training and organizational development services for large, complex organizations in the private sector, such as Exxon and other big oil-patch companies. He'd arrived early one summer in Washington from Kansas City as the sole emissary of his company, with a mission: win some new business, like those government contracts. But after six months of going to networking meetings and association events, federal contracting had him stumped.

Mike was frustrated. "Judy, trying to sell to the federal government feels like swimming in the ocean with no mileposts!"

I went back to my office and thought hard about that. I was bringing my clients the best tools and techniques, but had failed to bring them the boat they needed when they felt awash in a confusing sea of information and surging opportunities.

That conversation with Mike showed me that, more than just a boat, you wanted clear direction, meaningful milestones, and a way to achieve constant small wins and build momentum on the way there.

I'm here for you.

This book is for Mike Osredker... and this book is for you.

What's new in the second edition

- More about what it takes to actually win the business! Field intelligence from my last ten years of hands-on experience building relationships with federal buyers, and the players at all the layers!

- Stronger checklists to support business decisions in the federal market.

- Updates to regulations and programs, especially those related to small business and mentor-protégé.

- Mapping of the ten current-to-pending new public federal competitive intelligence platforms in GSA's Integrated Award Environment under SAM.gov.

- Updates to links and online resources

- More advice on specialty topics like GSA Schedules and certifications. As this book goes to print, the General Services Administration has begun to consolidate 24 of its Schedule Contracts in a transition planned for completion before the end of 2021. At that time, the published plans for consolidation were published at *http://bit.ly/GSA-Scheds-Consolidation* . Always check *https://gsa.gov* for the most current information.

What's It Take to Win a Government Contract? The Facts

Nearly 700 successful small business contractors had this to say about that:

- *Start small and work your way up.* 50% of firms said their first win was as a prime contractor, and valued at under $100,000; only 26% won a contract worth over $100,000 the first time around.

- GSA Schedule contracts can be key to success – but they *aren't the only path* to growth in this market. In fact, GSA Schedules account for only about 10% of the total federal contract spend. If you're obsessed with getting a GSA Schedule contract but haven't done the research to see whether the federal buyer you have in mind actually *uses* GSA Schedule to buy what you do, drop everything and get that research done before you invest one more dollar in your GSA Schedule proposal.

- *Be persistent.* Data shows companies made an average of 3.1 unsuccessful bids before winning their first one.

- Expect to invest *time.* On average, successful companies took **12 months** to win their first federal contract.

- Be ready to invest *money.* Those unsuccessful bids – which everyone must expect – are just part of the time and money federal contractors invest. They reported an average spend of **$128,628** on the way to that first contract. That figure is 49% higher than responses just three years earlier.

- *Seek subcontracts and teaming* as well as contracts. 19% of businesses made their first win as a subcontractor, 15% were a prime but subcontracted out some of the work, and 6% won first as a teaming partner. 62% of active small business contractors have pursued teaming arrangements with other small firms, compared to only 36% of non-contractors.

What do successful companies have in common?

Fit: 34% of active contractors decide to go after government business based on fit; they're convinced that a specific agency has a need that their product or service will meet.

Alignment with Growth Plans: As you're about to find out, this is going to be a long, expensive undertaking. How does doing business with government align with your company's mission, your vision, your resources, and your capacity?

Established Core Competency: Pick a narrow core competency. If they're meeting you for the first time, and especially if your company is small, when you say, "We do everything," primes and buyers hear "We don't know what we're doing." Federal buyers and prime contractors are both highly risk averse, which is a polite way of saying they don't want to take on a new supplier if the one they already have is good enough. They want what you're best at, especially if you're *the* best at it.

Commercial Track Record: If you haven't been a prime contractor before, then you can show that you're the low-risk choice by presenting your strong record as a subcontractor or commercial supplier. Similarly, becoming a subcontractor is simpler if you can show off your success on big commercial projects or ones for big-name companies. The federal market is an incredibly tough market for startups and one-person companies that want to grow. The very new companies and solo-preneurs who win federal contracts without a commercial track record typically have either unique niche expertise, trusted insider relationships, or likely both.

Financing: In order to win, and after you do, you'll have to pay bills and staff for weeks or months before you get your first contract payment. Meet with your banker when you decide you're going to pursue federal business. A line of credit doesn't guarantee working-capital financing. Just because you have a $40,000, $50,000, or $100,000 line of credit does NOT mean that your bank will turn around a couple million in financing over the weekend just because you won a big contract. Start early to find out what kind of collateral, paperwork, assurances, audits, review, approvals, and time it will take to get financing.

That's more likely to be successful than screeching into the bank with a screaming emergency, unable to make payroll. Explore whether and how your bank could finance a project if you do win. If they can't, then start looking for alternatives. Some banks specialize in contract financing.

Asset-based financing is a lot easier to get if yours is a brick-and-mortar-based company. If your company provides professional services, you might need to look beyond a traditional bank.

Learn more about factoring, which is monetizing the cash flow from your contract up front -- at higher interest. It might not be your first choice, but it might end up being your only alternative.

Using This Book: What's Special

A Structured Approach

You'll get seven chapters to guide your journey into the heart of what it takes to win federal business. This organized approach encourages momentum and prevents overwhelm. When you always know the next practical step you can take, you keep moving toward your goals!

Key Concepts

Each chapter gives you the essentials that successful companies master as they launch and grow their federal business.

Research Data & Top Expert Insight

Anticipate the time and resources you'll need based on hard statistics and data on what real companies experience on the road ahead. You'll see who wins, who loses, and what works, from new studies and leading specialists in diverse aspects of government business.

Learn from Real Business Owners: Profiles in Success

Other business owners – small- and minority-business owners, veterans -- have generously shared the candid truth about their journey, their challenges, their mis-steps, and the tactics they used to win government business.

Exercises

You'll get the tools I use when I work with my clients. If you decide to hire someone to handle some of these points, you can use these tools to guide their work, set reasonable expectations, and be confident that you're getting good value from the people you hire to help you.

Checklists and Tip Lists

You've probably heard of proposal checklists, to make sure you include everything your buyer asks for. I've shared some of my other favorites, with plenty of point-form lists to make technical material easier to work with.

Resources

This market and its players, rules, and tools, keep changing. Technology keeps driving that change ever faster. So the book includes links to free and low-cost resources that you can use along the way. If you're reading this book in electronic form, web sites and links in blue are live.

So. Ready to uncover *your* unique advantage in winning federal business? Successful companies do seven things.

It all starts with being in the right place, headed the right way, the right right reason. That's the first chapter: Strategy.

Let's begin together.

Acknowledgements (Second Edition)

When I wrote the first edition, people would ask me, "How long did it take to write the book?" Now the answer is, "Thirty years."`

The first edition was built on curiosity and trust: the curiosity of thousands of people who came to me for help in this market, and the trust you placed in me to find answers and resources for you. You remain my best teachers. Your questions drive my passion to find the most practical, effective tools and information I can give a business owner who wants to grow their federal business.

Particularly special kudos to Curt Adams, then Senior Director of Member and Chapter Services of the Armed Forces Communications and Electronics Association (AFCEA). He bought a thousand copies right out of the box, before there was a box and before there was a book, from a first-time author, and put them into the hands of small businesses across the country.

Teaching is still a ton of fun for me, and spurs me to make sure I'm sharing the most current data and best practices with you. I thank those who have invited me to speak repeatedly between 2011 and 2018, particularly Pam Eason at the Women's Business Enterprise National Council (WBENC); Scott Semple and Scott Denniston of the National Veterans Small Business Coalition (NVSBC); Candace Waterman and Lin Stuart of Women Impacting Public Policy (WIPP); and the Association of Procurement Technical Assistance Centers (APTAC and the individual PTACs).

Among the PTAC counselors, I'm especially grateful to Anna Urman, Sherri Komrosky, Rick Palmer, Veronica Doga, Lenora Leasure, and Jane Dowgwillo, all of whom marked up the first edition when it was time to find the many rules, references, and technical details that needed an update. Any errors and omissions are my responsibility.

True experts learn constantly from others. The very best experts aren't the ones who always say, "I know it all." They're the ones who know when to say, "I don't know, but I can tell you just the person you should be talking to." My list of go-to gurus begins with my original mentor, government-contracting guru and radio host of "Amtower Off-Center," Mark Amtower. My guides on procurement law and regulation are Pam Mazza and Jon Williams of PilieroMazza and Maria Panichelli of Obermayer. Kudos to them and their colleagues for unstinting generosity to the small business contracting community. Lisa Dezzutti and Aaron Heffron of Market Connections were similarly generous in sharing their research on top federal contractors' marketing strategies.

I add a special thank you to former Contracting Officer Stacey Coolican for her loving care and detailed review of this edition. Contracting is all about details, and her keen eye helped me get those right.

This edition's revised content on federal sales and marketing reflects the extraordinary insight that Federal Sales Sherpa Eileen Kent brought to our in-depth collaborative service to over 70 companies...and to endless hours she spent coaching me on sales and relationship-building in my own business.

Once again, the editing talents of David McLoughlin made this a much better book than I could have brought you on my own. A giant thank you to Nat Gertler for book design, layout, and production of both print and e-book versions, and to Sarah Gertler for cover design and image selection.

This second edition is happening because thousands of people bought the first one. To you who bought that one, from a first-time author, thank you. For that matter, to you who bought this one, thank *you*. Autographing books is the second-best part of writing a book. The best part about writing this book is when someone comes up to me with a dog-eared, stickied, highlighted copy of that auto-graphed book years later and says, "This really helped us!"

My husband, J.J. Gertler, remains the wind *above* my wings (because, as pilots know, that's what creates lift!) with a constant stream of support (including but not limited to editing) not just for this book but also for Summit Insight, the business on which it is based.

Acknowledgements (First Edition)

Most of what I know about government contracting, I learned from my teachers – that is, everyone who asked me a question, and needed an answer, and it had to be right...because the answers so often begin, "Well, here's what you asked for, but there's more you'll need to know..." I'm grateful to over 6,000 teachers who chose to ask me their questions – starting with my colleagues at the Canadian Embassy in Washington in 1988 and rising even faster from clients and friends since I started private practice in 2003.

This book is grounded by the stories of government contractors. As readers, please join me in thanking Mike Osredker, Marissa Levin, Kathy Kastner, Lisa Dolan, Linda Lazarowich, Carolyn Sawyer, Deborah Stallings, Gabe Batstone, Colin Hung, Neeld Wilson, Mike Boehmer, and Martin Saenz. While the chapter on teaming is based on insights from executives of many systems integrators, two stand out above all the others: Diane Dempsey of BAE Systems and Ludmilla Parnell of General Dynamics Information Technology.

Teaching is vital to how I develop my work, my tools and my insights. I thank those who have invited me repeatedly: Jim Regan at the Procurement Technical Assistance Center (PTAC) at George Mason University; Linda Denny, Liz Cullen and Betty Cole at the Women's Business Enterprise National Council (WBENC); Barbara Kasoff and Michael Fravel of Women Impacting Public Policy (WIPP); Curt Adams, Tammy Goehring and Sheila McCoy of the Armed Forces Communications and Electronics Association (AFCEA), Bridget Bean of the Small Business Administration (SBA), and Diane Sears, Molly Gimmel, Leslie Curran, Tya Bolton and Courtney Nicholson in particular with the National Association of Women Business Owners (NAWBO).

Nobody knows it all. The best experts admit readily that half the battle is knowing where to look (and who else to ask) for the answers. Topping that list is Mark Amtower. As author and government contracting guru, he's been my no-nonsense sage and mentor on many levels for as long as I've been doing government contracting. He also spent at least five years encouraging me to get this written, reminding me that the marketplace always has room for another good book.

At the American Small Business Coalition (ASBC), Guy and Maggie Timberlake have created a community where I find a constant source of inspiring questions as well as knowledge, support, and technical experts. Courtney Fairchild of Global Services kindly reviewed the chapter on Process – but any errors that remain (there or elsewhere in this book) are entirely my responsibility. Aileen Pisciotta provided legal review on intellectual property. Larry Hugg and Dori Kelner of Sleight-of-Hand Studios did a great photo shoot and book design.

Two people got me out of the doldrums at critical points. Seth Godin offered kind insights in person, and gave me a vital kickstart with his book, Linchpin. Preparing for my interview series with Jon Hansen, host of PI Window on Business, finally got me unstuck from the chapter on Process. As a first-time author, I also had the great good fortune to benefit from the generous and gracious guidance of experienced authors Sam Horn, Michael Levin and Jill Konrath.

In the wake of their advice, I really needed an expert to hack the manuscript down to size. I am indebted far beyond any accounting to my copy editor and longtime friend, David McLoughlin – a debt I look forward to repaying on the installment plan for many years to come – even if I put back in stuff that he took out.

Jonathan Levin of Clearpoint Communications and Jennifer Abernethy ensured that I had (and used) the effective social media tactics I needed. And – did you know? – many authors have to close down their businesses, sometimes for months, in order to concentrate on getting a book finished. The stalwart support, skill, and bottomless patience of Dawn Middlestead, my virtual assistant since 2005, meant that I could keep the business running while I was writing.

I'm more grateful than I ever manage to express to my family: my mom Bernice, my sister Karen, and my brothers Lorne and Dave for their ideas, prototypes and most of all cheering and moral support.

Finally, this book would not have come to be without the unfailing faith, energy and talents of my champion (chief editor, book shepherd, technical consultant, sounding board, production manager, eternal muse) and husband, J.J. Gertler. I simply could not have imagined a better partner in my wildest dreams.

Chapter One: Strategy

Your federal strategy starts by answering critical questions that get to the heart of your plans to grow your company. This chapter presents the hard-hitting questions you'll need to ask your team as you begin your quest for more government contracts – and gives you the tools to find the answers. Get ready for straight talk – and candid insight – into how you can lay a foundation to win new government business in the year ahead.

By the end of Chapter One, you'll have a much better idea whether or not this giant customer makes sense for you.

What You'll Do

- Evaluate Strategic Fit
- Understand & Affirm Your Core Business
- Set Goals & Metrics
- Identify Critical Resources
- Address Constraints
- Assess Your Strategy
- Make a Go / No-Go on Selling to Government

Part 1: Overview

Concept – Why Sell To Government? The Opportunity

Government – federal, state, and local – buys just about everything. The question is not so much whether government buys what you've got, but whether you want to do what it takes to reach those buyers.

The federal government spends between $400 billion and $500 billion ($471 billion in FY2016) on contracts for goods and services. (In Part Two, you'll learn how to find out how much federal buyers spend on services or products like yours, and what else you need to know before you begin). Moreover, the total purchasing power of over 80,000 state and local buying authorities tops two *trillion* dollars.

Combining all levels together, the American government is the world's biggest buyer. Who knew?

Who sells to government? All kinds of people – quite possibly including your competitors. What are their secrets to success?

Strategic fit is absolutely critical. How will the effort to pursue, win, and perform for this new and demanding customer – whether that's Northrop Grumman or the Department of Homeland Security – be in harmony with the direction you plan to take your company?

If you don't already have a reasonably strong business plan, believe me, selling to government is going to make things harder, not easier.

Selling to government may be the biggest challenge your business has ever taken on. If you're ready, winning this business can catapult your company to the next level of success. If you're not ready to take on federal business, the effort just to pursue, never mind to perform, a federal contract can put your business out of business.

If your focus is fuzzy, if your mission is mundane, if your finances are weak, if your strategy is sloppy, if your back office is out to lunch, and certainly if your performance is sub-par, that's going to show up big time when you start out on the road to win government business.

I've never heard anybody say they deliberately went after government contracts because they wanted to get their business into shape. But if you're successful, that can be another benefit for you.

Venture capitalists have told me they often like to see young, strong businesses plan to win government business in order to drive growth that will make the company attractive to buy. And I have definitely heard dozens of companies say, "Before we did our GSA Schedule proposal, our pricing and discounting were somewhere between inconsistent and nonexistent. That proposal forced us to get our act together and create more consistent business practices in the commercial market, and strengthen our internal corporate management. ALL our customers appreciated that, and we're more profitable as a result!"

In addition to being the world's biggest buyer, and one that is often very loyal to vendors who provide good service and delivery, government is also one of the most demanding customers, and one of the least forgiving if you don't perform well.

If you've been meaning to get around to updating your business plan, beefing up your back office, or improving your infrastructure, this is the perfect time to do it. Getting ready to sell to government may turn out to be the best thing you ever did – even if you decide, long before the end of this book, that you have no intention of EVER selling to government after all.

EXERCISE ONE: Gut Check. What's Special About These Clients?

A Quick Market Comparison: Government and Commercial Clients

The chart below is a starting point for a discussion with the team that's going to be tackling and supporting your effort to win government business. If you're just thinking this through on your own, you can work through the right column. To use this chart for a planning session, you can start with a blank chart topped with just the headers, and ask your team to fill it in, based on their experience or perception of the market. How do government buyers stack up against commercial customers?

Buyer Characteristic	Government	Commercial	Which One You'd Rather Do Business With: Government / Commercial / Both
Process Predictability	The buying process is published in the Federal Acquisition Regulations and the solicitation – in other words, it's transparent and predictable. Clear, published rules enforced by law. You know who's making the decisions and how. And, win or lose, you're entitled to a debriefing to find out how you did.	Varied, unpredictable. Who knows how they pick winners? If you think your loss was unfair, it's hard to litigate if you don't know what rules the buyer was supposed to be following in the first place.	
Power of Repeat Business	Complacency will lose you the business... but, do a good job and your success can keep on rolling. Government buyers are reluctant to change contractors if what they have is working well.	People do business with people they like and trust... but commercial companies can also be more willing to take a risk on a new vendor. So it can be easier to get in, but you may have to work harder to *stay* in.	

Buyer Characteristic	Government	Commercial	Which One You'd Rather Do Business With: Government / Commercial / Both
Reliability of Payment	If you did your job and the invoice is correct, they're good for it. They print the money. And they have to pay you a penalty fee if they pay late.	What percentage of your commercial contracts do you allow for bad debt?	
Payment Time Frame	The rules require federal buyers to pay a *correct, complete* invoice in 30 days, and to honor discounts offered for prompt payment. Although that doesn't *guarantee* you'll be paid on time, it's reasonably likely.	Many small businesses face challenges from delayed payment by commercial customers, especially large primes.	
Reliability of Client – Will They Be In Business?	244 years and counting	They come, they go. Even giant car companies can go under.	
Right of Appeal	Right and process of appeal guaranteed by law	No guarantee of being heard, nor of a consistent dispute resolution process	

Buyer Characteristic	Government	Commercial	Which One You'd Rather Do Business With: Government / Commercial / Both
Reputation Enhancement	Imagine telling a prospect, "The Navy is my customer"! Government contracts, even small ones, pack prestige.	Contracts with big-name companies get attention; less so, work with a client no one's ever heard of.	
Buying Cycle	12-month fiscal-year cycle means that you could face 18 to 24 months of marketing expense and time before a solid flow of profitable sales can begin. It can be harder to build friendships with your government buyers, not least because they have to be above reproach. Ethics rules dictate who you can and can't talk to and when, and even whether you can buy them lunch.	Because businesses aren't bogged down by that huge public buying process, they can make decisions fast if you have what they want. Long-term sales can build from long-term relationships, and vice versa.	

Buyer Characteristic	Government	Commercial	Which One You'd Rather Do Business With: Government / Commercial / Both
Fast-Track Purchasing Ability	Government buyers are extremely risk-averse. Even for small purchases, they first choose suppliers they know and trust. Most agencies have Simplified Acquisition Procedures (SAP) for smaller purchases. If you know the rules, you can ask the buyer to tell you more about how they use SAP.	If they want it, they buy it, in accordance with their internal purchasing procedures.	
Estimated Buying Power/ Market Size	World's biggest buyer: well over $400 billion at the federal level alone.	Some are big, some are small. However, none of them buys $400B worth of anything.	

MAKING THE GRADE – EXERCISE ONE:

This exercise calls for a quick gut-check. Which market would you rather be in? What do you like about each? And what has you worried?

- If you're charged up about taking on a giant new customer, great – proceed to the next chapter!

- If your review has left you with more questions than answers, that's okay too: write 'em down. We're on the way to answers.

PROFILE IN SUCCESS: Marissa Levin

Meet **Marissa Levin, CEO of Information Experts in Reston, Virginia,** an award-winning provider of strategic and creative marketing communications and marketing and education services since 1995. Today, Information Experts is a multi-million-dollar company for commercial and federal organizations. In 2008 her flagship government contract, with the Office of Personnel Management (OPM), was worth over $6 million. Government contracts helped her company into the ranks of the INC500, which recognizes America's fastest-growing companies.

- **What spurred her federal pursuit?** A focused strategy for corporate growth. "After 9/11, we nearly went out of business," she said. "So we turned to the business in our own backyard," and started to go after government contracts.

- **How did she get started?** "We got on several GSA Schedules; built strong partnerships with large integrators; and [did] a lot of marketing, including through many 8(a) shows produced by private-sector companies as well as events sponsored by government agencies themselves."

- **How long did it take to win her first contract?** That happened surprisingly fast: "We were invited by the Environmental Protection Agency (EPA) to bid on two task-order competitions for creative work...because we had strong commercial experience." EPA was also looking for qualified 8(a) companies. But Marissa cautions that her initial experience isn't the whole story – "Steady profit took us a big investment of time and money."

- **What did it take to build that $6 million success?** "That took us nearly two years of getting to know the customer and what they wanted, and building trust. When the time came for the proposal, we had eight people working full time for six weeks and spent well over $200,000 – and that wasn't billable time!"

- **What was her biggest challenge?** Financing! "From the day you win, you have to start executing! But you then have to bankroll your employees for 60 to 90 days," before you might get your first payment. Without financing, that large contract could put you out of business! The day she won the OPM contract, Marissa declared in triumph to her new client, "My living room has no furniture in it, but I have this contract!"

Marissa's story highlights keys to success. Those keys are about to be yours.

Part 2: Strategic Fit

Marissa Levin's story shows the power of a good strategic fit. She invested time and money to learn how government did business – an investment that made good business sense because she'd thought it through. Once she made that commitment, she built relationships, figured out her competitors' weak spots, and attacked the market with tight focus on getting every advantage possible with prospects that offered the most potential.

How could YOU do that? Time to roll up your sleeves and figure it out. If your company has a current strategic plan and a planning process you like, then, for goodness' sake, start there. I'm not going to tell you to re-invent something that already works. On the other hand, if you *don't* currently have a suitable strategic plan, or if you're looking for some questions and ideas to get the ball rolling, then the rest of this chapter can help.

In my experience, when clients work through these questions, they can take anywhere from three hours to a day, depending on things like the size of the company, the number of key players who design and execute the strategy, the sophistication of their existing business plan, and the impact that a decision to pursue government business will have on the company as a whole.

EXERCISE TWO: The Right Stuff

Do you have the Right Stuff to win government contracts? Here's one way to find out.

Get together with your key managers – including executive leadership as well as sales, marketing, finance, and production. (If that's just two people, total, this is going to be either a really long meeting... or a really short one.)

Brainstorm, and ask yourselves: "Why do we want to sell to the government?" Then compare your reasons to the lists below.

List A: Some Potentially Really Bad Reasons to Chase Government Business

- I heard the government has a lot of money. There has to be some for us.
- Thousands of federal opportunities are published every day! We just have to get busy and send in some proposals.

- I just got back from a seminar about this, and they said all we have to do is follow the rules and we can win.

- The government has to buy from us because we're a small/woman-owned/service-disabled veteran-owned business.

- Our business needs a big contract to bring in some fast cash.

- I'm hurting for business, and a government contract could save me.

- I just came up with this great idea for a product the Army's gonna love.

- Government does a lot of stupid things, and our company's ideas could fix a lot of things.

- I heard that if we get 8(a) certified, the government has to buy from us.

- Our competitors just got a GSA Schedule, and we need to keep up.

- I'm a service-disabled veteran and just started my company because the government has to buy from us.

- My sister just got out of the Navy and needs a job; she can sell for us.

List B: Much Better Reasons to Focus on Winning Government Business

- They're the world's biggest buyer.

- We've got a great track record selling to Fortune 500 companies, so government could be a natural next step.

- Results of competitions and the rules of the game are in the public record.

- I'm passionate about using our proven expertise to save lives and keep soldiers safer.

- We've pinpointed a problem, and proved we can solve it, for a government buyer who has money to fix it.

- Government publishes tons of info about buyers and competition.

- They print the money – and pay their bills.

- If we win that Marine Corps contract and perform well, that'll build our reputation with those Fortune 500 companies we want to win!

- If we do a good job for that first Air Force base, they'll want to tell their friends... and we'll be in a good position for repeat business, too.

- We've been subcontracting to Lockheed for years, we've got strong end-user relationships, and we're ready to take it to the next level.

MAKING THE GRADE – EXERCISE TWO

Which sounds more like your list?

- If you have more "A-list-type" items, then you've probably started to feel uncomfortable. Good. You should, because you're recognizing that you may be taking more risk than you thought. But don't worry; you're now going to get what you need to mitigate that risk. The next exercise will be absolutely critical for you – please keep going.

- *If you're lining up with the "B" list, your reasoning for market entry is probably sound, and Exercise Three will build on that foundation.*

EXERCISE THREE: Mission & Vision

This is another discussion you should have internally. Why? Because you care about the success of your company, and so do your employees and stakeholders. Your key company players need to buy into your company's commitment of time and resources to go after government business. Otherwise, you can expect resentment, sabotage, and just plain failure to deliver results.

    a. Mission: Why does your company exist? What do you deliver, whom do you serve, and how?

    b. How would serving government clients fit with that mission?

    c. Vision: What do you want to create in the world?

    d. How does serving government clients contribute to realizing that vision?

    e. Think for a moment about the government departments, agencies, or buyers you would most like to do business with. If you were to win contracts with them, would performing and delivering on those commitments be consistent with the direction you have already defined for your company?

MAKING THE GRADE – EXERCISE THREE

The potential for government contracts to build your long-term business needs to be consistent with where you plan to take the company. Do the first two exercises give you a sense that pursuing federal business would be central to the journey your company is on?

▶ *NO – Then stop now. It's okay not to do this.*

Why would you spend ANY scarce resources – talent as well as time and money – on a venture that's just a distraction from your main line of business?

If you have no idea why your company would want to win government business, OR you really don't like anything about the federal government but would take their money if they offered you a contract, OR you figure you'll just throw some small change and leftover marketing money at a well-meaning employee who keeps bugging you about getting a GSA Schedule (whatever that is) just to make them stop pestering you about it...

... then I'd like to suggest that pursuing government business is not going to be good for your business. At least not now. If your answers change, maybe government business can become a good idea later. In the meantime, you can pass this book along to a friend who's asking questions like yours.

▶ *MAYBE – Then proceed with caution.*

If pursuit of government contracts would represent a major change in direction for your company, are you ready to do that, and is this the right time? Who needs to support that change, and are they on board? This book is here to help you figure this stuff out before you go charging ahead.

▶ *YES! – Then let's get into the details. What's next?*

Even these short exercises show you and your team that this is the right time to put more focus and effort into the federal market. The investment of time and money to develop this business gets everybody excited and ready to dig in for the long haul and kick some butt. Time for Exercise Four.

EXERCISE FOUR: Assessing How You Fit This Niche

4-A WHAT'S YOUR CORE CAPABILITY?

This is the foundation for everything that comes next. You will win more business faster in the federal market with a narrow focus on a product or service that you deliver or perform superbly well, and which represents a unique and top-quality solution to a federal buyer's problem.

What's a core capability?

Here's what it's NOT:

"We do everything, just ask us."

"We do everything Oracle."

"C++, C#, J2EE, COBOL, ASP, ASP.Net, VB.Net, JavaScript, PHP, Perl, Python, TCL, .Net, XML, XHTML, SOAP, WSDL, UDDI, COM+, CORBA..."

Your core capability answers the question, "What do you do?" by starting, "We specialize in..."

Your core capability describes what you do, and the outcome for your customer, that represents most of the value your company creates.

In three steps: When you consider your relationships with your best customers or clients today:

1. What do you do better than anyone else? Of all the things you do or make, what product or service do you provide so well and with so much value that clients consistently pay you fast, ask for more, and refer their friends to you?

2. What problem do you solve for them, and how do they benefit as a result?

3. Why did your customer choose your company to solve that problem rather than a competitor, and/or instead of doing the work themselves?

MAKING THE GRADE – EXERCISE 4-A

Your clients are the best ones to tell you how well you did here. If you haven't already gotten in touch with one or two of your best customers to ask THEM these questions, then it's time you did.

If you did well, then your perception of your strengths will match theirs reasonably closely – and you'll probably find out some things you never realized about why they like you.

Pay attention to the SPECIFIC WORDS your clients use! Your own marketing language isn't as important as the terms that your clients are using to describe their pain and your solution. When you use their language, you help them see and hear themselves when you communicate your value to them.

Sketch out a table like the one below, and jot down the key words from Exercise 4-A in box A.

		Clients	
		Current	**New**
Offerings	**Current**	A. Current Offering Current Client	B. Current Offering New Client
	New	C. New offering Current client	D. New Offering New Client

The hardest position move in this chart is diagonal, direct from Box A to Box D. Would winning federal business represent that move for you: selling something untried to a risk-averse customer who has never bought from you?

A two-step approach might actually get you there faster. Options:

- A to B to D: Start by helping your new federal prospect get to know the service or product that your current clients love most. Maybe the federal buyer would like to try what you do now without any adaptation. As you get to know each other, then you might get the chance to tweak your commercial offering to better meet your federal buyer's unique needs.

- A to C to D: You might be able to collaborate with one of your current clients, who already knows and trusts you, to develop and test an adaptation or variation of your offering that would not only expand your effectiveness in serving today's customer, but create a track record for something that would be an even better fit for your new federal prospect.

4-B WHAT'S YOUR CORE OFFERING FOR YOUR FEDERAL BUYER?

Think about those clients for whom you solved a problem like the one you think your prospective government buyers may have.

Government buyers are notoriously risk-averse. They want to know that you've already solved their problem, just yesterday, for someone who looks almost exactly like them. Commercial customers need to fix many of the same problems that governments do: increase skilled employee retention, or lower costs, or improve effectiveness. Your commercial customers also might love you for other things that government doesn't care about – for example, most notoriously, "increasing profits."

Sort through your core offerings to pick the ones that your top-priority government buyers would find most attractive. Federal buyers respond strongly – and are willing to pay -- for a well-defined offering that your past performance gives them confidence will solve their problems with low risk.

How much do you think you'd need to adapt what you offer, and how you talk about it, in ways that fit what government buyers say *they* need? Expect to evolve. Even if you think your commercial offering is absolutely identical to what you want to offer government, look and listen closely. These buyers generally perceive themselves and their missions as unique – and they're right.

Any time you're marketing to government buyers, and particularly when your offering isn't a commercial off-the-shelf product or service, focus your conversation on THEM: their experiences, their vision, their missions, their challenges. You don't want to start out saying to your federal prospect, "...and I know our regular stuff will suit you just fine." Even if that turns out to be true, you need to take the time to listen to them. Share your insights and experiences respectfully, especially if you have an approach that's different from the way they do things now. Change is hard for everyone. Changing from a vendor they know (even one who is serving them poorly) to a new contractor (even one who offers a proven product or service) represents risk. You know you're on the right track when you hear, "Yes,

I really want that thing/seminar/expertise your commercial customers are raving about! Let's try it here!"

The table below might be one way to review each of your proposed offerings to new government buyers, and think about which ones would take the least – and most – adaptation from the way you're reaching today's buyers, whether commercial or government.

Your Commercial Offering	Government Buyer's Need and Profile	Importance to New Government Decision-Maker	Potential Adaptation Needed	Effort/ Resources Required to Adapt
		High/Med/Low		
Product or service				
Why your client buys it from you				
How your client buys from you **(Purchasing/Contract type)**				
Marketing tactics				
Channels and partners – direct or teamed?				

Part 3: Business Plan Elements

The next analysis tools are basic ones you're probably familiar with from your current business plan. I've just adapted them as a way to think about the effect that pursuing government business might have on your strategy.

EXERCISE FIVE: The Mix – Government and Commercial

This exercise helps you figure out:

- How much government business do you think you want to win, and by when?

- How much can you actually perform?

- What do you need to step up to that level of performance?

- Can you get what you need to do the job?

- After everything you may have to spend to develop the business... would this be profitable?

Most companies that sell to government aim for a balance of work between that market and their regular commercial clientele. Why? To spread the risk, more than anything. Just as a commercial client can close or relocate or be bought out, a government client can end a program or change its requirements. Furthermore, it takes time to develop government business – it's not a tap you can turn on overnight.

I can guarantee two things: it's probably not going to happen the way you plan, and your chances of success are much better when you set goals than if you don't. So, look into the future, and jot down some ideas for the mix you're going to aim for. Big-picture is fine for now. You'll get the chance to figure out what's going to drive that business a little later.

% or $	Now	Year 1	Year 2
Commercial			
Government (as Prime)			
Government (as Subcontractor)			

EXERCISE SIX: Capacity Forecasting

So you want to step up to win those levels of government contracts? Great!

- Current Capacity: For each product or service you want to offer the government market, how much can you deliver today?

- Years 1 & 2 Forecast: With your current growth plans, what would be the maximum capacity or biggest project you could deliver to government buyers in each of the next two years?

- Years 1 & 2 Scalable: What constraints limit your current forecast capacity? And if you could address those constraints, how big a project or job could you deliver?

Product/ Service Offering	Current Capacity	Year 1 Forecast	Year 1 Scalable	Year 2 Forecast	Year 2 Scalable
1					
2					
3					
4					

EXERCISE SEVEN: Critical Resources

What resources do you have now, have access to, and/or think you need to find in order to support that growth? Even if you've got questions rather than answers ("Legal? Why would I need a lawyer to sell to the government? I only want to sub-contract!"), just jot down the questions. Don't worry – this is just a first cut. When we do this again later, you'll have more answers to your questions and a better ability to plan for what's ahead.

Successful companies get the inside scoop on both the resources they need and where to get good help from other companies in similar industries that are already selling to government. Why would potential competitors help you? "Compete today, team tomorrow." People help their friends, and you never know when you'll need a good partner who can do something you can't. (Where do you meet people like that? You'll find out in Chapter Six, Relationships.)

	Required – Estimated Cost – Availability		
Additional Resource	**Today**	**Year 1**	**Year 2**
Full-Time Client Service/ Production Staff			
Outsourced Client Service/ Production Staff			

	Required – Estimated Cost – Availability		
Additional Resource	**Today**	**Year 1**	**Year 2**
Administrative Support • pre-proposal financial review • pre-contract audit • proposal production • contract administration • client relationship management • marketing support			
Delivery Channels			
Product/Service Development			
Management			
Financing • equity • asset-based • other debt instruments			
Legal • certifications • teaming support • proposal/contract review			
Outside Technical Support • business management • government contracting expertise • proposal preparation • marketing adaptation			
Production Capacity • expert staff • office space • manufacturing and assembly			
Business Development • forecasting • competitive research			
Marketing			

Additional Resource	Required – Estimated Cost – Availability		
	Today	Year 1	Year 2
Sales			
Relationships with Channel Partners			
Relationships with Government Buyers <ul><li>initial introductions</li><li>business development</li><li>client relationship management plan</li></ul>			

How did you do with Exercises 4, 5, 6, and 7?

- If these exercises seemed like a tedious waste of time, and you want to skip right to where you can find the RFPs to start bidding on, I hope you'll stick with me just a little longer. Bidding is expensive. Your patience will bring you more profit, because the cost of every win includes the cost of every losing proposal along the way to that win.

- If these exercises have given you new things to think about, or reminded you of business growth issues that you need to address, great! You want to have confident answers to those questions before you get any more deeply invested in the federal market. Early-stage clarity can keep you focused on a few high-potential opportunities, and on projects at a scale where you can perform well if you win. Great performance, even on small opportunities, positions you for bigger projects.

- If these exercises simply validated or strengthened strategies you've been working on – terrific!

Part 4: Strategy Snapshot

What criteria does your company use to evaluate new opportunities? If you have a decision process that works well for you, great! This next section might be a refresher. If not, then I hope you'll get some ideas to tweak or even to create your own best practices.

Strengths, Weaknesses, Opportunities & Threats: A Classic Analysis Framework.

This is one of the first ones I learned, and still one of my favorites.

Strengths and Weaknesses are **internal** to your company. These reflect your company as it is today. They are things within your control, and reflect choices you make, conditions you created and, most importantly, things you can change. Consider each in view of what it would take to explore, pursue, win, perform, sustain, and build business serving government clients and buyers. The examples below should look familiar: they're the same things you've been thinking about throughout Chapter One.

Strengths	Weaknesses
Some typical considerations:	Some typical considerations:
• Commercial client track record • Reputation in marketplace • Subcontracting experience • Financing • Development & Adaptation Capacity • Production & Delivery Capacity • Knowledge of target government agency • Geographical Proximity to customer • Agency Relationships • Customer Contacts • Teaming Partner Relationships • Competitive Analysis • Government Contracting Expertise • Government Sales Experience • Eligibility for set-asides / special preferences	• Start with the flip side of the strengths list. • If it's not one of your strengths, it's probably a weakness you need to deal with.

Opportunities, Threats & Obstacles are **external** to your company. They're not things you control. They are based on your observations and analysis of the business environment, the potential customer base, the competition, the market factors that affect your prospects' interest in doing business with you, and your ability to reach them.

Opportunities	Threats & Obstacles
Some typical considerations:	Some typical considerations:
• New Administration / Congress: looking for new ideas	• New Administration = new regulations; budget cuts or changes to DoD and civilian agencies affect opportunities that you or your teaming partners are focused on
• New programs or initiatives (e.g., Mentor-Protégé Programs; increase in Immigration Enforcement)	
• Urgent military or disaster response requirements	• Urgent requirements favor established suppliers who already have contract vehicles
• Long-term needs forecast to grow (e.g., qualified employee shortage, rehabilitative care for returning veterans)	• Change in government agency mission
• Reorganization (e.g., new buildings, temporary moves, Base Realignment and Closure of military facilities)	• Reorganization (e.g., Base Realignment and Closure relocates military facilities)
• Media / public pressure to fix problems	• Fixing problems can divert program managers from ongoing programs and delay planned procurement
• Competitor leaving the marketplace	• Tendency toward giant contracts or "bundling" makes it hard for smaller companies to enter the market
• Budget cuts demand more cost-effective solutions	• Credit crunch makes it harder to get financing
• New contracting preferences or vehicles that give your company an advantage	• Focus on insourcing

Key Success Factors
Key Success Factors are things you can and must do to:

- Play from your strengths
- Address weaknesses that can prevent your success
- Seize opportunities that offer the most potential for success
- Develop ideas to neutralize threats and overcome obstacles
- Ensure profitability over selected time horizon

Recommendations/Issues for GO / NO-GO
Based on your company's track record in opening up new market niches:

- What would tell you that it's worth your time and money to explore your prospects among federal buyers?
- Conversely, what are the danger signs that experience tells you to look for?

And finally – Your Initial Go / No-Go

This chart is one way to record your discussion.

First, list the factors for and against going after government business, based on what you know at this early stage. Those are the right and left pairs of columns.

Second, it's still early going – there may be things you need to find out before you can make a Go / No-Go decision. List those too. Those are the center columns.

Third, all factors are not equal! Give each factor a weight, from 5 (most important) to 1 (least important).

Con – I've Got a Bad Feeling About This	Factor Weight 1-5	Caution – Things We Have To Find Out	Factor Weight 1-5	Pro – Let's go for it!	Factor Weight 1-5
TOTALS					

MAKING THE GRADE – INITIAL GO / NO-GO

How does it look to you? The weighted totals can help you size up your current situation.

READY FOR THE NEXT STEP? STRATEGY CHECKLIST

- ○ Be in this market for winning reasons
- ○ Commit to realistic goals – a minimum of two years
- ○ Draft a quarter-by-quarter work plan tied to those goals
- ○ Get management support for the resources you need for the job
- ○ Set interim goals & milestones for regular reviews

Find Out More

Visit *www.GrowFedBiz.com* for bonus materials like:

- Government Contracts Made Easier: The Strategy Workbook
- Top Online Resources For All Seven Steps

Chapter Two: Focus

*I*n *the federal market, focus or go broke.*

Your best federal prospects are often related in some way to the best clients and contacts you have today. In truth, it is possible to win a federal opportunity by responding to a notice you see for the first time, from an agency where you've never done business, a few days before the deadline. But those wins are rare. Rather than pumping out proposals for people who have never heard of you, your time and money are almost always much better spent on research and calls to get to know those buyers long before they publish requirements. You want your *company to be the one they have in mind when requirements hit the street.*

What You'll Do In This Chapter:

- Define Your Core Competency
- Characterize Your Ideal Federal Buyer
- Find Your Target Federal Agencies
- Narrow The Field
- Review The Forecasts
- Draft Your Priority List

"Every week I get dozens of bid notices from federal agencies that need what we do.[1]! What's the matter with you? We're wasting time. Let's get bidding!"

Does this sound like someone you know? It's easy to get excited by the sheer magnitude of the opportunities. And no wonder! The constant message many small business owners hear is that federal buyers across the country are able, willing, and eager, to award work to small businesses. That message makes many people impatient with courses and books about federal contracting. They want to jump right into making proposals.

This story is typical of what happens when you do that:

A business owner once told me she had won her first government contract. After I congratulated her, I asked her how many proposals she had made before her first win.

"Thirty-nine," she said with a triumphant smile.

I'm glad that I was momentarily too stunned to point out to her that the cost of winning included the cost of preparing the other 38 losing proposals.

Research[2] shows that successful federal contractors need to have the resources to stay in the game long enough to start winning more often. Here's what I mean:

- The average small business that is new to federal contracting bids three times before their first prime contract win. That's a 25% win rate.

- Experience and focus bring more success. Active contractors surveyed reported an average 55% win rate on prime contract proposals and 85% on subcontracting proposals.

Want a better-than-average win rate? Act like a winner. Winners know when to say, "No."

Have the courage, patience, confidence, and savvy, to pass on a bid where you don't know the buyer, the budget, the incumbent, and the project history. If this really is your ideal federal agency, and you've stumbled into a large-dollar-value solicitation on no notice, odds are good that they're still going to need what you do after that particular requirement has been awarded...and poor that you'll win if they've never heard of you. Instead, do some more research and uncover the players at all the layers of that acquisition. Start to get to know them for the next time around. We'll talk more about how to begin those conversations in Chapter Six, *Relationships*.

---

1   FedBizOpps.gov, the federal publication of record for contract opportunities, will be migrating into an application domain called "Contract Opportunities" on *www.beta.SAM.gov* . This site will become *www.SAM.gov* once the migration project is complete, which is forecast to be late 2020. Keep reading for more details. I'll get to that.

2   2013 OPEN for Government Contracts Survey: Trends in Federal Contracting for Small Businesses

Even if you say, "Oh, I only want to subcontract," well... prime contractors behave much like their federal buyers. And they are almost as risk averse. They expect you to arrive with a clear understanding of which of *their* customers already know you and like you, and how much you know about specific federal buyers, their problems, and how you solve the problems those federal buyers have. (We'll talk more about what primes expect from you in Chapter Five, *Teaming*.)

Long before the RFP comes out, winners pinpoint the people, in a specific agency and program and office, who have the need and the funding and the authority to say, "Yes. Let's do business," and get to know them.

Success in government contracting comes from building relationships with government buyers who get to know you so well that they realize they can't imagine life without you.

"Well, okay," you say. "But I can't do that with everybody!"

No. You can't. If you want to be successful, you won't try to. *"Everybody" isn't your customer.*

Please, please, please: do *not* get seduced by Contract Opportunities. Stop crawling around there, hunting for solicitations and writing as many proposals as you can. For now, the only way I want you to use Contract Opportunities is as a market research tool. DO NOT BID ON ANYTHING YET. If you are already churning out proposals based purely on federal bid notices, STOP NOW.

When I teach, I often ask the class: "Hands up, everyone who has ever submitted a proposal in response to something they saw for the first time as an RFP online... when you haven't met the buyer, you don't know the incumbent, you don't know the budget, you don't know the problem they're trying to solve, and you don't know what's driving the requirement."

There are always a few hands.

"And hands up if you've ever won that job."

Very few hands remain.

"And roughly what percentage of the time does that happen – how often do you win when you're bidding on something like that?"

The answers? Five percent, tops. Those wins are usually for lower-dollar-value requirements, particularly for off-the-shelf products or easily defined services.

You might think, *if I could win twenty percent of the time, that wouldn't be bad.* Remember: the cost of winning ONE includes all the time and money you spent on the FOUR you lost. Eighty percent of your effort has very little payoff.

Professional federal-proposal writers (yes, there is such a profession) have win rates greater than 85%. They get that good in part by saying "no." They get that high win rate by only bidding on opportunities that experience tells them the client has a high probability of winning.

If the first time you hear about your perfect project from your dream client is when it's posted online less than 30 days before bid deadline, chances are good that you don't know enough about the project to win.

SECRETS OF THE PROS

- Create – and use -- a Bid / No-Bid Checklist.

- Keep fine-tuning your checklist based on your experience. What do your wins (for the sweet-spot jobs, not the ones you wish you hadn't won) have in common? Look for those factors when you're evaluating good fit.

- What do the jobs you LOSE have in common? Why did you lose? If you can't fix those faults, then requirements you can't meet are warning signs that suggest high risk of loss.

It's rare to win a prime contract through a competition when the only thing you know about the requirement is what's in the published RFP. That's especially true if you have no past performance relevant to the project you're bidding on.

So why *would* a company submit a proposal when they know only what's published in the solicitation? Business owners often tell me:

> "To put our hat in the ring."

> "To let people get to know us."

> "To meet people at the debriefing."

> "You can't win what you don't bid."

Continuous bidding to buyers and agencies where you don't know anyone is an expensive way to market. A single major proposal can cost you over $65,000 in time and sweat equity. The theory of "hat in the ring" is based on the idea that if you bid unsuccessfully, the buying officials are required and even interested in meeting with you afterward.

The reality is that's not so. (How unfortunate to see a beautiful theory mugged by an ugly gang of facts.) For starters, not every competition requires a debriefing.[3] There's no guarantee either that you'll get a post-bid meeting of any kind, or that, if you get one, that meeting will include everything and everyone you want to know.

---

3   Read more about debriefings in the next chapter.

Unsuccessful proposals are an inevitable cost of federal business. Yes, you will write some proposals for people you haven't met. And even when you *do* have lots of customer insight, you can still expect to write – and lose – a couple of proposals for buyers who like you, but haven't yet done business with you, before they first award a contract to you.

Suggestion: you can minimize that inevitable cost, especially when you're getting started. Put your time and money into researching, and building relationships in, a select few agencies where your prospects are strongest. You'll protect your profit, as you're getting started, by making conservative bid / no-bid decisions. You'll boost your revenue when you win more of what you do bid.

As you grow, and establish track record in a couple of agencies, you may reach a point where you win a contract that puts your company in a limited pool of pre-selected vendors who are always invited to bid on a steady stream of task-order requirements. At that point, you'll need a separate bid strategy just for those situations, when success requires you to respond fast, with minimum cost, to the maximum number of jobs you can perform well.

SOME TERMS YOU NEED TO KNOW

- Prime Contractor (or "Prime"): A vendor that holds a contract, signed by a warranted federal contracting officer, that defines the terms and conditions under which the prime agrees to provide the government with specific goods and/or services.

- Subcontractor (or "Sub"): A company bound by a contract that defines the terms and conditions under which the sub agrees to provide a prime contractor with specific goods and services that the prime in turn uses to meet the government's needs on its own prime contract. The subcontract agreement usually mirrors at least some of the provisions of the prime contract with the government customer.

- Supplier: A company that provides goods or services to its own customer, but those goods and services are not direct inputs to the performance of the government prime contract. For example, a company that provides internal audit services unrelated to any specific contract to a prime contractor would be part of that prime's general overhead, not a subcontractor.

- Past Performance: experience in delivering the product or service you're proposing. The strongest, most credible past performance to cite is as a prime. But past performance can be at any level of contracting, prime or subcontractor, in the government realm. And, finally, if your only experience is as a supplier outside government contracts, then you can cite THAT as your past performance.

Suit Up, Everybody

It's time to give you some protective gear, in the form of intelligent questions and substantive sources to answer them, before you venture out onto one of the most deceptively dangerous business battlefields in the world: "Contract Opportunities."

The next time somebody – especially a federal official – answers your question about opportunities in their agency by saying, "It's all online," or "It's all on SAM. gov," realize that they're speaking in code. What they're *really* saying is, "I'm not going to tell you anything more useful until you ask more intelligent questions."

At that point, if you *have* done your research into what that agency does and how they buy, and have the opportunity to follow up, that's your cue to ask *one* intelligent question. Their response will show you whether they're willing – or able – to offer you more.

If you *haven't* done that research, or have no idea what to ask next, just smile politely and say, "Thank you." You can certainly ask for a business card and follow up when you have something more specific. You'll avoid the public embarrassment of showing everyone around you how little you know.

Furthermore, the next time a federal buyer says, "That's not how the government does it…" remember that what they're really saying is "That's not how *I* do it." Hundreds of acquisition regulations give each contracting officer tremendous discretion to choose among dozens of options to make purchases and award contracts. To be successful, you'll get to know how each individual buyer likes to do business…and make it easy for them to reach you the way that person likes best.

If you're thinking, "Every minute I sit here reading this, there are dozens of new RFP's being published. They're perfect for us. I want to get going!" that's the voice of scarcity talking. If your big call to action is the fear of missing opportunities, pause a moment to consider how that balances against your fear of missing cashflow.

Not concerned? Got oodles of cash? Okay, off you go, into one of the world's most competitive business arenas, armed with everything you know right this minute. Have a great time, and don't forget to write (proposals, not postcards).

Our kit includes gear for intelligence, communications, protection, defense, and capture. But also subtle, persistent tactics to build relationships. Success come not just from the gear…but in using it the right way.

Part 1: Define Your Core Offering

What will you sell to your federal buyer? If your company already has a tightly focused offering, that's easy. But a surprising number of companies – both large and small – that have grown their revenue and customer base over the years have ended up with an ever-expanding sprawl of offerings. If that diversity of offerings represents a "one-stop shop" or vertically-integrated supply chain, great. Often, that's not the case.

When you're selling to government, someone is always asking you about your core capability. Your answer needs to center on the problem you solve best, for clients with whom you've earned a track record doing just that. In other words, the products or services that drive the best results for your best clients today are your best choices to offer a federal prospect you'd like to win.

When you're starting out, you may feel your experience is not as strong as you'd like it to be. If, as a result, you're tempted to respond with a long list of all the things your company does, you're not alone.

You'll be more likely to engage the right people with a *short* list focused on things you do well and that matter to those ideal prospects. The point of defining your core competency narrowly in this step is not to limit your possibilities for profit. Nobody wants to limit you! The idea is to *focus your effort on the business you are most likely to win*. That lowers your cost of pursuit, and increases your profit when you *do* win.

"But wait," you say. "My company has much more capability than that!"

"Capability" isn't the same thing as "Competency." Capability means you *could* do something: you've got all the parts, but you might not have shown that you *can* do it. Core Competency is where Capability meets Past Performance: you've *shown* that you can do it – and do it very well.

A lengthy list actually marks you as a novice. Someone who "does everything" specializes in nothing, and drives away exactly the people you're trying to impress, especially at a first meeting. Worse yet, people have short attention spans: by the time you get to the thing they might care about, they may have long since stopped listening.

Why don't they want to hear the long list? It's not their job to figure out where you fit in their universe: it's up to *you* to understand them well enough to communicate why you matter to them. Even if you truly ARE good at a lot of things, solid research will help you focus your conversations on what's most important to your prospect… and the reason why that person will keep you top of mind.

Cracking the Code

My favorite kind of research is taking people to lunch. In this case, it was a breakfast, and it was with Nick Wakeman, then a senior editor at Washington Technology. He was talking about how to open doors to meet the senior military brass. This was something I definitely wanted to be able to tell my clients about, so I was taking notes.

"It's easy," he said. "The General told me, 'I always have twenty minutes to hear a company's capability brief.'"

I put down my pen. "Wait a minute," I said. "I want to be sure I heard this right: I can call up his office and just get an appointment because the General's going to give up twenty minutes to hear my capability brief?"

"No," said Nick. "You didn't hear me. The General said, 'I always have twenty minutes for someone who *can solve my problem*.'"

I've heard federal vendors' capability presentations that could be summed up: "Here is what *I* do! How could you use me? Call me if you want some." The vendors who make those presentations are often puzzled and frustrated when buyers and primes never call back. Your government buyer doesn't have time to figure it out for you. You can also bet your bottom dollar that they're not sitting around listening to your capability presentation thinking, "Wow, this sure is interesting; where could I use something like that?" They've got too many other things to do.

In other words, your government buyer, the first time they buy from you, will choose you to solve *one* problem. That is, if they are confident you can do it.

Contracting officers are under pressure to compete every requirement, and to give lots of opportunities to small business. Yet in 2018, 25% fewer vendors were winning contracts than in 2010. You'd think buyers would welcome new vendors. Here's the reality: if they've never heard of you before, when you walk through the door, all they see is a great big ball of risk.

They don't like risk. Federal buyers don't like it, and prime contractors like it even less.

You might expect that government buyers would want to work with the vendors with the best offerings and prices in town. Yet they are some of the most risk-averse customers in the world. So they're often quietly reluctant to consider you as a new vendor, at any price.

What breaks down their risk aversion? Past Performance. When a government buyer (or prime contractor) says, "Tell me about what you do," what they're really asking is, "Show me how you've solved a problem a lot like mine, for someone who looks a lot like me, yesterday afternoon."

What products or services represent your top-performing offerings – the ones that your top clients buy most, that represent your best performance, that generate meaningful profit, and that are the reason why your company is in business?

Go back to that list of sweet-spot clients. Your records show the products or services they bought from you. That list represents your candidate core competencies. You'll narrow that down further based on the top priorities of your federal prospects.

Review and, if need be, edit, your profile in SAM.gov to make sure it includes the North American Industrial Classification System (NAICS) codes and Product Service Codes (PSCs) that you consider best correspond to those products and services. You'll refine those in Step 4, Competition, but, for now, these represent your sweet-spot offerings.

Part 2: Characterize Your Ideal Federal Buyer

We'll start by doing this qualitatively, and then refine it quantitatively.

Buyers matter because there's no such thing as doing business with "the government." You're doing business with *people*. Individual buyers, program managers, and contracting officers draft the Statements of Work, Requirements Packages, specifications, performance work statements, and evaluation criteria they'll use to choose their vendors. They develop those based on factors that include their own research, field experience, budgets, and needs for inter-agency coordination...as well as what they learn from, and the trust they develop for, their vendors.

Whether you sell a service or a product, you *must* be able to identify *which government buyers are most similar to your sweet-spot clients today.*

Long before a formal competition begins, you need to find and get to know the buyers who are (or could be) most keen for what YOU have to offer. Even – and especially – when they're already doing business with your competitors.

Here's how to find your answer.

Ask yourself: Who are the clients you love to serve in your business *today* – your most ideal customers so far?[4] Those clients might be commercial customers, or in state or local government. Maybe they're in a different federal agency from the one where you want to win work; maybe the same one. Whether the work was as a prime or a subcontractor, pick the ones you've had good experiences in serving.

List them. Don't worry if the list isn't very long. Look at what have in common. For example, maybe:

- They're a long-time / repeat customer.
- Your profit margins are good.
- They come back for more and grow their business with you.
- They pay you on time.
- They refer their friends.
- At the end of the job, you and your team can say, "YES, this is what we're here for."

Then look at what your current sweet-spot clients have in common. For example, maybe:

- Their industry: maybe they're in financial services, or health care, or construction, or social services. What's the mission or purpose of your core clients' organizations?
- They tend to be concentrated in a geographic area or region: where?
- You solve similar problems for them. How would you characterize that?
- The projects or orders are of a similar magnitude. How big?
- Their first contract or order is for...what?

That leads you to the key question: Which federal agencies, locations, offices, might have the most in common – in terms of mission, location, size, scale, and scope -- with your best clients today? Write down your best guess. That'll help you narrow down your choices in the next step.

---

4   If you've never considered who your company's perfect clients would be, take a look at a great book that's JUST about this: *Attracting Perfect Customers*, by Stacey Hall and Jan Brogniez.

Finding Your Target Federal Agencies

You need to know:

- What's your target customer's mission?
  Every federal Department publishes its mission (and much more) on its web site. Buyers from each Department will expect you to have read that information, and to be intimately familiar with it, long before you come calling.

  Why? Because if you don't have time to learn about them, they definitely don't have time to learn about *you.*

- What specific programs does the Department run?
  Now that you've thought about which Departments have a mission that your products or services can support, you need to find out how each of those Departments is organized. What programs do they run? Who manages them?

- How big is the program?
  Maybe you define your sweet spot in terms of scale: if you know you can handle a project that requires up to 50 of your people, you're not going to look for anything bigger than that. And what's your surge capacity? If you were suddenly faced with the prospect of serving another client as big as your current biggest client, how quickly could you staff up, or how fast could you ramp up production to deliver a big order? While government purchasing can seem to take forever, government buyers often want immediate delivery once they choose a vendor.

- What are their problems and challenges?

  › Mission-specific factors?

  › Scaling up for an expanded mission?

  › Delivering a mission despite budget cuts?

  › Recent criticism?

- How would they benefit from solving those problems?
  What function, capability, unique characteristics, benefits, or results will someone get when they do business with you? What will get better for them?

- What products and services do they buy in order to do that job?
  What have they been buying, and what do they plan to buy?

- Who are the players at every layer?
  Just as you don't "sell to the government," you don't "sell to the Marine

Corps" either. A human being puts their signature on that contract with you...and their career is on the line every time they do. In fact, there are *five* people you need to meet, in every agency, for every opportunity that arises. We'll meet them in Chapter Six, Relationships.

How Opportunities Rise From Relationships

Let's say Sarah retired from the Marine Corps as a logistician after two tours of duty in Afghanistan. She's kept in touch with her buddy Jada, a reservist with the National Guard. Last time they got together, Jada was telling her that in a recent disaster-response situation, the Guard units needed to set up a command post in a new location but there were never enough generators to go around, particularly to power wide-area lighting either indoors or outdoors.

That got Sarah's attention. Today, Sarah works for a company that supplies rugged, lightweight, high-lumen portable lighting systems powered by featherweight rechargeable solar batteries. Those lights would be ideal to improve perimeter security and operational readiness.

Jada knows incident commanders who would be keen to try a proven, reliable system. And Sarah knows they'll want to see some track record in training environments first. Sarah's next move is to follow up with the Industry Liaison director at the National Guard Association for advice on how to get a couple of demonstration projects going to support her marketing.

Start thinking about federal agencies and buyers in terms of:

- the jobs they do (their missions); and

- the products and services they need to serve citizens and deliver those missions.

Think every agency needs what you do? How can you narrow your focus?

Before your first proposal, I want you to know four Winner's Secrets:

1. How you can get in on the action long before the formal competition opens;

2. How much these buyers spend every year on what you do;

3. What their buying plans are; and

4. How to focus on prospects that you can actually develop and win.

The exercises coming up will give you the answers.

EXERCISE ONE: FOCUS with USA.GOV

- **What it is:** As if the federal government were all in one office building, and gave you access to all the federal departments' basic information at once.

- **Why it's useful:** Whether you want to refresh your memory about whether the Forest Service is part of the Department of Agriculture or the Department of the Interior or find out what the Department of Energy really does, *www.usa.gov* is your starting point.

- **Where to go:** Right up top, under "Government Agencies and Elected Officials," are options for "A-Z Index of U.S. Government Agencies," plus links to state, local, and tribal governments.

- **What to do:** Select for "A-Z Index of U.S. Government Agencies." Choose a department that you think offers you some good prospects. Go to that agency's web site; search the site for their mission. How does your offering support that mission? If you don't know what an agency does, this is a perfect time to read their web site and learn more.

  While you're at it, take a few minutes to explore your own state and local links, too. Your best opportunities might be in your own backyard.

- List the agencies you think you could serve, and their missions.

- For the top three to five agencies on your list, dig deeper. In each agency, go online and drill down to pick no more than three programs among their various bureaus, offices, or commands that you think have the best fit with what you could do for them.

- Remember to look past Washington DC. What buyers are located near you? What about buyers in cities where you are already spending time and money traveling for business today?

- Sort your list into priority order (top prospects first), based both on who's spending and on how likely you are to spend time where they are.

PROFILE IN SUCCESS: Neeld Wilson

Service-disabled Navy veteran Neeld Wilson, the President and aquifer engineer of GEAR Engineering in Orlando, was frustrated! He had heard all about how government agencies had a commitment to award more contracts to veteran-owned business. So he set out to focus on winning government contracts to grow his company.

He set out across the southeast, investing over $60,000 of working capital to attend small business procurement conferences and meetings. Military and civilian agency reps all told him, "Yes, we love veteran-owned business! We want to do business with you!" By September, he had racked up thousands of miles…and a whole lot of nothing.

"That was my profit for the whole year," Neeld said to me. "What can I do?"

In short, being a veteran-owned business wasn't a strategy.

When we looked at his strategy, it was clear that his first big challenge was FOCUS. He'd been traveling far and wide, but not spending enough time and effort in any one place to develop relationships with specific buyers who needed his company's services.

After I suggested he focus more tightly, Neeld realized that, back in Orlando, there were some high-potential buyers really close to home. He picked just four of them, and called on them again…and again…and again.

After a few months, he said, "Our challenge was breaking into the federal marketplace, and although I did not want to hear the things I needed to do to get into the marketplace… (I'm) now submitting multiple bids, getting phone calls from large businesses wanting to work with small businesses, and being personally invited by federal folks to come visit them."

Nine months later, in one day, he was awarded his first two federal contracts, one prime and one subcontract, together worth nearly $500,000.

Research and focus turn effort into relationships and wins. Here are the basics.

FREE FEDERAL CONTRACTING MARKET INTELLIGENCE TOOLS

The General Service Administration's (GSA) Office of the Integrated Award Environment (IAE) administers ten federal procurement and awards processes that are used by people who make, receive, and manage these programs. Prior to 2019, these systems were:

- **CFDA.gov** (*Catalog of Federal Domestic Assistance*)

- **SAM.gov** (*System for Award Management*)

- **FBO.gov** (*Federal Business Opportunities*)

- **FPDS-NG.gov** (*Federal Procurement Data System - Next Generation*)

- **WDOL.gov** (*Wage Determinations OnLine*)

- **eSRS.gov** (*Electronic Subcontracting Reporting System*)

- **FAPIIS.gov** (*Federal Awardee Performance and Integrity Information System*)

- **FSRS.gov** (*Federal Funding Accountability and Transparency Act Subaward Reporting System*)

- **CPARS.gov** (*Contractor Performance Assessment Reporting System*)

- **PPIRS.gov** (*Past Performance Information Retrieval System*)

To streamline processes and eliminate the need to enter the same data multiple times, GSA is consolidating the information and functions of these ten systems into a single platform, eliminating data overlap while sharing the data across the award lifecycle.

The Office of the IAE is merging these ten "legacy" sites into one system—the System for Award Management. A single homepage and single sign-on will open comprehensive search tools across multiple applications. A single reporting tool and workspace will give users access to the information they need to make, receive, and manage federal funding awards for contracts and other programs.

You can see – and, as they are ready, begin to use – the successor applications at *http://www.beta.SAM.gov.* Once the migration is complete, users will have access to the functions and data provided on the legacy sites through the home page *www.SAM.gov.*

This system migration has a planned completion date of late 2020. Old and new systems will run in parallel until the new system is approved for cutover and the old one decommissioned. Until transition is complete, you can check the project status at *https://beta.SAM.gov/help/whats-next*.

Key transitions on "New SAM"

Once the migration is complete, what were once separate websites will become applications on the new platform. Publicly available data from seven legacy systems and reference information will be accessible through their corresponding successor application domains:

- SAM.gov (*System for Award Management*) – Entity Information

- FBO.gov (*Federal Business Opportunities*) – Contract Opportunities

- FPDS-NG.gov (*Federal Procurement Data System - Next Generation*)– Contract Data

- CFDA (*Catalog of Federal Domestic Assistance*) – Assistance Listings

- WDOL – Wage Determinations

- CPARS – Past Performance

- eSRS – Sub-Awards

- FPDS Organization Data – Federal Hierarchy

Okay, it's time. Let's meet Contract Opportunities...carefully.

Introduction to Contract Opportunities

- Yes, Contract Opportunities is the "publication of record" in U.S. federal procurement. Competitive opportunities estimated to be worth more than $25,000 are supposed to be published there.

- Published opportunities (also called "Solicitations") take many forms. Some solicitations launch competitions of various kinds. Others announce pre-competition activities that are critical to success on the formal competition. You'll read more about those in Chapter Three: Process.

- Free opportunities sent right to you: Contract Opportunities lets you set up a profile to receive electronic notices of federal opportunities that fit your criteria. Be aware: several companies offer paid subscription services to send you this same information for a fee. The federal government does not charge for this data feed. To set up your own free feed, follow the user instructions on the web site. *Time Investment: 30 minutes*

Secrets of Contract Opportunities:
Get In On The Action Before The Competition Starts

Government buyers do a lot of work before the formal competition – not only to develop requirements, but also to make sure they're asking for something vendors can actually deliver. None of these activities promise that there will be a procurement. But if you DO respond, and if the buyers like what you offer, they may very well consider your unique capabilities and write the statement of work or requirement definition in a way that favors your company.

Participation in these pre-solicitation activities is vital to position your company to win. To put it another way, if you've competed unsuccessfully on an opportunity, and wondered if the solicitation was "wired" for your competitors, consider that those competitors may simply have been marketing long before the RFP came out. That marketing might have resulted in a statement of work or a requirements definition that included some key words that uniquely described their approach or product, though often without naming the company or product specifically!

Sharp marketers find ways to get buyers to specify some unique aspect of their products or services without necessarily mentioning the item or company by name. That's a perfectly legitimate way to market. You can do it too, by participating in:

- **Request for Information (RFI):** Agencies use these for market research, to find out (before competition begins) about vendors' abilities to meet the buyer's needs. RFIs help buyers learn whether the requirement can be met by items already sold in the commercial market, and about the practices and standards of the firms, businesses, or organizations that would respond to the requirement.

- **Sources Sought:** These are used as an advance notice of buyers' interest when market research efforts suggest that there aren't enough qualified companies to create adequate competition. They're also used to help contracting officers find out whether there are enough small businesses to merit setting aside the contract for small (or 8(a) or woman-owned or HUBZone or Service-Disabled Veteran-Owned) vendors. (We'll talk more about these set-asides in Chapter 3, Process.)

  Sources Sought notices give vendors a heads-up about potential opportunities, and open the door for you to submit information that will let buyers evaluate your capabilities – in other words, to influence the specification that may be developed. Sources who respond are usually added to the appropriate solicitation mailing list.

- **Draft RFPs:** Agency buyers issue Draft RFPs to get vendors' feedback on whether the anticipated requirements and procurement process are defined in a way that encourages fair and open competition, and are sufficiently specific that vendors will be able to respond.

Sometimes buying agencies will hold a pre-bid conference or Industry Day to discuss the draft RFP. Sometimes notices for those events are published in Contract Opportunities on beta.SAM.gov; other times, just the companies who took part in other pre-solicitation activities are invited.

Even though you've heard me discourage you from responding to every RFP that comes along, I want you to think about responding, *selectively*, to these pre-solicitation opportunities.

Why?

Because if you let government buyers know that you're capable of meeting their requirement, you are more likely to get invited to participate. You can influence how the final requirement is defined, which strengthens your competitive position. And if your company is eligible for federal contracting preferences or set-asides, and fits the requirement, you *really* want to be sure to respond. That way, the contracting officer knows there are enough capable small businesses to warrant a set-aside.

"What if I can meet some, but not all, of the requirements?" people ask. At the very least, that's still a chance for relationship-building with both the buyers and potential partners. Ask the point of contact, according to the process specified in the notice, for clarification.

- Pay attention to how the notice is worded. If it says, "Only respond if you can meet all the requirements," then act accordingly. If you submit something that explicitly doesn't qualify , despite the instructions you've been given, the contracting officer gets a poor impression of your company.

- If the notice *doesn't* specify whether they'll accept a partial response, then check with the point of contact about whether they would welcome your response anyway.

- If you meet some but not all of the mandatory requirements, then

  › research partners whose capabilities complement yours, and with whom you might team.

  › get in touch with the point of contact listed in the pre-solicitation notice and begin to build a relationship. Start by explaining that you know you don't meet these requirements, but you wonder whether they might be willing for you to get to know each other for related future requirements. Work up to asking for recommendations of other people they think might want to meet you, including both federal buyers as well as other incumbent vendors they trust who might be potential teaming partners.

EXERCISE TWO: Browsing Pre-Solicitation Activities

Time Investment: 30 minutes

Why do this: To find out about opportunities, and how you might position to win, before the competition opens

Where to go: *beta.SAM.gov* or *www.SAM.gov*

What to do:

1. Set your search criteria fairly broadly at first. Enter in the windows or drop-downs one or more of:

   › Keywords: choose a few related to your core capabilities; and

   › Type: choose "Pre-solicitation" or "Sources Sought." That will show the items we talked about a moment ago: Requests for Information, Draft RFPs, and Sources Sought.

2. Review the results of your searches. Are you finding a lot...or not many? Narrow or expand your search terms as need be. Which terms consistently bring up opportunities that might be the best fit for your company?

3. If you're not finding much...relax. First, this isn't the only place to find opportunities! What would a federal buyer be purchasing before, or after, they needed services or products like yours? If a federal buyer were buying from one of your competitors, what might they be purchasing? Try searching on these "shadow" terms, and see what comes up.

4. Which opportunities are in agencies you know well, where you have relationships? Agencies where you have relationships, or have friends who can introduce you, might be good starting points.

   If you have *no* relationships with people in federal agencies, here's the easy way to begin. Pick out any pre-solicitation opportunity that looks attractive. Read it right to the end. You'll find a *point of contact*: usually a name, title, and either or both an email address and phone number. This is often your first clue to the set of people you'll need to meet in that buying organization.

5. Keep going. Who are *all* the people who buy what you do? When you keep combing through the notices, you'll start seeing the same names come up, over and over. Start building your list of the people you probably want to get to know.

6. If you were totally committed to the federal market, which opportunities would you respond to? Pick out the five or six pre-solicitation opportunities that are most attractive. Why did you choose those? How much time

and resources would it take you to respond to each? Who in your company would write the responses?

7. Select notices and opportunities you want the system to follow, and how often you want to receive notifications about each. Remember, this notification system is free! You don't need to pay for a bid-matching service or a consultant to do this for you.

What Next:

- Remember, this is a research exercise. If the only thing you know about the opportunity is what you see in the solicitation notice, then you don't yet know enough about the opportunity to submit a proposal.

  Consider getting help from your nearby Procurement Technical Assistance Center (PTAC) with your research. Find yours at *www.aptac-us.org*. Their help is free or low cost, and trained teams offer counseling, contacts, and courses in federal, state, and local government contracting.

Part 3: Narrow the Field – Where Your Sweet Spot Hits Buyers' Hot Spot

Now you're looking to find where your sweet spot (as expressed in combination of your key words, North American Industrial Classification System (NAICS) codes and Product Service Codes (PSCs) meets government buyers' hot spot (where they have already spent money, and will spend more).

"HOW BIG IS THE MARKET FOR WHAT I DO?"

It's a legitimate question, but the top-line answer isn't very useful. How different is your strategy if the answer is a billion dollars, $40 billion, or $400 billion? Once you've established that the government buys what you offer, you need the details.

Who's buying? How much are they buying? How are they buying? Who are they buying from?

In the commercial market, companies spend thousands of dollars on market research to identify competitors, buyers, and who's buying and selling how much. It's hard to find out exactly how much the market is worth, the identity of the top-ranked buyers, the position of the key vendors, and when current contracts expire.

One of the fabulous things about federal contracting is that public money means public information. Government publishes its past spending and procurement plans as well as its competitions and contract awards.

Imagine what you can do with that information! With answers to those questions, you could:

- Identify your main competitors...and potential teaming partners.

- Find out how much money your top-priority agencies spend on the things you do.

- Start to research potential opportunities, long before even pre-solicitation notices get published!

EXERCISE THREE: Know How Much These Buyers Spend Every Year On What You Do

In the federal market, that information is available to you free, online, right now. Because this is the most valuable free business research tool in the federal market, and it's about to change, grab the quick video tour I've left for you on my web site, at www.growfedbiz.com with the search term "Contract-Data"

Where to go: _www.fpds.gov_, migrating to https://beta.SAM.gov, where you'll select "Contract Data"

What you'll do: Research Past Contract Awards

Time investment: 30 minutes

Did you know?

The federal government collects and publishes – online, no charge, 24/7 – over 250 pieces of data on every federal government purchase against a contract worth more than $10,000, going back well over ten years!

Why is this helpful?

1. You can find out the market size, and identify the top buyers, for products and services similar or related to yours.

2. You can find out which departments are buying from which vendors, and who's purchasing how much.

3. When you view the individual contract data, you get contact information on the vendor. That's especially useful if you want to explore teaming.

How to start: Enter the key words that relate to your product or service.

Once the search results come up, go in and fool around. Seriously. Point, click, let your curiosity go wild. You can't break it, and you're going to find your 30-minute intro tour just flies by!

Look at your options for output:

- You can scroll through and drill down into individual contract details.

- If you want to see the patterns in the data (like who's buying how much, from whom, how often, and using what contract vehicles, for instance) use the export options to output to Excel and go at it offline.

What to look for: Remember that "Agency" can be a single organization (e.g., the Small Business Administration), or a part of a larger department (e.g., the Federal Bureau of Investigation within the Department of Justice, or Customs and Border Protection within the Department of Homeland Security).

Tips:

- After you've satisfied (or whetted) your curiosity about this one contract, I recommend that at this point you export your search results to Excel.

- More detail takes more work, whether you do it yourself or get help from a Procurement Technical Assistance Centers (PTAC) or consultant. You will get the most valuable intelligence by downloading the full set of contract data and then analyzing the buyer patterns by using pivot tables.

- Understand what you're looking at. The user manual also includes the data definitions of all the data.

- Look at data from the last few fiscal years. Is spending rising or falling for products or services like yours?

- Unless you're searching for info on a specific recent action, make sure your market research includes both the current fiscal year to date *and all* of the fiscal year most recently completed.

Remember, *a disproportionate amount* of buying gets done in July through September, so if you select only the current fiscal year's data, you won't get the full picture of agency buying. Also, while contract data is supposed to be entered all year long, as buying takes place, DoD may delay publication of its purchasing data a minimum of 90 days to protect information about operations tempo. (In other words, the military isn't keen on somebody counting up their cash-register receipts, looking at what they bought, and deciding they're provisioning for an outing.)

What next?

- Review contract expiry dates. Working backward, you can estimate when contracting offices and buyers might be starting to think about the follow-on competition to renew or extend their supply or service.

- If you see a contract expiring in the future for an opportunity you'd like to pursue, start to research the network of contacts involved in that buying decision. Check the buying agency's forecasts to find out about their plans.

- Again, many PTACs will help you to do this free of charge. Find yours at *www.aptac-us.org*.

Research Results Summary Worksheet

	Product/Service Keyword1	Product/Service Keyword 2 …
	$ % share	$ % share
Prospect Agency 1		
Prospect Agency 2		
Prospect Agency 3 …		

How to choose which agencies to focus on? Look beyond the big spenders. The best opportunities might not be just in the agency that spends the most money on what you offer. A few other considerations:

- People do business with people they like. Look at the buying patterns in agencies where you have some contacts or past performance already.

- Don't get lured by the big top-line spend. The agency that spends less than top dollar might also have the greatest need for what you do. A smaller agency might also mean there is less competition, and it may be easier to navigate contacts and build relationships.

- Your best prospects may be closer than you think. Who's spending the most in cities, states, or offices close to where you are located? Buyers who have met you and gotten to know you are more likely to choose you.

- Which competitors are already doing business with your target agencies in locations near you?

- Pick no more than three Departments to focus on, based on your sweet spot and their spending. In large Departments like Defense (DoD) or Health and Human Services (HHS) or Homeland Security (DHS), focus even more tightly. You might find plenty of opportunity in just one component like National Institutes of Health (NIH) within HHS, or Customs and Border Protection and the Coast Guard within DHS. Remember that every agency you choose represents a commitment on your part to literally thousands of dollars and months of time to develop relationships ahead of requirements. You can only do that effectively in a few agencies. Go narrow, go deep.

These are the agencies where you can expect to spend your time and effort, developing initial small opportunities (including micro-purchase and simplified acquisition, which we're about to cover in Chapter 3, Process) and getting to know the people you need to meet, which we'll talk about more in Chapter 6, Relationships, and Chapter 7, Marketing and Sales.

Part 4: Review the Forecasts – How to Follow the Money

Why go through all this work? Because that's how people find out about opportunities *before* they're published online. It's more productive to invest time in narrowing your search than to write dozens of proposals for projects you know nothing about and have no hope of winning.

Did you know?

- Most federal agencies publish acquisition forecasts online, and revise those forecasts at least a couple of times a year. Link to them from *https://acquisition.gov.procurement-forecasts* .

- These forecasts list planned acquisitions months or sometimes years in advance of the formal start of the acquisition process (about which more in Chapter 3, Process).

- The forecasts might not include anything specific to what you do. Don't panic! Read the list again, and consider which forecast items might suggest the buyer would need what you do in order to carry out that project...or might need what you do after that project is completed.

- Just as important as the forecast of purchasing is the contact information posted alongside the planned project. You'll want to follow up with the person who's listed there, and not only to check the current status of a project you want to bid. You can also ask them who else you might ask about similar opportunities coming up that haven't yet been published.

- The most current information about a specific acquisition nearly always comes from following up within a personal relationship, whether with the agency small business specialist, program officials, or your own friends and network.

- Even if the agency forecast is not comprehensive, the Congress must pass the bill that funds the agencies' programs. Searching the agencies' Fiscal Authorization, frankly, is no fun and takes a lot of time, but it's a lot easier to do once you know which of the agencies' programs you're focused on. (More about this in Chapter 3, Process.)

- Some agencies' forecasts focus just on opportunities that the buyers intend to award to small business. Others aim to publish their whole procurement plan.

- And top-level military service departments (Army, Navy, Air Force) are too large to publish a comprehensive forecast. Most often, you have to search the small business forecast at the level of individual program or command or military base.

  › On the other hand, the Department of Homeland Security publishes as much of their buying plans as they can, set-asides and beyond.

  › The General Services Administration has said that their small business forecast includes planned solicitations for purchases of goods and services as well as projects managed by the GSA Public Buildings Service. They update it a couple times during the year. See *www.gsa.gov/smbusforecast.*

EXERCISE FOUR: Acquisition Forecasts

Finding their buying plans for the current fiscal year

Time investment: 30 minutes

Why is this helpful?

If you look up the forecasts, you can focus your efforts on agencies that have money in the budget to buy what you've got. You can also pick out procurements planned as set-asides for preferences that your company qualifies for.

Where to go:

- DoD and the military services (Army, Navy, and Air Force) publishes separate acquisition forecasts, broken out by command or organization. Access those via *https:// business.defense.gov/small-business/acquisition-forecasts/.*

- For federal civilian departments and agencies, start at *https://www.acquisition.gov/procurement-forecasts* . If you don't find the forecast for the agency you're looking for there, then head over to that agency's web site and start with its Office of Small and Disadvantaged Business Utilization

What to look for: A forecast typically covers planned purchases worth more than $150,000, and includes:

- What products and services the agency plans to buy – description, NAICS code, and Product/Service Code (a system the government uses to classify procurement)

- How much they plan to spend on each purchase

- Who will do the buying – names, phone numbers, and emails

- When they plan to buy

- How they will seek vendors – the acquisition strategy or type of contract

- What kind(s) of small business preference(s) they plan to use

What next:

- Highlight the requirements you could meet – if the competition hasn't begun.

- Determine whether you could meet ALL those requirements, or whether you'd need to team.

- Go back to USASpending.gov and look up related past purchases the agency may have made, and who the current and recent past vendors are.

- Plan to attend the agency's small business outreach briefings to learn more about keys to successful business development with that agency.

- Get in touch with the published point of contact to set up a meeting to learn more about this specific procurement, explore related opportunities and ways to meet other key contacts, and present your capabilities and past performance.

Things to remember

- Forecasts are driven by the fiscal year. Federal agency buying forecasts are typically strongest – that is, most full of substantive information about opportunities that haven't yet been awarded and are far enough out that you can do pre-RFP marketing – in the *early* part of the fiscal year.

- There are no government-wide standards for procurement forecasts. Not all forecasts come out at the same time, are updated with equal regularity, or include the same information.

- While the government *encourages* agencies to publish procurement forecasts, particularly in support of achieving their small business contracting goals, agencies are not *required* to publish such forecasts. And they're not required to link their forecasts to the Acquisition Central website.

EXERCISE FIVE: Draft Your Priority List

Focusing on prospects that you can actually develop and win.

YOUR FORECASTING WORKSHEET

List potential opportunities from agency forecasts and budgets that may fit your sweet spot.

Agency	Project & Office / Location	Why It Fits Your Sweet Spot	Need to Team? Y / N	Project Value (Your share)	Key Competitors

GO / NO GO CRITERIA

When you decide to pursue one of these opportunities, you've also got to budget marketing money to go after the business. Every company that wants to win government business, large or small, prime or sub, has to make those decisions. If you don't put marketing resources behind your effort, you are not going to win. Period.

So there's a serious limit on the number of opportunities you can pursue at any one time. What's your limit, and how will you choose?

There are simply too many government contract opportunities to pursue them all. One of the major reasons why companies fail to win government contracts is because they spread their efforts so thinly across so many projects that they never make enough progress to win any single one of them.

Your company probably has a checklist for deciding whether or not to pursue an opportunity. That process saves time, encourages objectivity, and lowers conflict among team members grappling for limited marketing resources.

If you don't have such a checklist, then entering the government market is a really good time to set one up. Here's an example; as you can see, the point is just to have a consistent way of choosing what to go after and what to leave alone.

Criterion	Score (1 - 5)	Weight	Weighted Score	Maximum Possible
Past Performance with this client		5		25
Relationships with decision makers		4		20
Understanding of client needs & drivers		5		25
Knowledge of procurement process & budget		3		15
Past performance with this type & size of project		4		20
Presence / experience in project geographic region		3		15
Client perception of competitive differentiation		4		20
TOTAL SCORE				140

Next: Refer back to your strategy worksheets. How much government business did you aim to win – this year, next year, the year after that? And, based on your company's win record as you enter new markets, what value of business do you think you'll have to pursue in order to achieve those goals?

Now, choose potential projects that add up to that amount... bearing in mind your capacity and resources. If you can't afford to perform the contract, there's no point in pursuing it and no point in hoping to win it.

Based on that evaluation process, which projects do you want to win, and by when?

• How much performance capacity do you have – that is, how big a job can you do?

• How much money and person-time can you devote to pursue each project – whether you win or not?

• How much financing will you need (and be able to get) if you win? Remember, you must be able to afford to perform the work – to pay your people and pay for whatever other production inputs you need – *and* to stay in business until you get paid. No, the government check will not bounce, but you get paid after you perform, and after you invoice, and then sometime after that...even if all goes well.

- Choose milestones and decision points for Go / No-Go on each project

- It takes trial and error to figure out how many projects you have to put into the top of your pipeline to reach the goal you set for winning business. That ratio improves with experience.

Projects in Priority Order	Critical Activities Key Dates/Milestones	Capture Activities, Responsibility, Progress

If you've followed along and taken all the exercises in Chapter Two, it's probably taken you a lot longer than you expected. I guarantee that the time you invested in going through all this will save you thousands of dollars and months of time on the road ahead.

READY FOR THE NEXT STEP? FOCUS CHECKLIST

O Define Sweet Spot / Core Competency

O Find Government Buyers' Hot Spot: Who Buys That?

O Narrow The Field: Where Does Your Sweet Meet Their Hot?

O Review The Forecasts: What Will They Spend That YOU Could Win?

O Draft Your Priority List: What Can You Afford To Go After?

Resource Summary

• U.S. Government Top Level: *www.usa.gov*

• Federal Contract Notices: *www.beta.SAM.gov* and eventually *www.SAM.gov*

• Past Contract Awards: pre-migration, *www.fpds.gov* , post migration *www.beta.SAM.gov* or *www.SAM.gov,* select option for "Contract Data". *www.USASpending.gov* will give you award data but excludes contact data you'll need for lead generation.

• Buying Forecasts: *https://www.acquisition.gov/procurement-forecasts*

Chapter Three: Process

*G*overnment buyers have two problems: They need stuff – products, services, solutions. And they need an easy way to buy it. Winning vendors can get them the right stuff, right now. How many ways could a government buyer do business with you? Which of those is your shortest path to the sale? Success takes nailing the process: first, knowing the options your prospects can (and prefer to) use to do business with you, and, second, being set up to make it easy for them to buy from you.

This chapter gives you a practical introduction to things business owners need to know about the procurement process, some hands-on exercises to help you learn how to navigate, and suggestions for when you'll need to find out more and where to go to dig deeper.

What You'll Learn

- How to Follow the Money – From Congress to Contracts
  Where your prospect's money comes from and why you care
- Registrations, Certifications, and GSA Schedules
- How they differ, and what they're not
- Small Business Certifications and Preferences
- The Federal Acquisition Regulations: A Business Owner's Tour
- GSA Schedules: Hard Cold Facts
  › Seven Things You Must Know
  › Markers of GSA Schedule Success
  › Do You Need A GSA Schedule? How to tell

What You Really Need To Know About the Process... and Why

Federal procurement rules protect the interests of the *buyer* first and foremost. Your interests as a vendor aren't always the same as your buyer's. But think about it from your buyer's point of view. Who would you rather do business with: someone who's keen to help you follow the rules and make it easy, or someone who treats you like an adversary?

Your contracting officer is not your adversary. In successful acquisitions, buyer and seller are on the same team working toward the same goal: getting the products and services best able to meet the federal government's needs at a fair price via a transparent and predictable process.

About that "process": Did you know? Not every government purchase requires a full-blown, full-and-open competition complete with requests for proposals and an elaborate evaluation process! More about that later in this chapter.

A quick note: I want to make a clear distinction between three things that newcomers to the federal market often find confusing: Registration, Certification, and GSA Schedules. These three elements of the federal procurement system have one feature in common: *none of them guarantees you a contract.*

- *Registration* in <u>www.SAM.gov</u> is mandatory.

- *Small business certifications* can give you an advantage if you qualify, and apply, for them. They are not required to win federal contracts in general, and are not contracts in and of themselves.

- *GSA Schedules* are a kind of contract you compete for, but the Schedule Contract award itself does not result in revenue. They're not required to win federal business in general, although they can give you an advantage in reaching buyers.

We'll get to details about all three in a moment.

Part 1: How to Follow the Money: From Congress to Contracts

Sometimes purchases happen in a hurry. Some companies look like they're walking into opportunities that practically have their names written on them. Why?

Here's the essence of the answer: As Woodward and Bernstein knew, in Washington you have to *follow the money*. Understand where money comes from, and you start to understand why the process and the players behave the way they do.

Government activities require money. Expenditures have to be authorized and appropriated by the Congress.[1] The Executive Branch (aka the Administration) that supports these programs or activities has to ask Congress for funding. As early as the summer, some agency staff begin to prepare plans that become the basis of the budget that the President presents to Congress each January.

The House and Senate members, both individually and through various committees, spend most of the year reviewing that request. What Congress approves is usually different from what the President requests. Sometimes it's less, sometimes it's more... and sometimes it's completely different. The members, supported by Congressional staffers, hold hearings, draft, negotiate, and eventually approve the funds by authorization and appropriation.

In theory, by September 30th, the end of the federal fiscal year, Congress has passed the funding bills that let agencies begin their work for the new fiscal year that begins on October 1st. In practice, though, Congress often doesn't pass the funding bills for many agencies until later in the Fall or even into the new calendar year.

What happens then? Agencies need the approval of Congress to spend money, even if their new budgets aren't passed yet. More and more often, Congress bridges that gap with temporary measures called *continuing resolutions* (CRs). These resolutions approve limited operating funds based on a percentage of the previous year's funding. This has a heavy impact on prospective and incumbent vendors: under the usual CR rules, new projects can't be started as long as the CR lasts. Buyers might end up meeting new requirements by amending Statements of Work in existing contracts. And incumbents are challenged to plan work and order materials because they don't know how long the CR will last, with especial impact if the vendor was expecting increases in the new fiscal year.

On rare occasions, Congress refuses to pass a budget or a continuing resolution by the end of the fiscal year. When that happens, the federal government must close. Federal employees and contractors cannot be paid, for example, if appropriations have not been enacted. As the consequences of a federal shutdown are dire, there's heavy pressure on both Congress and the White House to resolve their differences quickly.

- Did you know? The longest shutdown of the federal government in history lasted 35 days, from December 22, 2018, to January 25, 2019, when the Trump Administration and the Congress disagreed about budget policy.

---

1   What's the difference between authorization and appropriation? Authorization writes the check; appropriation puts money into the account to cover the check. Using appropriated money without authorization is awkward, but using authorized money without appropriation is impossible.

Shutdowns hurt contractors. How would you cope if all your expected federal contract cash flow shut down with no warning, and with no predictable re-start time? How would you keep your contract staff? How much financing and cash do you have set aside for that kind of contingency? It's rare, but it *does* happen.

EXERCISE ONE: Where Does *Your* Prospect's Money Come From?

Let's try following the money.

Why would you do this?

To make sure you're calling on people who have money to buy from you.

Unlike in the private sector, your prospect's budgets are public information.

I often hear from business owners who say they have had months and months of meetings with government buyers, but "nothing ever happens." Most of the time, it turns out that the person doing the selling hadn't looked into the agency's funding or even asked their prospects about budgets. This vital information can keep you focused on winnable work. Expect to cultivate relationships over many months or even years with lots of people who have no money to spend right now to buy what you offer. Experience (and research) will teach you which ones are likely to get funded later, who never gets funding, and who's got money but also has another vendor in mind.

If you have never done this, I recommend that you do it just once, in order to understand which Congressional committees make the decisions on funding your agency... and to understand your buyers when they explain what's slowing down or even preventing their purchases.

Why?

No money, no contracts.

You'll want to be aware of the progress of your target agencies' budget bills throughout the year, to ensure your marketing effort and your relationship-building are focused on people who are managing funded programs, or at least on those with a very high probability of *getting* funding.

- If the agency doesn't have its budget, its purchasing authority is limited.

- If its funds have been delayed, or rely on continuing resolutions, buying can slow to a crawl, or purchases/programs can be cancelled.

- If the budget working its way through Congress now doesn't include funding in the upcoming fiscal year for activities that require your products or services, then buyers can't buy. Contracts you hold can be cancelled or postponed. On new programs, an opportunity you've invested months of time and effort to pursue can suddenly drop dead without hope of revival. The sooner you know something's not getting funding, the sooner you can spend your marketing time and money on opportunities that *are*.

- If Congress is deadlocked on the budget, the federal government can be temporarily shut down. Shutdowns are inconvenient and delay the payoff for those trying to get a government contract, but even a week or two of shutdown can create a major financial crisis for an incumbent vendor responsible for deadlines and employee salaries in the meantime.

Here's how you follow the money:

Step 1: Pick no more than three federal departments as your top prospective buyers. If you haven't thought much about narrowing your focus, now is the time. The easiest way to choose – just for this exercise – is to think about departments where you've got contacts who know you and your company, and like you, and would want to help you. Alternatively, if you have no prior federal customers, think about your best commercial customers today. Which federal buyers are most similar, in size and scope and mission, to the customers who love you best? Need details? Head to the listings of federal departments and agencies on *www.usa.gov*, and pick three.

Larger departments like Homeland Security or Health and Human Services have multiple components or agencies. Take a look at their websites to see how they're organized. Which offices manage the activities that generate the need for services or products like yours?

Step 2: What budget and programs did the President propose for those agencies? The White House Office of Management and Budget publishes those plans at *http://www.whitehouse.gov/omb.* See what information is available for each agency you're interested in. These documents show the big themes driving the President's spending priorities. Remember, though: "The President proposes; Congress disposes." The President does not always get what he or she wants.

Step 3: Go to *www.house.gov* and *www.senate.gov*. On each site, select "COMMITTEES" and browse until you find which House and Senate committees handle the departments/agencies of your choice. Remember that the authorizing committees specialize by topic, but the appropriations committees cover everything.

Step 4: If your marketing is focused on two or three departments, you might be reviewing the work of up to six committees: one in the House and one in the Senate for each agency; maybe fewer, if one committee handles several departments you're interested in. On each committee's website, select "LEGISLATION" and scroll through the bills that are in play. Which ones are clearly budget bills? In addition to the obvious budget bill, there might be other bills on topics that relate directly to funding opportunities you want to pursue. For the most current status on appropriations, go to *www.congress.gov* and click on "APPROPRIATIONS" under Bill Status; you'll get a table that shows you where all the money bills are in the pipeline right now, with links to each of them. While the bills themselves are arcane, they are accompanied, after passage, by a report that gets into more specifics, explaining the major cuts and adds.

Step 5: Look up the funding for the offices whose activities generate the need for what you do. That's especially important after a new Administration takes office. The budget bills show you whether Congress intends to expand, shrink, create, or totally eliminate the programs (and their managers and staff) that you thought might be prospects. Set your priorities accordingly!

Part 2: Registrations

You can't win the lottery without getting a number. That's true in government, too. You cannot be awarded a contract if you're not a registered federal vendor – and you won't even get very close, because most contracting officers will ask early on in the process if you are registered, and won't deal with you if you aren't. Here's what you need to know:

- You must be registered in the System for Award Management (via *www.SAM.gov*) before being awarded a federal prime contract.

- *www.SAM.gov* (you'll select the option for "Entity Information" after the SAM.gov migration) offers new users guidance on everything you want to have on hand before you register.

- If you gather everything you need[2] before you log on, it'll take you about twenty minutes.

- There is *no charge* to register in SAM. Beware of any solicitation email you get from anyone who tells you otherwise or offers you a paid service to help you register in SAM. Any email from a domain that ends in .org or .com is *not* coming from the federal government.

---

2   By 2020, the federal government aims to complete its transition away from use of the DUNS numbering system for contractors to a new government-owned unique entity identifier (UEI). The new SAM Managed Identifier (SAMMI), will be used within SAM and the Integrated Award Environment (IAE) as a primary key to identify every existing and new entity within SAM.gov. Historical contract data will still be searchable by DUNS as well as by SAMMI.

- Procurement Technical Assistance Centers across the United States offer companies in their region free assistance to register in SAM. Find the Center nearest you and learn more at *www.aptac-us.org*.

- As part of your registration, you'll read and certify that you comply with mandatory Representations and Certifications. When you submit your application, you certify that the information you've provided here is current, accurate, and complete, and that you also you agree to comply with dozens of mandatory regulations incorporated by reference into every federal solicitation, concerning everything from wage rates and equal opportunity to drug-free workplaces.

- ***Dynamic Small Business Search Profile Option:*** At the end of your registration process, you'll have the option to enter your "small business profile." Do it! The details you add here become part of the Small Business Administration's *Dynamic Small Business Search* system (*http://dsbs.sba.gov/dsbs/search/dsp_dsbs.cfm*), which government buyers and contractors often use to seek suppliers and partners. Contracting officers often search on key words and review the business description you publish here to get a sense of how procurement-ready you are. Make this profile keyword-heavy. Include quantifiable, provable, differentiators that make it easy to choose *your* business rather than your competitor's.

- Every business that creates or renews its Entity Registration in SAM profile must provide an original, signed notarized letter identifying the authorized Entity Administrator for the entity associated with that registration before the registration will be activated.

- After you submit your application, you'll first get an online acknowledgement. Expect to wait a couple of days for confirmation that your registration has been accepted, or for any other questions.

- Upon registration, you'll be assigned a unique Commercial And Government Entity (CAGE) code. Record that, and include it in your federal marketing materials.

- Keep your SAM Login and password in a safe place. If you lose your password, it can be difficult and time-consuming to restore access to your account...time you can't afford when you're in the final stages of submitting a proposal!

- You're required to renew your registration once a year. Better than that, update your record every six months, or more often if you're bidding frequently, so that you will show up in searches of recently updated records.

- Don't expect anyone to call you up and ask you to bid just because you're registered in SAM. It might happen, but it's rare.

Part 3: Certifications

The federal government seeks to achieve certain socio-economic goals through its awards for goods and services by establishing preference programs for certain American small business contractors. They have an overall goal to award 23% of contract dollars to companies that meet the definition of "small" under FAR Part 19.

- Small business certifications can give you an advantage in certain competitions. These certifications may be required for certain opportunities. If you're eligible for particular set-asides that your target buyers prefer, you'll want to apply for those certifications.

- Federal small business certifications don't require application fees.

- Some certifications are self-certifying. Other certifications require approval by the Small Business Administration or its designated third parties, or verification by the Department of Veterans Affairs. You can prepare your own application, or engage your Procurement Technical Assistance Center or other consultants to help with the application. You can market to the federal government without certification under any of its small business preference programs. In 2016, government-wide, almost 75% of federal contract dollars were awarded to "other-than-small" business.

- To assess its achievement, the federal government measures contract dollars *awarded* to a small business. Buyers have the authority to reserve (or "set aside") contracts for competition exclusively among small businesses as a way to help reach those goals, but may award work to a small business without set-asides.

Small business Certifications & Preferences[3]

If you haven't already looked into the rules governing preferences for small business and figured out which ones could give you an advantage, this is the time to do it. And no matter how small or large your company, if you're not eligible for an opportunity that falls under a set-aside, then you can do exactly what IBM and Northrop and Lockheed do: team with companies that are.

---

3   Small Business Administration (SBA)
    https://www.sba.gov/federal-contracting/contracting-assistance-programs

The Federal Acquisition Regulations (FAR) permit contracting officers to award sole-source contracts based in part on a company's small business status. The rules and limits of the value of the sole-source contract differ among the four set-aside programs. You may team with a small business partner that is eligible for a particular set-aside that your company is not, provided you comply with the rules on teaming and subcontracting.

First, the definitions....

FAR Part 19[4] gives you all the details on Small business Set-Asides.

In federal contracting, basic status as a small business is self-certifying – you just check the box on the solicitation document – and requires that the company:

- be established in the United States as a for-profit business
- be contributing to the US economy through direct material or labor or taxes,
- and have a level of revenue (for service businesses) or a number of employees (for manufacturers) that falls below the level defined in Title 13 Code of Federal Regulations Part 121 as "small" under the North American Industrial Classification System (NAICS) code of the item being procured.

Let me express that last point another way, because it's really important:

If a contract is set aside for small business, your eligibility to compete for it depends on whether your company meets the size standard that corresponds to the NAICS code for the product or service that the government is buying.

- "Small" is defined specifically for each NAICS code.
- For NAICS codes that describe *products*, "small" is determined by the number of employees at the company.
- For NAICS codes that describe *services*, "small" is determined by the level of revenue of the company.

You can see the full list of size standards in federal regulations published online at *13 C.F.R Part 121*[5].

Participation in a federal preference program does not automatically qualify you for state and local programs, or vice versa. Each state and many local governments have their own small business preference programs, certifications, and registrations. Even if you qualify for those programs, it's only worth your time and effort to apply for certifications or preferences with individual state and local governments if you intend to spend time and money to develop business with those governments.

---

4   Federal Acquisition Regulations Part 19 *https://www.acquisition.gov/browsefar*
5   *http://www.sba.gov/content/table-small business-size-standards*

Federal, state, and local small business certifications have one thing in common: certifications don't guarantee contract awards.

Let me say that again, perhaps a bit louder.

CERTIFICATIONS DON'T GUARANTEE CONTRACT AWARDS!

One of the biggest – and most costly – misunderstandings among small business owners comes from a mistaken sense of entitlement to government contracts. Yes, the federal government has goals to award contracts to small business. And they do track their progress. But no one is going to award you a contract *just because* your business is small, or woman-owned, or service-disabled-veteran-owned.

In 2016, the government overall met its 23% target, but missed some of its individual goals. 2017 awards to Woman-Owned Small Business slipped to 4.79%, below the 5% goal that it met the previous year. HUBZone awards achieved only 1.9% versus the 3% goal. (See the full details, including an agency-by-agency breakdown and statistics for each type of small business, online.[6])

Agencies are under scrutiny to make their best efforts to meet these goals. Failure to do so generally results in a bit of bad publicity, and pressure to do better next year.

The Federal Small business Contracting Programs

Thousands of small businesses meet the most basic definition of small business for government contracts. The federal government tracks the dollar value of contract awards to all these categories of small business. Contract awards to companies that qualify under multiple preferences are counted in each applicable category – for example, the value of a contract award to a female service-disabled veteran who owns a qualifying small business located in a HUBZone would count toward meeting four different categories of federal small business goals.

If the contracting officer considering acquisition strategies finds that there are more than two responsive ("adequately responds to the solicitation"), responsible ("qualified and capable of doing the work") prospective small business suppliers, the contracting officer is *required* to reserve (or "set aside") the competition for small business.[7]

Contracting officers may set aside contracts for all qualified small businesses that meet the size standard, or for those that qualify for one or more limited subsets of small businesses, which might specifically include:

- 8(a) Small Disadvantaged Business
- Economically Disadvantaged / Women-Owned Small Business (ED/WOSB)
- Historically Underutilized Business (HUB) Zone companies

6   https://www.sba.gov/document/support--small business-procurement-scorecard-overview
7   FAR Part 19.502-2

• Service-Disabled Veteran-Owned Small Business (SDVOSB)

Here's an overview of these programs. While generally none of these small business programs takes precedence over the others, there is a specific exception in law, and an exception in practice. If you might qualify for one or more of these preferences, you'll want to review the relevant rules closely before you apply or certify.

8(a)[8]

The 8(a) business development program is run by SBA to help small companies owned and operated by socially and economically disadvantaged persons develop their businesses – including but not limited to federal contracting.

The federal government defines who qualifies for the 8(a) program — including what counts as being economically and socially disadvantaged — in *Title 13 Part 124 of the Code of Federal Regulations* (CFR). You can also get a preliminary assessment of whether you qualify at SBA's Certify web site at *www.certify.sba.gov*.

The basic requirements for admission to the 8(a) program are that the small business be 51% or greater owned and controlled by one or more socially and economically disadvantaged US citizens and demonstrate "potential for success" – generally, but not necessarily, by showing a two-year track record of strong business growth.

Certification for participation in the 8(a) program is based on SBA's analysis of a comprehensive application that includes the personal net worth of the business owners, the size of the company, and a personal narrative that substantiates social disadvantage.

One benefit of the 8(a) program is the preference that qualified companies gain in award of federal contracts. SBA may act as a prime contractor to other federal departments and agencies, and award subcontracts – including sole-sourced – for performance by companies that SBA certifies as eligible under the rules of the 8(a) program. 8(a) companies are eligible for such privileges for up to nine years.

An 8(a) award represents especially low risk to the federal buyer because, when SBA acts as the prime under this program, SBA guarantees the performance of its 8(a) subcontractor. In other words, if the 8(a) company fails to perform, SBA agrees to find another company that can complete the work in its place.

8(a) contract awards are generally supposed to be made sole-source up to a value of $4 million for services or $7 million for goods, as determined by the NAICS codes assigned by the contracting officer. Contracting officers may, at their discretion, open 8(a) requirements for competition below that threshold.

---

8   Reference: Small Business Administration *sba.gov/federal-contracting/contracting-assistance-programs/8a-business-development-program*

Agencies must provide a sole-source justification and and approval (which contracting officers may refer to as "J&A") for any proposed 8(a) sole-source award.

Alaskan Native Corporations (ANCs) or Tribally Owned Native American Corporations have *no* dollar value limit on their sole-source 8(a) awards. That's also true for Native Hawaiian-owned Corporations – but only on their contracts with the Department of Defense. 8(a) companies owned by *individual* Native Americans or Alaskan Natives (as distinct from Native American Corporations or Alaskan Native Corporations) have the same limits as all other 8(a)s.

Once SBA designates work as appropriate for award to an 8(a) company, SBA strongly encourages the contracting officer to keep follow-on work reserved for 8(a) vendors. Contracting officers like the convenience of low-risk buying and the ability to award sole-source work with the least amount of justification of any of the four set-aside programs.

The ease of awarding 8(a) contracts often creates a practical preference for the contracting officer, even though no one small business program is given higher priority for contract awards than any other (except for purchases by the Department of Veterans Affairs from veteran-owned suppliers.)

These and related regulations about how and when 8(a) procurement can occur are complex and they change, so always check *13CFR 124.506(b)* for the most current details.

Women-Owned Small Business[9]

Under the Women-Owned Small Business Federal Contract Assistance (WOSB, occasionally called "8(m)") program, contracting officers may set aside opportunities for competition among certain women-owned small businesses.

Highlights of the program include that participating companies must:

- Be at least 51% owned and controlled by women who are U.S. citizens
- Have women manage day-to-day operations and also make long-term decisions
- Self-certify *or* be Third-Party certified to this effect[10]
- Provide supporting documents electronically in the SBA portal (*www.certify.gov*).

9   Woman-Owned Small Business References: Program rules - *https://www.sba.gov/federal-contracting/contracting-assistance-programs/women-owned-small business-federal-contracting-program*

10   As of 2019, SBA had authorized four third-party organizations to provide WOSB certification (see list at *https://www.sba.gov/federal-contracting/contracting-assistance-programs/women-owned-small business-federal-contracting-program*), and is revising the certification process. Always check for the latest procedures at *https://certify.sba.gov* .

Certification as Economically Disadvantaged Woman-Owned Small Business (EDWOSB) is open to a female business owner whose company falls under one or more of the NAICS codes designated for the EDWOSB program and who also certifies that her:

- Personal net worth is less than $750,000;
- Most recent 5-year average annual income less than $350,000;
- Fair market value of primary residence & business total under $6 million.

Section 811(m) of the Small Business Act of 2000 (15 U.S.C. 637), as implemented by 13 C.F.R. Part 127, allows contracting officers to set aside contracts for certified EDWOSBs and other WOSBs, if:

- The products or services they need are within one of NAICS codes[11] in which women-owned small businesses have been determined to be under-represented or significantly underrepresented;
- Two or more economically disadvantaged or otherwise women-owned small businesses can be reasonably expected to compete for the opportunity;
- The goods or services are offered under fair and reasonable pricing.

Contracting officers may award sole-source contracts worth up to $6 million for products and up to $4.5 million for services to qualified companies under the WOSB program.

Get the details on qualification and certification at *www.certify.sba.gov*.

Service Disabled Veteran-Owned Small Business (SDVOSB)[12]

SDVOSBs are eligible for set-asides as well as sole-source contract awards of up to $6.5 million for a requirement within the NAICS codes for manufacturing, or up to $4 million otherwise. Qualified veterans may self-certify their eligibility based on the definitions in FAR Subpart 19.14.

The Department of Veterans Affairs requires any company seeking a contract award based on its assertion of any kind of veteran ownership to verify that status through Vets First, a program administered by the Center for Verification and Evaluation (CVE at *https://www.va.gov/osdbu/verification/*). Those who qualify may display a "CVE Verified" logo on their marketing materials.

In 2016, the Supreme Court[13] directed the Department of Veterans Affairs to give first priority to Service-Disabled Veteran-Owned Small Business and Veteran-

11   *https://www.sba.gov/document/support--qualifying-naics-women-owned-small-business-federal-contracting-program*

12   References: Veterans Affairs website at: *http://www.vetbiz.gov/* and FAR 19.14 at *https://www.acquisition.gov/far/html/Subpart%2019_14.html*

13   In Kingdomware Technologies, Inc. v. United States, a decision colloquially referred to as "Kingdomware"

Owned Small Business for contract awards in all its purchasing contracting for goods and services.

Although the Department of Veterans Affairs has the highest goal of any federal department for SDVOSB contracting, statistics as recent as 2017 show that the VA awards over 70% of its contract dollars to companies that are "other than small."

Historically Underutilized Business Zone (HUBZone) Businesses[14]

SBA certifies and maintains a list of qualified HUBZone small businesses, and adjudicates protests of eligibility to receive HUBZone contracts. The HUBZone Program provides preferences to small businesses that obtain HUBZone certification from SBA based on these criteria:

- They meet the SBA size standards;

- They are owned and controlled at least 51% by US citizens, or a Community Development Corporation, or an agricultural cooperative or an Indian tribe;

- They locate their principal office within a "Historically Underutilized Business Zone," as defined at *http://bit.ly/HUBzoneMap*;

- At least 35% of their employees reside in a HUBZone.

Agencies find HUBZone goals the most challenging to meet, particularly because growing small businesses also find it hard to maintain their HUBZone status. Bluntly, when a company grows, promotes its employees, and hires more, people either want to move out of the HUBZone, or the company finds it challenging to locate enough qualified new candidates who live in the HUBZone. And if economic data shows that the geographic territory designated as a HUBZone prospers, then that area itself (and the companies located there) can lose designation as a HUBZone.

Keep on top of changes that the federal government makes to the certification process! As we go to press, for example, SBA is revising the certification process for WOSB, and more changes are in the works for SDVOSB. The most current information about those programs will always be in Federal acquisition regulation part 19. Don't guess. Check the FARS. Here's your reward for keeping up with the changes: treat a pending or recent change as an opportunity for a conversation

---

14   HUBZone References: SBA at
      https://www.sba.gov/federal-contracting/contracting-assistance-programs/hubzone-program

with your contracting officer (e.g., "Hey, I just read about this...what do you know about it? How would that work in your office?").

Next, the goals: Federal Small Business Contracting Goals

Category	Goal	Certification Process
Small Business Overall	23%	Self-Certifying
Small Disadvantaged Business Including 8(a)	5%	Self-Certifying SBA Certified
Women-Owned and Economically Disadvantaged Women-Owned Small Business	5%	Self-Certifying or Third-Party[1]
Service-Disabled Veteran-Owned Small Business (SDVOSB)	3%	Self-Certifying except for eligibility for contracts at the Department of Veterans Affairs.
Historically Underutilized Business Zone (HUBZone)	3%	SBA Certified

Each buying agency must aim to meet unique annual goals it negotiates with SBA for total awards to small business, and for categories within small business. In many agencies, their goals exceed the overall federal goals!

How are they doing? Check the scores!

The Small Business Administration publishes how well each federal agency is meeting its contracting goals for every kind of small business at: *https://www.sba.gov/document/support--small business-procurement-scorecard-overview*

As a result of these goals, a network of Offices of Small and Disadvantaged Business Utilization (OSDBUs, often called "OZ-duh-boos") for most departments or Office of Small Business Programs (OSBPs) for military departments spans every federal agency to help small companies pursue those opportunities and help agencies meet those small business goals.

Prime contractors are also accountable:

- Each must include in their proposals a small business subcontracting plan for any contract worth more than $700,000.

- The Small Business Jobs and Credit Act of 2010 gives the prime contractor just 12 months to engage your company in paid work on that contract.

- As a result, many large prime contractors have supplier-diversity programs and small business liaison program managers. Most also participate in Mentor-Protégé programs to achieve those goals.

About State, Local, and Commercial Supplier Diversity Certifications

While each supplier diversity certification – state, local, or private sector – has its own unique process, they have one thing in common with federal small business certifications: *none of the certifications guarantees business.* After you invest the time (and, whether in cash or imputed value of sweat equity, money) to get and maintain any certification, your certification only generates business if you invest even *more* time and resources, often over many years, to build the relationships required to develop opportunities.

Most, if not all, states offer state-specific certification programs for small business suppliers. There is no blanket application you can submit to get certified in all fifty states. Rather than being a problem, that forces most business owners to make highly practical decisions about where to apply. Very few small companies actively sell in every state.

In addition to their contractual obligations to federal small business subcontracting, hundreds of large primes make and meet ambitious goals each year to award millions or even billions of dollars in contracts to suppliers considered diverse in other respects.

If your company seeks work with a large prime, you might also qualify for, and benefit from, additional certifications that are recognized by commercial companies. The prime might even *require* your company to have additional private-sector certifications before it will consider you as a supplier on any contract.

In order to ensure the integrity of the supplier diversity process, many of the large primes are members of organizations including one or more of the National Minority Supplier Development Council (NMSDC), the Women's Business Enterprise National Council (WBENC), the National Gay and Lesbian Chamber of Commerce (NGLCC) or the National Veteran-Owned Business Association (NaVOBA). These organizations manage the applications and certifications of businesses that meet the published qualifications for their particular diversity.

The federal government doesn't recognize these other diverse certifications, but hundreds of prime contractors can and do.

Notice that none of these certifications are based on size! So while your company might outgrow your federal small business certification, you could maintain your status as a diverse supplier for the entire life of your business!

The basic eligibility and documentation requirements are fairly similar. The company must be 51% or more owned, operated, AND controlled by the diverse person or people. You can expect to provide personal identity and citizenship documents for the owners, articles of incorporation or formation, and recent financial statements and tax returns. You've got these. It just might take time to find them and make or scan copies.

Beyond the basics, many certifications require more information. That might include responses to a detailed questionnaire, résumés of key personnel, or a narrative that provides examples of how discrimination you experienced created a disadvantage that hampered the success of your business.

You will need to invest time to research which certifications your company is eligible for. You'll also need to invest time to apply for certifications and, if you're successful, apply for annual renewal.

Just because you *can* get a certification doesn't mean you *should*. For instance, when I was a contractor to the Commonwealth of Virginia, I applied successfully for certification as "Small, Woman-Owned And Minority" (SWaM). I didn't need the certification to win the business, which was sole-sourced. I got certified as a favor to my client, who wanted to count my contract award in their diversity spend. I didn't renew the certification once the contract was over, even though I could have, because I had shifted my business strategy away from pursuing state government contracts.

As of this writing, federal small business certifications do not require an application fee. Many other certifications require a non-refundable application fee as well as time to prepare the application.

Spend your time – and your money – where you'll get a return on that investment. Even federal certification applications can take time and care to get right.

You don't *need* to hire a consultant to apply for these certifications. Thousands of companies apply or renew successfully every year on their own or via help from PTACs.

But sometimes it makes a ton of sense to get help! Here's some advice from Heather Cox, President of Certify My Company, based on the hundreds of applications she's done for her clients.

Five Signs That A Certification Consultant Could Help Your Company

A large number of applicants drop out of the process long before finishing their applications. That failure to finish can represent millions of dollars of lost opportunity!

Worse: many business owners are denied certification for technical rejections due to incomplete or inaccurate paperwork. Sometimes, for instance, in applications for the federal 8(a) certification, the certifying body (in this case, the Small Business Administration) is looking for very specific kinds of narrative concerning evidence of how your experience of discrimination based on socio-economic factors damaged your ability to compete for federal contracts.

If your application is denied, you're often required to *report* that denial on future certification applications. The simple fact of denial can slow down a new application.

If you don't complete the application process, or don't understand and fix the problem that caused the denial, you can miss out on the powerful advantages that certifications can bring.

You can improve the ROI on the time and money you invest in pursuing certifications by outsourcing your diversity-certification process to a certification consultant who has a great track record in successful applications on behalf of their clients for the kind of certifications you qualify for.

Here are five signs that a certification consultant can help you and your company:

1. You have at least one partner that is not the same demographic.
   - The number one reason companies are denied certification is due to inconsistencies in the governing documents; even one paragraph can render a company ineligible. A qualified consultant will know what to look for and how to rectify inaccurate verbiage
2. Any of the company ownership is held in a trust.
   - As diverse-owned businesses become savvier and more sophisticated, the certification process becomes more complicated. Each certification has its specific requirements that pertain to trust agreements.
3. The ownership has changed at least once.
   - Ownership changes, regardless of the reason for the change, require additional documentation, and it is essential that the change documentation matches the past *and* current documentation and that it is clear the diverse person meets all eligibility requirements.
4. You are good at what you do.
   - Most business owners are exceptional at what they do, which is why they started their business to begin with. However, most

business owners are not great at paperwork. When was the last time you looked at your formation papers? Your governing documents? The certification process requires A LOT of documentation. Having an experienced consultant help you identify, collect, and review the necessary documents takes a large burden off an entrepreneur's ever-growing to-do list

5.   A corporate or government client requested the certification.
    *   If a client requests the certification, the last thing you want to do is tell them you were denied, even if it is because of a technicality (see items 1-3). Get it right the first time!

This is by no means an exhaustive list. And I recommend reaching out to a consultant before you start the process. Accomplished consultants are transparent and will inform potential clients if hiring a consultant is recommended or discretionary.

Certify My Company provides diverse businesses with the expertise, tools, and access to thrive in a competitive marketplace, and supports them through the arduous process of diversity certification. Find out more at <u>www.certifymycompany.com</u>.

Part 4: Procurement By The Numbers: *A Business Owner's Tour*

There is no great mystery to how the federal government buys goods and services – just an awful lot of detail. The secret to sanity is to know where to find and learn about the rules that apply to what you offer and the buyers you want to sell to.

One of the reasons many companies like to do business with the government is that the rules of the game are open for all to see – that is, the process is transparent. You know exactly what to expect, and you can expect a fair hearing if things go off the rails. In fact, many large corporations publish much less information about their acquisition processes than the government does!

Most importantly, to participate indiscriminately in competitions – put bluntly, to hunt for RFPs you think you can win, and pump out proposals – is almost always a waste of time and money. Your typical win rate will be under 5%. When you consider the average cost of a major proposal is about $65,000 (once you figure in explicit costs, opportunity costs, employee time, sweat equity, morale, and departure of talented employees discouraged by repeated losses), very few companies (large *or* small) can afford constant proposal losses.

The solicitation process is a formal and public communication channel. The contracting office will usually define how vendors may submit questions requiring clarification, but by the time the RFP hits the street, your opportunity to gather significant intelligence about what the buyer really wants is long gone.

Federal buyers need two things:

1. services and products to deliver their missions and programs;

2. a lawful, efficient acquisition process to get those products and services.

Successful vendors are ready to meet *both* of those needs:

- They identify a buyer with a problem, court them, get them interested in their solutions to both those problems, find out whether they have money to spend, and get to know the players at all the layers who are involved in the decision.

- They research past contract data to learn the kind of contracting method or vehicle the buying office and contracting office typically use to buy services or products like theirs, and discuss with the buyers which acquisition method the buyer is most likely to use this time. If the buyer likes the vendor, they'll choose an acquisition method that can make it easy for their preferred vendor to compete strongly for the opportunity.

- They ensure their company is able to participate in the kind of competitive process the buyer wants to use. We'll talk about these methods of competition in just a moment!

Tools You'll Need

The Federal Acquisition Regulations (FAR)

These are the basic buying rules for almost all[15] federal departments and agencies. You can see them all at *www.acquisition.gov*.

Agency Supplements

In addition to the FAR, every other agency has its own special requirements their buyers and vendors must also comply with. You'll find these in agency-specific supplements.

The best known is the Defense Federal Acquisition Regulations Supplement (DFARS – "Dee-Fars"), but you'll also find the Homeland Security Acquisition Regulations Supplement (HSARS), the Department of Energy Acquisition Regu-

---

15   The Federal Aviation Administration (FAA) has a complete exemption from the FAR. If you're doing business with FAA, you'll want to become "FAST" friends with the FAA's unique procurement rules – the FAA Acquisition System Toolset – at http://fast.faa.gov/. Several other agencies you might think of as part of the federal government, like the Office of the Comptroller of the Currency and the Smithsonian Institution, also have their own procurement rules outside the FAR.

lations Supplement (DEARS), the General Services Administration Acquisition Supplement (GSARS)... well, you get the picture.

You need to know the rules of the specific agency you're selling to. The good thing about becoming familiar with the FAR is that the agencies' supplements have a parallel structure – for example, just as FAR Part 19 contains the government-wide rules on small business, DFARS Part 219 is the corresponding section on DoD's small business procurement rules.

Link to the agency procurement supplements at
https://www.acquisition.gov/Supplemental_Regulations.

Buying By the (FAR) Numbers

We'll look at the process in three stages:

* Pre-Solicitation

* Formal Competition

* Post-Award

Pre-Solicitation

Let's take a few minutes and get in the flow of the rules. If you like structure, you'll love this part!

I suggest that you read this next section while you have the Federal Acquisition Regulations open in your browser or e-book. It's free (your tax dollars at work!) Pull up the table of contents at *https://www.acquisition.gov/browsefar* or download from amazon or iBooks.

a. Need

Government buyers' needs flow together from all kinds of sources.

Every government department has programs and offices that provide ongoing services to citizens, either directly or through carrying out the missions of government as authorized by Congress, and every one of them buys products and services from contractors in order to carry out their missions and mandates.

If you want to do business with an agency, you've *got* to know what they do. Select the agency you're curious about from the list at *https://www.usa.gov/federal-agencies/a* and thoroughly review its website. How is the agency organized? What are its offices and programs? Who are the key officials in charge of those programs? And how and why would your products or services help them deliver their services and missions better?

Many initiatives and programs are invented, designed, led, implemented, and continued (or closed) largely by the officials within the agency. Public consultation is often involved throughout the process.

Presidential priorities drive some big top-down requirements and create the mandates to establish certain programs or define military missions. Members of Congress include other provisions (called "earmarks") in funding bills that define pots of money to be used for specific purposes (for example, testing a new kind of unmanned aerial vehicle, or building a new office, or doing a type of research). Earmarks have officially been eliminated, but a good deal of Congressional bill provisions look an awful lot like them.

Whether there is an emphasis on doing the work with government employees or on relying as much as possible on contractors, the fact remains that the government will always need goods and services from industry to deliver those programs and perform those missions.

As a vendor, there are some things *you* need to do, too. *FAR Part 4, Administrative Matters*, explains critical applications and registrations you need to get started. They don't guarantee you'll win anything...but you are guaranteed *not* to win *without* them. Your friendly neighborhood contracting officer wants your paperwork, such as:

- A properly signed contract (*FAR Part 4.1*)

- Registration in the System for Award Management (*FAR Part 4.11*)

The contracting officer has to do their share, too. This part of the FAR includes government's obligations to:

- Safeguard classified information within the industry (*FAR Part 4.4*);

- Report contract actions to the Federal Procurement Data System (*FAR Part 4.6*) and track achievement on mandatory small business subcontracting plans (*FAR Part 4.14*); and

- KEEP your paperwork (*FAR Part 4.7, Records Retention*).

  b. Requirements Definition

Once agencies have their budget approvals, top officials can begin to implement their programs for the year. They pass along the budget allocations to program managers, who can then revise accordingly the plans for operations and procurements they originally prepared nearly a year earlier.

With the spending authority in place, the procurement process can move into gear. Program managers work with end users, contracting officers, and contracting officers' technical representatives to define exactly what goods and services they need (Statements of Work and Requirements Definitions, for example) and how they plan to buy (the Acquisition Methods).

c. Market Survey & Market Research

Government buyers have many options to find out about potential suppliers. FAR Part 7 spells out ways they can do that before they begin an acquisition. For example, they can publish a Request for Information (RFI) to survey industry capabilities. It's a way for government to ask questions like, "We think we might want vendors to help us solve this problem or meet such-and-such a requirement. What do we need to know if we were going to do that? What's realistic to ask for, and where's the leading edge? What capabilities, specifications, or quantities does your company or industry readily supply in the commercial market, and what's simply not available, or is only in the developmental stage right now, but might be ready in a few years?" (See details in *FAR Part 15.2.*)

An RFI does *not* mean the government has any commitment to buy anything. So why should you respond to RFIs? Easy: they are one of the formal ways that winners influence the development of the specification. Even after you might have had months of informal discussion with contracting officers and program managers, they still need to be open to hear from vendors who might not have had the chance to meet with them. RFIs make that possible. And if you *aren't* the vendor with the inside track who's been making calls all this time, then the RFI is your chance to get on the buyer's radar, to make them sit up and take notice and invite you to tell them more about an approach they might not have considered.

Did You Know? The Rule of Two

As noted, if there are two or more small businesses that appear capable of meeting the contract requirement at a fair and reasonable price, the contracting officer *must* set aside that contract for small business.

In practice, most contracting officers want to have more than two apparently qualified competitors, so that, when the auditors come by, their files look absolutely perfect, with full and open competition documented.

So, be generous: bring a friend to the competition. Sure, on one hand, you have more competition....but perhaps you also have better odds of winning in a smaller pool of competitors.

Buyers also use "Sources Sought" notices, particularly to research whether there are enough qualified small businesses to justify setting aside the contract for small business.

If you're a small business owner, don't complain that not enough contracts get set aside for small business if you don't respond to the Sources Sought in your product or service niche. Far from wasting your time, your response to a Sources Sought tells the contracting officer, "Yes, I'm capable of meeting your need."

If you can fulfill *some* of the requirements but not all of them, take a look to see whether the contracting officer is interested in knowing that. Sometimes, based on responses to a Sources Sought, the contracting officer will structure a later procurement so that a supplier she likes can compete rather than be excluded.

Sources Sought are excellent market intelligence for vendors, too! While there is no guarantee that a Sources Sought will lead to a procurement, there's good reason to think that the point of contact is involved in all kinds of other buying activity, and would be a good person to get to know for future opportunities.

d. Marketing Ethics

You hear all kinds of things about what you can and can't do when you are marketing to government. Some people take government officials to lunch all the time, while others are met with scowls when they offer to pay for coffee. What gives?

The FAR says very little about how to market… but they're very specific about how *not* to. Here are the facts.

Part 3 of the FAR is about procurement integrity. Its full name is Improper Business Practices And Personal Conflicts Of Interest. Three reasons why you want to take a look:

Keep your contract

If you offer government officials gifts or hospitality with intent to get favorable treatment on a contract worth more than $100,000, your contract can be cancelled. (*FAR Part 52.203-3*)

In general, government officials can't seek or receive coffee, lunch, gifts, or entertainment from a contractor. (*FAR Part 3.101-2*) So don't offer. Individual agencies *are* allowed to have their own rules about this, so if you're uncertain, look up their rules online, and/or ask the contracting officer to confirm your understanding.

Protect your business secrets

Find out how to mark your documents to prevent the government giving competitors sensitive business information from your proposal. (*FAR 3.104.4*) This really can happen if you don't watch out.

Notice and avoid shady practices

Whether you're a prime or a subcontractor, ethics rules apply to you. Those rules prohibit things like kickbacks, contingent fees, and under-bidding today in order to raise prices after the contract is awarded. If you're even remotely concerned about whether a business practice is legitimate or not, run, do not walk, to *FAR Part 3*. It's short and very clear.

Formal Competition

e. Acquisition strategy and competition preparation

Whenever I teach an intro procurement class, someone complains that government business always seems wired for somebody else. "Would you like to know how to get sole-sourced?" I ask them.

Everyone's ears perk up, so I say, "It's in the FAR."

Is it legal to get sole-sourced?

Absolutely. In Fiscal 2017, 25% of all federal contract dollars were spent either "Not Competed" or "Not Open for Competition."

What are those allowable reasons, and how could you qualify? FAR Part 6 gives experienced contractors winning secrets, such as:

- When things *must* be competed, and what "Full and Open Competition" means. (*FAR Part 6.1*)

- The small business set-aside you might not know about. (Can you name all five? See *FAR Part 6.203*.)

- When federal buyers can sole-source: The Seven Justifications (*FAR Part 6.302*).

  › Only one responsible source

  › Unusual/compelling urgency

  › Industrial base mobilization/maintaining critical capability

  › International Agreement

  › Authorized by law

  › National Security

  › Public Interest

- How to justify being sole-sourced. (*FAR Part 6.303*)

All that being said, sole-source represents a *lot* of work, and risk, for the contracting officer. They're under constant pressure to maximize competition. Remember your job, as a vendor and as their teammate in the acquisition process: Follow the Rules, Make It Easy, Make Them Look Good. Sole-source can be done by the rules, but it's rarely easy for buyers. Furthermore, remember your adversaries. Competitors? They can hardly wait to attack a sole-source award they think is unfair. So sole-source might not be the easy route for either buyer or seller.

Keep digging into the rules and you'll see some perfectly straightforward options for competition that can lead an enthusiastic contracting officer your way.

- How to justify and approve limited competition. (FAR Part 8.405-6)

- When competitions must be based primarily on price. (*"Sealed Bidding"* – *FAR Part 6.4*)

FAR 7.105 says that buyers need an acquisition plan. This means that, before any buying begins, the contracting officers can already tell you some *very* useful things (if you know enough to ask), such as:

- how they'll invite and choose vendors

- what contract type they'll use

- how much funding they have

- the environmental or energy requirements

- logistics

- what property or data they'll provide the vendor

- the security and clearance requirements for facilities and personnel

- the timing and nature of acquisition milestones

If you can start chatting with the contracting officer early enough in the process, you and your buyer might discover some ways in which your company is a really strong fit for exactly what your buyer is looking for. If you're having that conversation before the requirements get written, you're making it easier for them to define the requirement in a way that makes it easy for them to choose you.

Certain kinds of acquisitions – for example, construction, engineering, services, research and development, information technology, and utilities – have uniquely defined contracting processes. You need to check out the FAR and see whether there are special rules that apply to your industry, products, or services... and, if so, become intimately familiar with those rules.

Even if a purchase must be competed, you can still find out about opportunities long before the formal competition begins. For one thing, *FAR 5.404* encourages federal agencies to publish procurement forecast information. Find those forecasts online 24/7 at *Acquisition Central.*

Acquisition Methods and Strategies

Your federal buyer not only chooses the supplier they want; they also decide the acquisition method and type of contract they'll use to pick the buyer. That choice can depend on things like value of the purchase, the agency regulations, and simply the way they like to do things. They can make small purchases with minimal competition. They can pay small *and* large contracts using credit cards. They can amend the scope and terms of an existing contract to add new suppliers, products, or services. They can order from a pre-negotiated contract that has set the terms and conditions of sale but guaranteed the vendor no business at all. They can get three quotes by phone and then award to the vendor they had in mind from the start.

Which acquisition strategies might government buyers use to purchase goods or services like yours? Remember that contracting officers must give priority consideration to certain sources of supply and certain methods of competition before conducting a competition that is open to all vendors.

Mandatory sources: Before running a new competition, contracting officers must consider whether the buyer's needs can be met by products or services offered under existing contracts (see FAR Part 8 for details). They must consider, in priority order, whether the buyer's needs can be met by:

› UNICOR (Prison Industries),

› Ability One (Workshops for the Blind and Severely Handicapped),

› The Government Printing Office,

› Vendors who hold GSA Schedule contracts, or

› Vendors participating in other indefinite delivery contract vehicles.

Small business Set-Asides (FAR Part 19): Not only can (or, in some cases, must) the contracting officer set aside the contract for competition limited to small business, the contracting officer also has the option to further limit the set-aside to specific kinds of small business, including Service-Disabled Veteran-Owned Small Business (SDVOB), or Small Disadvantaged/8(a), Historically Underutilized Business (HUB) Zone, Women-Owned or Economically Disadvantaged Women-Owned, or plain ordinary Small Business.

Even given those requirements, contracting officers have many options open to them. Federal buyers award thousands of contracts totaling billions of dollars each year as single transactions. These one-time buys can range from a few dollars for supplies or parts to a multi-million-dollar consulting services project.

Savvy vendors engage buyers in conversation early to explore the rules that would make it easiest for the buyer to do business with them while still meeting the government's competition requirements.

Contracting officers' options include:

- Micro-purchase: If the purchase is worth less than $10,000, a government buyer may purchase products or services sole-source, without competition, from vendors that are registered and active in SAM.gov. (see FAR Part 13.2.)

Did You Know? An Easy Way to Win Your First Contract

Imagine winning your first federal contract without writing a long, complex proposal.

Contracting officers can place small orders for products and services for minimal, and often no, competition. If your offer falls below the Micro-Purchase Threshold (currently $10,000), there is no requirement for set-asides, either. Large and small companies alike can win business this way.

If the value of a requirement is between $10,000 and $250,000 (that is, greater than the Micro-Purchase Threshold but less than the Simplified Acquisition Threshold), the Rule of Two applies. That requirement is supposed to be set aside for small business (again, so long as two or more such businesses are capable of doing the work at a fair and reasonable price). If your business is small, you can compete on that work.

Where are those opportunities published? Under $25,000, they don't have to be published anywhere. These opportunities are developed in conversation between buyer and vendor.

The contracting officer may make Micro-Purchases and Simplified Acquisitions with procedures as simple as getting three quotes over the phone…if they want to do it that way. Contracting officers have enormous discretion over how they buy what they buy.

And so long as the contracting officer is buying commercial items, they can use such simplified procedures on purchases as large as $7 million, sometimes even more!

If the opportunity is worth more than $10,000 but less than $25,000, the contracting officer doesn't need to publish the notice on Contract Opportunities in SAM. gov. While they *might* do that, most won't. Although they are under pressure to compete every opportunity, they also don't have the time or desire to sort through thousands of offers! The language you'll see in the FAR advocates competition "to the maximum practicable extent."

In other words, contracting officers have a *lot* of discretion! They could also simply post a hardcopy notice on a public bulletin board, post something on the buying command's online list (not on SAM.gov at all) or make three phone calls! Think of it from their point of view. If you were the buyer, what would *you* rather do? And why?

If you're just getting started, and a contract worth from $10,000 to $25,000 appeals to you as the vendor and to the contracting officer and program manager, then you'll want to take a look at *FAR Part 5.101* to see what options might meet the FAR requirement for open competition, while staying below the radar of your own competitors.

***Simplified Acquisition Procedures (FAR Part 13)*:** In FY 2017, federal buyers awarded $22 billion, both competitively and non-competitively, using Simplified Acquisition Procedures (SAP).[16] That's up 300% from 2010, when awards under SAP were just $6 billion! Expect that number to grow even faster in the years ahead.

Much of that $22 billion was awarded to small business, but not all.

Simplified Acquisitions below the $250,000 threshold are supposed to be set aside for small business – *if* the contracting officer believes that there are two or more responsive, responsible small businesses capable of doing the work at a fair and reasonable price. That doesn't happen 100% of the time.

Furthermore, buyers can – and do -- use Simplified Acquisition Procedures for much larger purchases, if they want.

If you know how the FAR on Simplified Acquisition work, you can make it easier for a first-time government buyer to give you a try, and you could supply the government without doing a massive proposal! Wouldn't that save you a lot of time and money?

For example, buyers don't have to invite vendors in writing. FAR Part 13 explains how they can ask for an offer by phone or look up your published list prices. Contracting officers can ordinarily meet their requirement for "maximum practicable competition" on purchases below the Simplified Acquisition Threshold by seeking offers from suppliers in their local area. Unless certain exceptions apply, the contracting officer should seek offers from at least three sources, and, "whenever practicable," from two sources that didn't take part in the previous solicitation.

Simple procedures, big bucks. Get to know these rules well. Check the data to see which of your prospects uses that kind of acquisition procedure. As you get to know each buyer, long before you pitch them on something, make simplified acquisition part of the conversation. Don't try to tell them how to do their jobs! But *do* show you know a little, and ask them how it works in their office.

16   Source: The Federal Procurement Data System (*https://fpds.gov*)

Other kinds of acquisition processes include:

Broad Agency Announcement (BAA) (FAR Part 35.016): This kind of solicitation is usually open for many months. Buyers use this method to solicit technologies in development, and find new solutions to urgent problems. It's most popular with the Department of Defense & Military Services (*https://www.darpa.mil/work-with-us/office-wide-broad-agency-announcements/*); the Combatting Terrorism Technical Support Office (*www.tswg.gov*), which evaluates technology for multiple defense and security agencies; and the Department of Homeland Security (*https://baa2.st.dhs.gov/portal/BAA/*).

Invitation for Bid (IFB), also called Sealed Bidding (FAR Part 14): In this kind of competition, the lowest-priced, technically responsive bid by a responsible company (that is, a firm capable of doing the work) wins. This method is used most often by government buyers who can define their needs precisely.

Negotiated Contracting (FAR Part 15): Buyers most often use this acquisition strategy for large systems and complex requirements. Negotiated Contracting can begin with a Request for Proposal (see FAR Part 15.203) or an Unsolicited Proposal (see FAR Part 15.6).

Negotiated contracting can result in a one-off award, or set up a framework for multiple purchases from a single vendor over time, or create a qualified short list of vendors who compete for certain requirements over time.

You'll also hear people talk about "contract vehicles." Think of contract vehicles as a metaphorical "bridge"[17] between buyer and seller for times when the buyer needs or expects to go back to the same vendor multiple times.[18] Think about all the different kinds of bridges you've ever seen: pedestrian bridges, bicycle paths, superhighway overpasses, rope bridges, suspension bridges, and even covered bridges.... Each one is built to do a specific job suited for a specific location, to carry a specific kind and weight of traffic.

Similarly, the federal the buyer chooses the "bridge" or contract vehicle they want for each specific transaction. Each seller has to be positioned on the other side of the bridges their buyers are likely to want to use, ready for the way each unique buyer wants to do business.

Sometimes, you'll hold the prime contract: that's like owning the bridge to a buyer who wants to visit you often. If someone else holds the contract that the buyer wants to use, or that buyer doesn't visit you very often, you can still do business. Subcontracting is like borrowing someone else's bridge. If you do that, expect to pay a "toll" (that is, margin) to use the bridge.

---

17   For the record, there is actually a type of contract known as a "bridge" contract, but that's not what I'm talking about here. Go with me on the visual image of the metaphor for a moment, okay?

18   Special thanks to Eileen Kent for the bridge analogy!

When you've got your own contracting vehicles in place, and agreements in place to subcontract on other vehicles, you've made it easy for the buyer to use the one she or he prefers. By making it easy for your buyer, you get:

- Lower business development costs

- Greater probability of winning

- Faster return on investment

- More margin and more profit

- ...And, best of all, a buyer who's on your side

Indefinite Delivery, Indefinite Quantity (IDIQ): This kind of contract vehicle may be awarded to single or multiple vendors. Government uses IDIQs when buyers have an idea of the kind of thing they want, but not how much of it or when they'll need it. In other words, vendors go through all the effort to respond to an RFP, win a contract, and are guaranteed... absolutely no sales at all.

> An IDIQ means that when the buyers who are authorized to use that contract want those products or services, they can limit their search (and time and effort) to vendors who hold that contract. First, there's a contract award; then those vendors compete to be chosen to carry out Task Orders (for services) or Delivery Orders (for products) that are covered by that contract. Some IDIQs are government-wide or open to agencies that have chosen to participate; others may be used only by a single program, office, or agency. You've got a government contract (yay!), but the government will place an order on it only if and when they feel like it.

Blanket Purchase Agreements (BPA; FAR Part 13.3): Contracting officers can set up BPAs to facilitate repetitive buys of a commonly used product or a frequently needed, low-priced service when the individual purchases might fall below the Simplified Acquisition Threshold but the total value of purchases might be much higher. An agency can use BPAs to set the Simplified Acquisition Threshold higher than $250,000...sometimes as high as $7 million or even upward of $20 million.

GSA Schedule Contracts (FAR Part 8.4): GSA Schedules are a type of IDIQ. If your target agencies use GSA Schedule contracts to buy products and services like yours, then you want to be intimately familiar with the ordering provisions outlined at FAR Part 8.4. A contracting officer can also set up a BPA based on your GSA Schedule pricing, making it even easier to make multiple purchases under your contract. (More about GSA Schedules in just a moment.)

Government-Wide Acquisition Contracts (GWACS) are another type of IDIQ. They can be used by all civilian and defense agencies and are intended solely for information technology products and services. Many federal agencies administer such contracts. Contractors that win a GWAC must then compete with other GWAC holders for task orders that are issued under that GWAC. In other words, even after they win the GWAC, they must develop business and write more proposals to win actual revenue-generating work. Buyers consider GWAC-holders to be pre-qualified and lower-risk sources because they have already been vetted through the competition to win that contract.

f. Solicitation

Let's say you're a prospective vendor and you've been busy marketing and researching and building relationships. The buyer is interested, and has money and is willing to spend... but no matter how many times you read through the rules, it looks as though none of the conditions for sole-source purchasing or any form of simplified acquisition are appropriate.

Contract Types

A government buyer must have a contract – a legal agreement between buyer and seller – to do business with you. The government uses several types of contracts; even a government credit-card purchase is a contract.

Contract types include (but aren't limited to):

- SmartPay government credit card: rules, policies, and limits vary by agency

- Fixed-Price: used for commodities and well-defined requirements. May include Economic Price Adjustment.

- Fixed-Price Incentive with or without award term

- Cost-Reimbursement with or without incentive fees, award fees, or award terms

- Time-and-Materials

- Labor-Hour

- Letter Contract

- Cost-Plus-Fixed-Fee: most commonly used for research and development

- Indefinite Delivery Vehicles (also known as IDIQ – see above)

It's far better to take part in a solid competition than to push for a sole-source acquisition that has a weak justification and leaves the contracting officer (and you) at high risk for protest. Competitive, long-lead marketing strengthens your reputation as a wise, confident, and savvy supplier, and supports the contracting officer and buyer to lower the risk of getting tangled in costly and time-consuming protests.

If your competitors think you won business through an unfair sole-source award, they will find you. Maybe not this time, but eventually. When unfair or unethical procurement practices unravel, they can get ugly and public in a hurry – sadly, and sometimes especially, when you've developed opportunities through contacts with longtime friends. Entirely ethical and above board is the only way to go.

Let's say the contracting officer must solicit offers. They've done the market survey, gotten the results of a Request for Information, run a Sources Sought. They've determined that there *are* more than two potentially responsible small businesses that could meet the requirement, and have decided to set aside the competition for small business.

They've decided which acquisition strategy to use, and published the solicitation. Now the final stage of competition begins.

g. Response to the Solicitation[19]

Yes, even if you are selective, even if you're lined up for sole-source, you can expect to prepare some kind of response or proposal.

Whether it's a Request for Proposal, Request for Quotation, Invitation for Bid, Task Order, or Delivery Order, you *do* have to ask for the business... and that means a response to the solicitation – or, in other words, a proposal.

You might be submitting to a prime contractor, or contributing a section to the prime's submission, or submitting directly to the government. No matter how effective your marketing and relationship-building have been, you can't win the business if your proposal is *non-responsive* – that is, if you don't provide what the solicitation asks for, when (on time), how (in the specified format), and where (right person, right office).

What's in a federal solicitation? FAR Part 15.204-1 spells out exactly what you can expect to see. And that's how you can expect to put together your submission.

Table 15-1—Uniform Contract Format

Section	Title
Part I—The Schedule	
A	Solicitation/contract form

---

19   Remember: although early-stage solicitations like Requests for Information or Sources Sought can sometimes require as much effort as an RFP and still not result in a contract award, your participation in carefully chosen ones is a valuable way to build awareness of your company's capabilities, meet buyers, shape requirements, and position yourself for future awards.

Section	Title
B	Supplies or services and prices/costs
C	Description/specifications/statement of work
D	Packaging and marking
E	Inspection and acceptance
F	Deliveries or performance
G	Contract administration data
H	Special contract requirements
Part II—Contract Clauses	
I	Contract clauses
Part III—List of Documents, Exhibits, and Other Attachments	
J	List of attachments
Part IV—Representations and Instructions	
K	Representations, certifications, and other statements of offerors or respondents
L	Instructions, conditions, and notices to offerors or respondents
M	Evaluation factors for award

How do people cope with that?

If you haven't had much success with your proposals, or have never done one for a government project, you've got two choices: do it yourself, or hire somebody.

There's no shame, and there can be a lot to gain, when you hire a seasoned proposal writer to support your bid. After all, you've put a lot of time into your marketing efforts. Now you want to win the business. Most of us are not professional proposal writers. We're technical and subject-matter experts and entrepreneurs. The proposal is no place to start shortchanging. What you learn from the first couple of proposals can give you enough of a template and a process to decide whether you want to build that expertise in-house, seek a different consultant, or hire that person back.

You're going to spend time and you're going to spend money on writing proposals. How much of *both* did you spend last year? What was your win rate, and your return on investment? If you're new to federal contracting, how much will you budget in the year ahead, and what's your goal for win rate and ROI?

These are key performance indicators to gauge your company's progress in the federal market. If you don't know these numbers, find out what they are right now. Track, and work to constantly improve, these indicators. Expect to shift your mix of time and money as you seek the best possible win rate and ROI.

ROI is driven by both total outlay and win rate. Global Services Inc., a professional services company specializing in federal proposals, earned its 84% win rate writing federal proposals for hundreds of clients by being good at what they do... and being selective about what they bid. I encourage you to use those criteria when you're comparing prospective proposal consultants to help you: what percentage of projects do they turn down, and what's their win rate on proposals for services or products *like yours*? Where to find a proposal writer? Start by asking friends who have succeeded in winning government work in industries like yours. Alternatively, check out LinkedIn Groups including *RFP (Request For Proposal) Professionals*, the *Association of Proposal Management Professionals*, and the *National Contract Management Association*.

Some things to ask when you're hiring a proposal writer:

- What's their experience with federal contracts, and with the agency you want to work with?

- What's their win rate?

- How much lead time do they generally require before the proposal deadline?

- What will your responsibilities be for proposal input?

- What client references do they have in your industry? Get names and numbers, and call their references.

- What steps are involved in their proposal process?

- What additional charges can you expect for production of the finished proposal?

Some things to consider if you plan to write your own proposal:

- Who on your team has the most experience with federal proposals?

- Are the right people available, with enough hours to do the job well?

- Can you afford to spend the resources to bid, given that you might not win?

- What's the risk of submitting a weak proposal, due to lack of experience, and giving the buyer a poor impression of your company?

- If you're writing your own proposal to keep your costs down, but you don't have a lot of experience, make the most of free and low-cost resources. There are lots of options, depending on how you like to learn, including:

- Most of the Procurement Technical Assistance Centers (_www.aptac-us.org_) and dozens of private sector consultants offer courses in proposal writing.

- Many websites offer templates, models, and checklists that can save you time. Make sure that your templates are specific to _federal_ buyers, and be sure that, when you use a template, you review it carefully to make sure you've customized it for your opportunity and your buyer.

- LinkedIn groups are another source of expertise. Get a look at _Carl Dickson's resources and related LinkedIn Group_, and the templates and tools he offers online at _www.CaptureManagement.com_.

- Consider hiring an established proposal writer who has a high win rate in your target agency and your industry either to review your most recent proposal or even to write your next one. What you learn can give you a strong model with many elements you can re-use.

- That being said, remember that each proposal is unique. _Never_ cut and paste a response from a past proposal to a new one until you have carefully read the solicitation and edited the recycled text so that it's _precisely_ relevant to the new requirement.

- There will never be one perfect template for your company and the agency whose business you want to win. You're probably going to be some distance from perfect through your first couple of attempts. Build your own proposal library based on experience, and expect to adapt even a winning proposal next time around.

You've Submitted. Now What?

- Make sure the point of contact listed in your proposal can be reached by phone and email. Respond promptly to any correspondence from the contracting officer. They may have questions or need clarifications on your proposal.

- The contracting officer and the agency team will evaluate all the proposals. Depending on the competitive process, they may narrow the range and negotiate with a short list of finalists.

- Eventually, they'll select a contractor and announce the results.

Post-Award

Whether you win or lose, get a debriefing as soon as possible.

What's a debriefing?

FAR Subpart 15.506 Post-award debriefing of offerors.

(a)(1) An offeror, upon its written request received by the agency within 3 days after the date on which that offeror has received notification of contract award in accordance with 15.503(b), shall be debriefed and furnished the basis for the selection decision and contract award.

The debriefing is supposed to cover:

(1) weaknesses or deficiencies in your proposal;

(2) how your cost, pricing, technical qualifications and past performance stacked up against the winner;

(3) how your offer was ranked overall against your competitors;

(4) the rationale for the award;

(5) the make and model of commercial item to be delivered by the successful offeror; and

(6) "reasonable responses to relevant questions" concerning whether the rules that were to govern the specific competition were followed.

Find out more about debriefing – such as what isn't included, when you can get a pre-award debriefing, and when and how either you or the contracting officer can delay the debriefing – at FAR Subpart 15.5.

A formal debriefing is *required* in only two situations: for procurements under FAR Part 15 - Contracting by Negotiation, and for task or delivery orders exceeding $5.5 Million under FAR 16.505(b)(6) when the agency receives your written (emailed) request within 3 calendar days after you receive:

- Notification of exclusion from the competitive range (FAR 15.505) or

- Notification of Contract Award (FAR 15.506).

If you win an Indefinite Delivery Vehicle contract (that is, if you're one of many vendors who are eligible to compete for multiple opportunities to supply products or services under a base contract), you aren't always entitled to a debriefing on the results of competitions for individual orders under those contracts.

Not all task orders are created equal: companies with a General Services Administration schedule contract are not entitled to a debriefing from an agency if they lose a bid for a task order.

If you've bid an opportunity that is *not* under FAR Part 15 and *not* a task/delivery order over $5.5M under FAR 16.505(b)(6), then a formal debriefing is *not* required.

Vendors who make an offer under Simplified Acquisition Procedures may request a slightly more formal structure called a "Brief Explanation," described in FAR 15.503 (b) (1). At a minimum, it includes:

- (i) The number of offerors solicited;

- (ii) The number of proposals received;

- (iii) The name and address of each offeror receiving an award;

- (iv) The items, quantities, and any stated unit prices of each award. If... impracticable at that time, only the total contract price need be furnished... [h]owever (it)...shall be made publicly available, upon request; and

- (v) In general terms, the reason(s) the offeror's proposal was not accepted, unless the price...readily reveals the reason...

Five Reasons To Seek A Debriefing

Even if the contracting officer isn't required to provide a formal debriefing, you can – and should – always ask for *feedback* on your proposal. Whether you win *or* lose!

1. Pre-Protest: If you know you're going to protest an award, you must file a formal protest no more than five days after the earliest debriefing date you were offered. After that, your opportunities for redress become more complicated and your chances of overturning the award decrease. Take a look at FAR Part 33 – ahead of time – so you have a good idea of exactly what you're going to do if you're concerned about the outcome.

2. Fact Finding: You might have concerns but not *know* whether or not you want to protest. Get the debriefing anyway, to discover everything you can about the competitive and evaluation procedures that were used, and how those compare to the FAR that governed the acquisition.

3. Lessons Learned: If you went to the effort to submit an offer of any kind – whether a complex proposal or a simple quote – you want to learn as much as you can from the time and money you invested to make the offer. If you know you do not want to protest the award, make that clear when you request the debriefing. That will help set a relaxed tone and make conversations easier.

   BONUS: You can also ask the contracting officer if you can debrief them to help them with lessons learned! Many COs have never worked in industry and may be genuinely curious to learn more about what you went through to prepare your offer.

Did you lose?

- At a minimum, you probably want to know what you could do better next time, and to be confident that your offer was treated fairly.

- A contracting officer who sees you as a qualified bidder they'd like to do business with may choose to coach you through a couple of informal post-award conversations to position you for future success.

Did you win?

- No proposal is perfect. There are always things you can do better. Asking for a debriefing or feedback shows humility, gratitude, and a willingness to listen. All essential for building trust and success.

- Next, you want to know whether your offer was definitively superior, or whether your victory was a squeaker. If your margin of winning was narrow, you're going to have to make an extra effort to prove yourself from the moment you start to perform.

  Was your win a surprise to you, when you didn't know the buyer? If they didn't know you either, imagine how they feel. What if you won on a technicality, but weren't the company the buyer really hoped would win? You really want to uncover any concerns they might have right from the start. A smart vendor will address those concerns immediately to keep the business, win any option years, and position for an eventual re-competition.

4. Marketing: The contracting officer can invite a variety of officials to the debriefing. That's your chance to meet decision-makers and -influencers face to face. You can ask about others who are involved in buying services or products like yours. You can inquire about similar opportunities that may be coming up.

   You can also ask for a follow-up meeting to get to know each other better. In short, this can be the beginning of a beautiful relationship! As you'll see, more than one of my clients has won opportunities based on relationships that got started with a debriefing.

5. Help Defend the Award: If you won, but the award is likely to be protested, then a debriefing can serve the purpose of a rehearsal to help the federal contracting team prepare for debriefings they can expect to have with unsuccessful offerors.

PROFILE IN SUCCESS: Krug Furniture

GSA's Furniture Commodity Center (now the Integrated Workplace Acquisition Center) denied an award to Krug Furniture, citing eleven different deficiencies in their proposal. Krug thought that GSA had misunderstood their offer, and so Mike Boehmer, Krug's Director of Sales for GSA, asked for a debriefing.

A whole team attended the briefing – contract specialists, managers, and even the head of the Furniture Commodity Center. They took his request very seriously.

As GSA went through the list of eleven deficiencies, they actually reversed their views on ten of them... but hit one no-go: GSA required offerors to submit testing data from Underwriters Laboratory, and Krug had submitted testing data from a different organization that the company was confident would be accepted as equivalent. It was not. The solicitation meant what it said.

But something else happened along the way: Krug got to know many key players in GSA that day. Mike and his team made a strong positive impression because they came in well prepared, engaged in the discussions with a positive attitude, and accepted the results with grace. In short, they made friends who wanted to help them succeed with future proposals.

And succeed they did. Krug has sold over $100 million in furniture since then to federal buyers.

Contract Execution and Administration

Once you win, you've got more responsibilities for performance and contract administration... and remember, if you don't invoice correctly, you don't get paid. In fact, sometimes even if you *do* invoice correctly, something goes wrong and things get held up. Want to get paid on time? The contracting officer will continue to be among your best friends even after you sign on the dotted line.

Performance

Post-award, the FAR continues to light the path to success. Your win is the beginning, not the end, of the game. After all the work you've done to win, your ability to grow your federal business is firmly rooted in how well you perform.

Sort of like elections, the next competition begins the moment the last one ends.

Modifications/Updates: Successful contractors get regular feedback from their clients about how well they're performing, and are also alert for the need for opportunities to fine-tune their deliverables to better meet the client's new and emerging requirements.

Oh, and if you don't perform well, the government can unilaterally terminate your contract.

Your contract may include provisions for additional task orders, options, or recompetes. However, you only get paid for delivering what's in the statement of work and has been authorized. Be alert to the need to use contract modification procedures or to formally exercise contract options before extending your performance or delivery.

Part 5: More About GSA Schedule Contracts!

Curious about GSA Schedule contracts? Considering getting one for your company? You're not alone!

GSA Schedules open exciting opportunities. Hundreds of companies drive multimillion-dollar revenue with these contracts. Those companies make significant investment up front to support that success. Conversely, thousands of companies spend tons of time and money to get a GSA Schedule only to win nothing.

When could a GSA Schedule be right for your company? Here's some things to consider.

What's a GSA Schedule?

Let's start at the beginning. The US General Services Administration (GSA) is an agency of the US federal government. GSA aims to offer the best value and efficient administration of the goods and services most suitable for the federal government to perform its missions, and the acquisition services and management policies that are required to do so.

GSA plays an important role in billions of dollars' worth of goods and services contracts. GSA's operations are headquartered in Washington DC, and include dozens of offices across its eleven regions. Its operations include the **Public Buildings Service** (which owns and leases over 376.9 million square feet of space in 9,600 buildings in more than 2,200 communities nationwide) and the **Federal Acquisition Service**, which manages the government's acquisition regulatory process and administers the GSA Schedule contracts.

GSA Schedule contracts enable all authorized government buyers (military and civilian at the federal level, and some state and local) buyers to purchase certain categories of goods and services that are already available in the commercial market easily and quickly, by negotiating government-wide terms and conditions.

GSA is rarely the end user or consumer of the items and services that are sold through these contracts, nor does GSA generally warehouse things. With a GSA Schedule Contract, you're almost always using this contract to sell to other agencies. GSA's role is to negotiate and administer the contract that they and other agencies use.

Learn more about GSA Schedules starting with
https://www.gsa.gov/acquisition/purchasing-programs/gsa-schedules

GSA offers a free *Vendor Toolbox*: resources to help you decide whether getting a GSA Schedule contract is in your best interest.

Fast Facts You Need To Know About GSA Schedule Contracts

- Federal buyers don't have to use GSA Schedules. **Only about 10% of the total federal contract spend is made using GSA Schedules.** Buyers have *many* options. Contracting officers use the contracting vehicles of *their* choice – not yours.

- Yes, a GSA Schedule can give you an advantage. Some buyers like to use GSA Schedules – but not all of them! Does yours? Only the past federal-contract data can give you the definitive answer. If your target buyers use some other contract vehicle, then you might not want to pursue a GSA Schedule.

- No, the government does not require your company to have a GSA Schedule contract in order to win federal business.

  o The government does not charge you money to submit a GSA Schedule proposal.

  o However, the proposal is complex.

  o It requires price, technical, financial, and management information about your company, including recent invoices to substantiate pricing. Your proposal becomes the basis for negotiations that, if successful, set the terms of your contract.

  o Some companies prepare this proposal on their own. Others get free advice from the GSA Contracting Officer or the local Procurement Technical Assistance Center. Still others hire a consultant that specializes in preparing and negotiating GSA Schedule proposals. No matter which approach you choose, this proposal represents an investment of months of time and thousands of dollars of cash or sweat equity.

- **There is no guarantee that any buyer will use your GSA Schedule contract to purchase from you.**

Whether you prepare the proposal on your own, hire a consultant to help, use a combination of your own resources and subject-matter experts like those at the PTAC, or even just get advice from your contracting officer, your response represents a considerable investment of time and money. To make your decision on that investment with confidence, first research:

- whether the government uses GSA Schedules to buy products and services like yours;

- how much of them the government buys using GSA Schedules; and

- how much of them the government buys using *other* contract vehicles.

GSA offers a free online readiness assessment for vendors considering the Schedules program. Visit *https://vsc.gsa.gov/RA/toolBox.cfm*

You don't "apply" or "register" for a GSA Schedule Contract. GSA Schedule Contracts are awarded through a competitive process. Interested vendors review the appropriate solicitation and, if they wish, submit a proposal.

As part of the proposal process, GSA also requires vendors to complete its online training at *https://vsc.gsa.gov/* about how vendors will be expected to manage their contract and comply with the terms and conditions.

If you're working on your GSA Schedule proposal but don't yet have a contract, you can and should still be marketing and developing leads and interest while you're working on it.

If a buyer wants to use a GSA Schedule to purchase from you before you have your GSA Schedule, you can subcontract through a partner who does hold an appropriate GSA Schedule. The General Services Administration may need weeks or months of lead time to modify a GSA Schedule to add a subcontractor, so be sure to have your partners in place with lots of lead time.

Contract awards are based on how well your proposal responds to GSA's solicitation and how well you fare in subsequent negotiations. If your proposal is accepted, and your negotiations are successful, you'll execute a legally binding contractual agreement between your company and the General Services Administration.

Remember, a GSA Schedule is an actual contract, but for indefinite delivery and indefinite quantity (IDIQ – there's that phrase again) of specified products or services. In other words, it makes no guarantee of how much any buyer might want to purchase, or when. Think of it like a hunting license: Just because you get a hunting license doesn't mean you're gonna bag a moose. Once you get the contract, you will need to spend time and money marketing and selling to buyers.

Your GSA Schedule contract *does* establish the terms and conditions, including sales goals, under which you agree to offer the goods and/or services covered by that contract.

The contract award begins with a five-year base period. You may be eligible for up to three 5-year renewal options, if you meet your sales goals and other obligations. In other words, you might hold this contract for up to 20 years.

GSA can – and, more often these days, does -- cancel Schedule contracts with vendors who don't sell at least $25,000 on their contract in the first 24 months.

GSA permits vendors to modify the contract to add, change, or remove items, as well as revise prices, during the life of the contract.

Negotiating the right price on your GSA Schedule is important. That issue alone is one reason why many companies choose to work with a GSA Schedule consultant.

- Federal buyers can negotiate other deals based on your GSA Schedule pricing.

- Your published GSA Schedule prices are ceiling prices for what you can charge someone who's buying from that contract. You'll want to learn more about how you can offer spot discounts, and what kind of action triggers a price-reduction clause to everyone who can buy from your GSA Schedule.

- Your GSA Schedule pricing must be based on actual past invoices.

- GSA will want a price that's as good as, or better than, the price you offer your best comparable commercial customer.

- After a contract award, your entire contract, including your unit pricing, is published on the GSA e-library, where both buyers and competitors can see it. If you feel uncomfortable with that prospect, consider the upside: you can also see your competitors' GSA Schedule pricing.

There's no submission deadline. If you decide you want to pursue a GSA Schedule contract, you can start any time, and take as long as you like. If you tend to get things done better when you have a deadline, then decide when it's important for your company to get this finished. Lack of a specific deadline is one of the reasons why hundreds of companies take years to get their GSA Schedule proposals finished...and why many other business owners realize they're only going to get that job done by hiring help (about which more shortly.)

Whether you do this on your own, get some help, or hand the whole job over to a professional, read the information on GSA's website before you begin. You'll find free online education about the Schedules program. Some of that education is mandatory for GSA Schedule contract holders prior to award; however, you can take the classes even if you don't have a GSA Schedule.

If and when you decide you're ready to begin, download and respond to solicitations that match the products and/or services you offer.

Which one (or ones) fit what you offer? Review the full list online.[20] Schedule contracts for medical, dental, and veterinary products and services are administered by the Department of Veterans Affairs.[21]

Once awarded and executed, each GSA Schedule contract has a unique identifying number. If you hear people asking you about a "GSA Number", that's what they're talking about. If you win more than one Schedule contract, each one will have its own number.

Companies may hold multiple GSA Schedule contracts. You might want to consider making such an investment if contract data shows that your target buyers make significant use of GSA Schedules to buy what you do *and* you're ready to apply sales and marketing resources to win business on each Schedule.

You can be a subcontractor to a GSA Schedule vendor. Not ready for your own GSA Schedule, but your buyer wants to use that vehicle? Data might show that your target buyers make heavy use of GSA Schedules. If so, *and* if the buyers you're talking to are eager to buy that way, but you don't have a Schedule contract, you can negotiate a subcontract with another vendor who does. If that's your plan, then you'll also want to research which GSA Schedule contractors your buyer already does business with.

These are multiple-award contracts. GSA negotiates Schedule contracts with thousands of companies offering products and services that buyers might consider alongside yours. Each winner invests a lot of time and effort to submit and negotiate a proposal. Once you win a GSA Schedule Contract, there is no guarantee that anyone will invite you to bid or to supply a requirement. It's up to *you*, the vendor, to let them know they can use this contract to buy from you.

There is no minimum company size requirement to submit a GSA Schedule proposal. But GSA generally requires vendors to provide at least two years' worth of invoices to substantiate the prices you propose to offer. Every company, large or small, that invests the time and money it takes to win a GSA Schedule can expect to spend significant sales and marketing resources to get a return on that investment.

It's a door opener and deal closer. Some prospects or primes may ask whether you're on GSA as an indicator of your level of experience with and commitment to government business.

When government buyers have money and know what they want, Schedule contracts let them buy quickly, and meet the requirements for a competitive process from among Schedule contract holders with minimal effort.

A GSA Schedule contract positions you as a lower-risk choice. Government buyers know that GSA has reviewed and approved every Schedule contract holder's

---

20   *http://www.gsaelibrary.gsa.gov/*
21   *https://www.fss.va.gov/*

management, pricing, and financial information. Even if they don't *use* that contract to buy from you, it makes them feel safe to *consider* you, especially if you're new to them.

Similarly, your GSA Schedule contract gives you credibility when you're approaching a prime contractor: again, lower risk. Got solid sales on that contract? Even better!

Hard Cold Facts

In 2016, the federal government awarded $14.75 billion in business through its GSA Schedule 70 contract, for information technology. Let's take at some statistics about that one contract.

4,924 firms offered their solutions through that contract. Of those:

- The top 100 firms – just over 2% of awardees – won a whopping 66%, clocking in at $9.7B. **The Top 100 share has not changed since at least 2004.**

- 3,213 other firms – 65% of awardees – shared the remaining 34%, just $4.8B.

Doesn't add up, you say? Indeed it does not. Because 1,611 firms – 32% of awardees – sold $0.

Zero. Zip. Zilch. Nada. Nothing.

Minor good news: the percentage of vendors who *did* win work through this contract rose about 12% between 2004 and 2016.

If the others had just sold nothing, that would be bad enough. Here's what these numbers don't tell you: how much they spent **just to have the privilege of winning nothing whatsoever**. Each one of those 1,611 disappointed contract holders probably spent:

- Anywhere from $5,000 to over $30,000 in consulting and legal fees (or the equivalent in internal sweat equity) and six months to a year of elapsed time to prepare and negotiate their offers;

- Anywhere from $30,000 to $200,000 in marketing and sales staff; and

- Well over $50,000 in specialized marketing activities for the federal government niche, including websites, trade shows, conferences, meetings, and memberships.

Even using very conservative estimates, those unsuccessful companies collectively spent upwards of two hundred million dollars and got nothing in return. Why would they do that?

- Fear: of missing an opportunity

- Hope: in what someone sold them as a fast track to easy sales

- Ignorance: of alternatives that might have been equally, or more, cost effective

And you know what? I run a small business. I've made bad choices for reasons like that. And sometimes that's how we all learn. But I'd rather you save your painful learning for something more soul-enriching, save your money for something either more fun or profitable, and just let you get this lesson without the pain.

Markers of GSA Schedule Success[22]

80% of active small business contractors surveyed who hold GSA Schedule contracts have annual revenues of over $1 million, and derive 47% of their annual revenues (at least $500,000 per year) from their federal contracts. Only 58% of active contractors not on GSA Schedules have total annual revenue of more than $1 million. Federal business accounts for only 33% of their revenues.

Do GSA Schedules drive growth...or do more companies tend to pursue GSA Schedules once they pass the million-dollar mark? Maybe a bit of both.

More GSA Schedule contract holders are located close to Washington DC than elsewhere. 44% of active contractors in the South Atlantic region (MD, DC, VA and east-coast states down to Florida) are on the GSA Schedule. Mid-Atlantic (NJ, NY, PA) and East-South-Central (AL, KY, MS, TN) regions account for just 16% and 19%, respectively, of GSA Schedule contract holders.

Those stats might simply reflect that once a company decides to get a GSA Schedule, they often establish operations closer to where many of their buyers are.

Do You Need A GSA Schedule? How To Tell

Whether and when to get a GSA Schedule is a high-stakes business decision. Don't let someone pressure or persuade you to make that decision before you've reviewed detailed federal contract data that shows you how your target buyers actually purchase.

A consultant who insists that you really, really ought to have a GSA Schedule, but doesn't show you hard data to back up that recommendation, might not have your interests in mind. Similarly, don't be surprised if a federal official will talk in general terms about how important GSA Schedules are. GSA encourages new vendors: it wants government buyers to have a competitive range of items and prices to choose from. Small business advocates across government want to show

22   Reference: Strategies for Success from Federal Small Business Contractors – A Research Summary for the American Express OPEN for Government Contracts: Victory in ProcurementSM (VIP) for Small Business Program

that they did everything possible to open access, including via GSA Schedules, for small companies to participate in government opportunities.

You might need a GSA Schedule if...

- Serious prospects are asking, "Are you on GSA?"

- Your competitors are on GSA...and you're losing to them because buyers strongly prefer to use the Schedule.

- You are willing to invest time and money to learn how Schedules work and what marketing techniques are effective, and then hire experienced help while you do it.

- You sell products or services to the commercial market, preferably in the USA, and can show a minimum of two years' worth of corporate financial records, preferably audited ones, to GSA.

- The prime contractors you want to work with require it for teaming.

- You are tired of giving up your margin as a subcontractor to the primes or partners on a growing volume of business.

Don't rush to get a schedule if...

- Your prospects can and will use other contract vehicles – whether to you directly or via subcontract to someone else.

- You lack resources for proposal development and the negotiation, administration, and marketing of your Schedule contract.

- You can spare the margin to sell through a channel partner's schedule while you build volume and credibility.

- Your usual order size for products is under $10,000. If so, buyers can use Micro-Purchase procedures – they don't even need to compete the purchase! – and SmartPay (the government credit card).

- You don't expect to win business worth at least $25,000 via this contract in one of the first two years. If you don't sell at least that much, GSA can cancel your contract, or decline to renew it.

Do You Need A Special Consultant To Get A GSA Schedule?

Should you hire a firm to help with your GSA Schedule?

Maybe! GSA knows that many vendors hire consultants to write their GSA Schedule proposals, negotiate, and even administer the resulting contract. They often remind vendors that you *can* do the proposal yourself.

Of all the proposals you'll submit in the federal market, a GSA Schedule can be one of the most important. Not many government contracts can run 20 years, and give you lots of opportunities to change your prices and offerings!

Five Signs That A GSA Schedule Consultant Could Benefit Your Company

If a GSA Schedule is right for your company, you need to ensure not only that you win a Schedule, but that the contract you negotiate is good for your company and works for your sales team. Winning a Schedule with too-low rates may be worse than not winning one at all!

These five signs will help you decide whether hiring a GSA Schedule consultant is right for your company.

1. **EXPERTISE: You have little to no experience with GSA Schedule proposals.** GSA Schedule proposals are unlike any other federal proposal. They are based on past performance, and require the correct analysis and proposal presentation for both the technical and pricing portions. Different Schedules and Special Item Numbers have distinct and very specific requirements, many of which are not clear from the Solicitation alone.

2. **ELIGIBILITY: You are not certain which Schedule(s) or Special Item Numbers to pursue.** You need to understand all of the potential GSA Schedules and the scope of each in order to determine which ones are the best fit for what you do, and whether you meet their requirements.

3. **RATE OPTIMIZATION: The final ceiling rates awarded for the GSA Schedule contract will have a major impact on the bottom line of your company.** An experienced consultant who has strong relationships with GSA's contracting staff and has negotiated thousands of proposals can result in higher rates (which means more revenue for you). Remember that the rates on your GSA Schedule affect the rates you charge to all of your customers – whether they're purchasing through the Schedule or not.

4. **BANDWIDTH: Your Company is busy with billable work, projects, and proposals.** Hiring an expert to take the GSA Schedule proposal process off your hands allows your team to focus on driving revenue and completing other tasks at hand.

5. **TIMELINE: Your Company needs the GSA Schedule contract awarded as quickly as possible.** GSA Schedule awards can take up to twelve months. If your initial proposal is rejected, the total time to award can be years. Submitting an offer that is 100% compliant the first time mitigates this risk and streamlines the process, resulting in the fastest award possible.

By Courtney Fairchild, President and CEO of Global Services. For more than 20 years, Global Services has prepared GSA Schedules and federal proposals for clients who have won over 2,500 contract awards totaling in excess of $20 billion. Find out more at www. globalservicesinc.com.

Part 6: First Look: Contract Opportunities (And Buyers!)

Enough, already. You want to look at some actual opportunities, and you promise not to run out and write proposals this afternoon?

The federal government is happy to oblige, and for free!

You might already have a subscription to a bid service. Many PTACs offer bid-matching or bid-search services.

Keep this in mind: No matter how perfect the opportunity looks, just because it lands in your inbox does not mean you should bid on it. In fact, if that's the first time you're hearing about it, you want to think very hard before you start writing a proposal.

Let's start by getting a sense of the flow of opportunities that federal buyers publish every day, so that you can get a look at notices of opportunities that might fit your company.

Here's how to do that.

Register & Set Your Profile To Receive Opportunities

Why do this: While you can browse opportunities without logging in, login lets you define specific opportunities that you'll receive automatically. This lesson gives you both the reassurance that you're not missing out on opportunities and the peace of mind to put them someplace safe so that they won't distract you until you're really ready to look at them.

What you'll need:

- Your entity registration already complete in SAM.gov
- Your login credentials for *login.gov*

Time Investment: About 30 minutes

Where to go:

- *https://beta.SAM.gov* , and select the domain Contract Opportunities

- Start with a broad search by keyword rather than by NAICSSort by date to begin with the most recent

- Notice how many entries come up: Dozens? Hundreds?

- Filter by type of solicitation.

    › Look at an example of each type of solicitation.

    › Notice the differences in the type of information each contains.

    › Some – but not all – types of solicitations notices display an option at the top to "Follow." Choose one or two that look interesting, and practice setting up how often you'd like to receive notification about them.

- Experiment with combinations of filters like type of solicitation, agency, publication date, set-aside, and place of performance.

- When you find a combination of filters that gives you a list that starts to look genuinely interesting, you can

    › download the search to .csv (which will also give you the option to name and save it)

    › or just save it.

What next:

- Consider setting up a FOLDER (or multiple folders if you have created several different notification searches) and a RULE in your email program to automatically file contract opportunity notices in that folder.

- Once you've got about 20 of those opportunities, review and sort out which ones genuinely fit your past performance and capabilities – and which ones don't.

- Refine your search criteria so you get more of what you want and less of what you don't want.

- Sort out which type of notices they are, and sort by how early in the buying process they are. The earliest stage can be general industry days or small business events. Next, RFIs or Broad Agency Announcements; then Sources-Sought, Draft RFP's, RFP's, and Combined Solicitation/Synopsis: any of those could represent something that hasn't been awarded yet and that, in theory, you might be able to win. Later-stage notices, that are almost always too late to run after, include "Notice of Intent To Sole-Source" and "Notice of Award."

- Review the ones that are the best fit. For each one, ask yourself, "Have I heard of this requirement already? Do I know the contracting officer? The small business specialist? The buying organization? The end user? The budget? The incumbent? The history?"

- If most of your answers are "No," then a proposal would probably be unsuccessful.

- If you see an exciting Request For Proposal that looks perfect for your company, but it's the first time you're hearing about it, odds are good that the buyer is already in touch with your competitors. While you could drop everything to write a proposal, the best thing you can do might be to follow up with the point of contact and get to know them better. Your chances of success are likely to be better on a future competition that on this one.

- Start collecting contact information from the most promising opportunities. Copy that information from the procurement notices and start to log those somewhere simple, like in a spreadsheet. Notice who the most active buyers are. Which points of contact come up again and again in your target agencies, buying what you do? *Those people* represent prospects you want to get to know. For now, just start logging those contacts. We'll start to sort out who's who in the chapter on Relationships.

Remember: LOOK, BUT DO NOT SUBMIT ANY PROPOSALS RIGHT NOW.

Review any attractive "opportunity" with care. Remember how much time and money it will take to prepare a proposal. This is still a research exercise. If all you know about the opportunity is what you see in the request for proposal, then you probably *don't* know enough about the opportunity to submit a winning proposal.

Acquisition Rules Change Constantly. Stay Current!

In most games, the rules don't change very often. In federal acquisition, the rules are the definition of transparent and predictable, but they also implement other policy objectives that the federal government wants to achieve when it buys things. That means the rules change constantly. Expect to invest time to stay current. Non-compliance with these rules, even if it's inadvertent, risks consequences that can range from not getting paid to disbarment from contracting altogether... or even jail.

Every week, the federal government changes and works on dozens of laws and rules that affect your federal business opportunities, for better or (possibly) worse, including things like:

- The threshold for Simplified Acquisition Procedures was raised in 2018 from $150,000 to $250,000, enabling federal buyers to make bigger purchases without complex competition requirements.

- The Micro-Purchase Threshold: Warranted contracting officers may make purchases of up to $10,000 and award the work without competition. The legislative authority to increase the Micro-Purchase Threshold to that level was passed in 2017; the FAR Council spent more than the first half of 2018 working on regulations to implement that change. Even when acquisition laws change to make things easier for everyone, contracting officers have to wait for final implementing rules to be published before using new procedures.

- The Small business Subcontracting Threshold was last raised from $650,000 to $700,000. Large businesses thus may win even larger contracts before they're required to have a subcontracting plan for small business.

- The Women-Owned Small Business (WOSB) Federal Contracting Assistance Program has been expanded and revised several times since it was launched in 2010. First, the initial dollar limitations on set-aside awards were removed. Authority for sole-source awards was not added until 2016! Then, there's this: not every woman-owned small business is eligible for the WOSB program. SBA specifies and periodically revises the NAICS codes covered by this program – which it did most recently in 2016 and will do again -- based on data showing industries in which women-owned businesses are less well-represented in federal contracting than in industry as a whole. If your NAICS codes are removed from the WOSB program, you might suddenly be ineligible for set-aside contract awards under the WOSB program.

- In 2016, the Supreme Court ruled[23] that the Department of Veterans Affairs must first offer all contract opportunities to veteran-owned and service-disabled veteran-owned businesses before considering non-veteran-owned suppliers. Implementing policies have been the subject of ongoing controversy both within the agency and among large and small businesses.

- In 2016, the Small Business Administration launched its "All Small" Mentor-Protégé program that complements and is in the process of replacing similar programs that had been developed by individual federal departments, and restructured related rules governing joint ventures and subcontracting. Such rules define the kinds of corporate relationships and affiliations that affect the eligibility of a small business in specific alliances to win set-aside contracts.

How to keep up? A few ideas:

- Regulatory changes are published each business day in the *Federal Register* (www.federalregister.gov). You can set up a free online account and electronic alert to send you daily notices of regulatory changes on topics and agencies that matter to you. That makes it easy for you to stay current, to offer comments on proposals and draft regulations, and know when new rules that affect you have come into force.

---

23   In Kingdomware Technologies, Inc. v. United States, a decision colloquially referred to as "Kingdomware"

- Set Google Alerts for keywords related to procurement law and regulation.

- Big time saver: Many law firms and leading industry associations whose clients and members are focused on procurement track and report on significant regulatory changes in their newsletters – a great benefit of membership. Find out what services your law firm or industry associations offer you, and subscribe.

Face it: your contracting officer specializes in the Federal Acquisition Regulations. They might even have a Bachelor's or Master's degree in acquisition policy! They're always going to know the rules better than you do, because they know something you don't: their *interpretation* of the rules. There are over 50,000 federal contracting officers. How many interpretations of the rules do you think there are?

That being said, your contracting officer expects you to know your way around the rules.

Some facts for starters:

- Rules let government buyers purchase from vendors they prefer.

- Government buyers have lots of options to buy from you.

- Rules strongly encourage competition.

- Those same rules also establish preferences that *limit* (but don't eliminate) competition.

- It's faster to use an existing contract than to start a new competition.

- Some acquisition methods are a *lot* simpler and faster than others.

- Not every acquisition goes smoothly. The rules explain how to protest, solve problems and resolve disputes, and define the rights and obligations of sellers as well as buyers.

Knowledge of the rules gives you power. When you know your way around the Federal Acquisition Regulations, or FAR, you can:

- Influence project specifications (entirely legally!);

- Schedule marketing activities for maximum impact;

- Disqualify competitors;

- Get paid on time (and even collect late-payment fees from government!);

- Ensure you're being treated fairly; and

- Fix the problem if you're NOT treated fairly.

If you *don't* learn the rules, you risk:

- Missing opportunities;

- Looking too inexperienced to be worth a second meeting;

- Making naïve price offers that give away your profit to the prime;

- Spending thousands to get on a bid team, but getting dropped from the contract;

- Not getting paid, or being terminated, for non-performance or non-compliance; or even

- Getting barred or sued.

And don't tell me you don't need to know that because you're just going to subcontract!

- Both federal buyers and prime contractors presume you know the rules.

- Many of the prime contractor's obligations under FAR flow down to subcontractors.

- Some partners take advantage of you when they realize you don't know the rules.

If government buyers want what you've got, especially if they have an urgent need, they can and will thread their way through the rules to find a way to make it easy to buy from you. In particular, they'll go out of their way to find an existing contract rather than start a new competition.

Remember: what you sell includes not only your products or services but the whole experience of doing business with you. Like you, government buyers are also under pressure to do more than they have time to do. That includes a whole lot of other job functions besides finding convenient ways to buy what you are selling.

Turn that pressure into an advantage by making it easier for your government buyer to do business with you! Government has a lot of different options when it wants to buy something. Some are faster than others. Each is ideal for meeting certain kinds of requirements.

> Know the rules, and research current contract vehicles your buyer might use to do business with you.

READY FOR THE NEXT STEP? PROCESS CHECKLIST

Know the rules of the game:

○ Where to find the rules that govern how you can sell

○ How your target agencies buy

○ Which contract types and/or GSA Schedules they use

○ Which rules have just changed, and which are about to

○ Which set-asides and preferences you can access

○ When (and how) to submit proposals

○ How to leverage the debriefing

Find Out More

Tap in-depth lessons, including tip sheets and worksheets, on demand at www.GrowFedBiz.com:

• Mighty Micro-Purchase: Sole Source Super-Power

• Simplified Acquisition: Simply Awesome!

• Never Lose Again: The Debriefing Workshop

Get discounts and access special handouts with the code **GCME.**

Other Resources

• National Contract Management Association www.ncmahq.org

Chapter Four: Competition

First, the good news: government almost certainly buys the kind of products, services, or solutions you offer. Next, the bad news: they're probably buying from someone else right now. Now you can change that. Once you're honest about what you do well (and what you don't), you master the power of unique value. That's key to sidelining your competitors.

What You'll Learn: How to use...

- Four research tools to check out your competitors
- Two short worksheets for competitive analysis
- One worksheet to organize your past performance records
- Four marketing power tools to help your company stand out

Market Research Essentials

I've heard hundreds of small, innovative companies give a breathless description of their product or service, and explain why government buyers might want to buy it. When I ask them, "Who's your competition?" they glance around to see if anyone's watching, swagger just a little bit, lean in, and tell me, "We have no competition."

Your federal government respectfully disagrees. The federal government rarely has a problem so new that they've never had to deal with it before. Problems, needs, specifications, and the leading edge of what industry can offer don't start from scratch; they evolve over time. That means that somebody's already spending their money, or has their budget already spoken for, to buy their idea of the best thing they can afford to do the job right now... and they're not buying it from you.

Yet.

"Oh," you say.

Now that you're getting to know "the process" (or, really, the options) for how federal agencies buy products or services like yours, it's time to find out who they're buying from today. Once you know your leading competitors, you can start to figure out why a government buyer should pay any attention to you when they're already buying from somebody else.

Good News

Okay, welcome to one of the *very* best things about doing business with the federal government: public money means public information. 535 members of Congress wouldn't have it any other way.

Did you know? Any time the government awards a contract worth more than $10,000, the contracting office collects over 248 pieces of information about the purchase. And then they publish it. Online. Right now. 24/7.

You have something no other government in the world offers its citizens: glorious, easily searchable, comprehensive detail on over 20 years' worth of past contracts. Until you learn your way around, you can get lost in there for days. Don't despair! You're about to learn how to turn this data into priceless intelligence that winning companies use every day.

Back To The Future

Why would you look at past contract data, when the federal government publishes hundreds of contract opportunities every day that you can bid on right now?

What's the opportunity if these are past awards? Isn't that business long gone?

Successful contractors focus on *who* is buying as well as *what* they buy...and build trusted relationships with those buyers long before new opportunities are published.

The *most* successful contractors often collaborate with buyers to understand future requirements and make it easier for the buyers to award work to the contractors they most want to work with.

How Winners Start Filling the Opportunity Pipeline Ahead of Contract Opportunities

Remember the searches into past contract awards that you did in Chapter Two, Focus?

Click on the contract number, for example, and the detail screen includes information about when that contract expires.

- Search and build a group of contracts that you might like to win if there's follow-on business or recompetes.

- Export that info to Excel and sort by contract expiry date.

- Work backwards anywhere from 3-18 months from contract expiry dates. The bigger the contract, the greater the lead time. That helps you estimate when those contracting offices and buyers might be starting to think about the follow-on competition to renew or extend their supply or service.

- When you find clues to opportunities you'd like to pursue, then check the buying agency's forecasts to find out about their plans (how to do that is in the next Chapter). Add the contacts you find in the buying forecasts to your list of contacts in that agency (see Chapter 6 "Relationships" for who to reach out to and how).

How to start

Create a new research worksheet, like the one below, to keep your research focused. There is so much data in these systems that it's easy to lose track of what you were looking for in the first place!

Expect to discover all kinds of new data (and more questions!) as you go along. A research worksheet will help you track the answers you started out looking for, as well as your new questions and finds.

Select your search criteria

The federal government uses two systems to code its purchasing data: North American Industrial Classification System (NAICS)[24] Codes and Product Service Codes (PSC)[25]. Both are useful, but even when you use them together, you'll also want to use other keywords and search terms.

- NAICS codes are widely used for many kinds of economic-analysis and data-collection systems. The codes are used by commercial and government users for everything from tax and corporate-formation filings to small business size-standard definitions. Because NAICS codes were not created uniquely to categorize government purchases, they can seem frustratingly general if you use these terms alone to research contract data.

- PSCs are a taxonomy unique to the federal government, organized in a way that reflects the type of goods and services that government buys. If you're not familiar with PSCs, set aside some time to review the PSC list (see footnote) and get to know this powerful search tool.

- If you search using both NAICS *and* PSCs, you'll significantly improve the precision of your search results. Get to know which ones might be used to classify your products or services. Search utilities offer drop-down menus that permit you to select multiple codes when you set up your search.

- If you're not sure what NAICS and PSCs to choose, search the contract records for a couple of your competitors. See which codes buyers chose for *their* contracts.

- Notice which codes account for about 80% of the value of buying what you do. While you think of it, make sure your Entity Record in SAM.gov includes those!

Select Fiscal Year: While the data is entered all year long, it's important to get a full 12 months of data, because federal purchasing surges in the fourth quarter of the fiscal year: that is, July through September. To get the most complete picture of the competition, unless you're searching for info on a specific recent action, begin your market research by looking at the fiscal year most recently completed.

Furthermore, the Department of Defense can delay publishing its contract data by up to 90 days, to protect intelligence on the tempo of its operations. For a full federal fiscal year of data for the year that ends on September 30th of one calendar year, you need to wait until just after January 1st of the next.

---

24   *www.naics.org*
25   *https://www.acquisition.gov/PSC_Manual*

RESEARCH TOOL #1: FEDERAL PROCUREMENT DATA SYSTEM (FPDS) / CONTRACT DATA

The legacy system FPDS and its successor, Contract Data, will let you query and peek at a variety of criteria using standard reports. If you invest about an hour to build a custom query form, you can extract much more detailed data that you can download for comprehensive analysis – which is what I do when I work with clients!

FPDS is currently being combined into SAM.gov. Once the full function and data of the Federal Procurement Data System has been migrated, you'll head to *www.beta.SAM.gov* under the "Contract Data" application. When all legacy systems have been migrated, you'll do that via *www.SAM.gov*.

While it's still in service, FPDS is a difficult and time-consuming tool to use if you want to make customized queries and you don't do it every day. But FPDS is the superior choice for free federal contract data for one key reason: FPDS data includes email addresses corresponding to the people who created, modified, or approved the contract transaction. That contact information represents leads, which we'll talk more about in Chapter 6 – Relationships – and Chapter 7 – Marketing and Sales.

Whether you prefer to learn how to use FPDS yourself rather than ask your PTAC for assistance, or pay for a subscription database that might make those queries easier, make sure your data source and your output file includes the contact information for the federal buyers.

After you submit your query:

WORKSHEET #1: RESEARCHING PAST CONTRACTS

My Research Questions:

    1.

    2.

    3.

    4.

    5.

My Search Guide:

NAICS Codes To Use For Search:

PSCs To Use For Search:

Other Keywords:

Top Competitor Companies / Dominant Vendors I want to review

Departments / Agencies I want to review

Summary of Research Results:

Top Buyers by Department/Agency	Dollars	% Share
1		
2		
3		
4		
5		

Top Competitor Vendors in each Agency	Large/Small	Dollars	% Share

› Review the top buyers and top sellers. Any surprises? While the report might simply validate your experience and intuition, be alert to discover buyers (and competitors) you'd never thought about!

› Click through on the names of specific vendors and buyers, to get more detail about the ones that interest you.

› Explore which pre-formatted standard reports meet your needs.

› Take a look at options for custom reports (both on-screen and exportable).

› Notice changes in fiscal-year buying patterns. Is your market niche growing, shrinking, or stable?

› Select any agency, contract, or contractor for a more detailed listing.

› Refine your criteria and narrow the search.

› Check out options to sort or graph the resulting data.

› Consider the value of sharing exported PDFs or extracts with colleagues or on social media.

› Finally, *do* export data to Excel for deeper analysis rather than work with the data inside the application.

RESEARCH TOOL #2: USASPENDING.GOV

The Department of Treasury, Bureau of Fiscal Service, developed and operates USASpending.gov. It publishes the GSA's IAE Contract Data (successor to the Federal Procurement Data System) with a different user interface, search tools, and data export utilities. It also offers unique graphical displays of the data.

This tool can be intuitively easier to use, particularly for data export. However, the data fields do not include information about who created, approved, or modified, the record. As FPDS does That means you'll need another data source to capture the critical intelligence that leads you to the individual people involved in awarding individual contracts.

RESEARCH TOOL #3: GSA E-LIBRARY

As you know now, federal (and some state and local government) buyers use the US General Services Administration (GSA)'s Schedule Contracts to buy certain commercial, off-the-shelf products or services from thousands of vendors.

Why is this helpful? You can see whether or not the federal government uses GSA Schedules to buy products or services like yours. And you can see your competitors' GSA Schedule Contracts products, services, and pricing. Would you compete with them on price? Would buyers pay a premium for your unique value?

Where to go: GSA Schedules e-Library: *https://www.gsaelibrary.gsa.gov/ElibMain/home.do*

How to start:
1. Choose (or search on) the category of products or services that you offer. You'll get a list of related Schedule Contracts and a description of what's included in each.

2. Explore! Click a Schedule ID for a list of the categories of products or services it covers.

3. Jot down the Schedule IDs that correspond to YOUR products or services as you consider whether or not GSA Schedules are a fit for you.

What to look for: Check out who's selling -- listed alphabetically, and searchable as well.
1. If any data is underlined, that means you can click for more information. That's how you get to individual vendors' *pricing, labor rates,* and *contract terms and conditions*!

2. Using the search box, type a competitor's name. See whether, and what, they offer through GSA Schedules.

3. Finish your lesson time exploring. Sort by City and State. See which companies have what kind of small business preference.

RESEARCH TOOL #4: CALC.GSA.GOV

Do you offer professional services? You can compare your pricing with what your competitors are already offering on GSA Schedules today. You can search based on labor category, filter by criteria like years of experience and level of education, see their terms and conditions, and export that data for competitive analysis.

Remember, when you do, that these are the *highest* rates your competitors are likely to be charging their federal customers. Their pricing inside a bigger project or proposal will probably be less than that. But this will at least give you some idea of how your pricing stacks up against theirs now, and get you thinking about how low you can go while still being profitable.

WORKSHEET #2: TOP COMPETITORS' DIFFERENTIATORS

You'll want to complete the first run at your market research before you work on this section. The text below will help you fill in the blanks.

Competitor	Their Unique Value Proposition (see Marketing Power Tool #4, below)	Your Competing Best Values (see Marketing Power Tool #2, below)

Four Marketing Power Tools

Once you've started to target opportunities by looking at where your competitors are – and aren't – selling, you'll need some ways to set yourself apart from them. This section gives you four of the most powerful tools in your government business development kit.

Past Performance

This is the first of four exercises[26] I give my clients in order to put your past performance to work for you today.

Past performance is the number one risk-reduction factor when you're meeting new federal prospects. Remember: they want to know that *you've* solved *their* problem for someone who looks *just like them…* and that you did it *yesterday afternoon.* Past performance is how you prove that.

A word about new or innovative products or services. When you say "new," they hear "might not work" or "might get into trouble" or "might cost lives." New suppliers can represent risks of non-compliance, extra time to explain processes, or simply more paperwork. To be successful, you have to do everything you can to show them, early and often, why you are the low-risk choice, and that you un-

---

26   Get all four exercises in "Attract Your Buyer: The Past Performance Workshop", available at *www.GrowFedBiz.com*

derstand how they do business. Those are real, gut-level concerns; they're not dismissing you capriciously. You need to address those concerns to develop a relationship and trust *before* they'll consider you as a vendor.

Let's say you're smart and ambitious. You're an enthusiastic small business with great ideas, competing against bigger, more experienced companies. You've got some past performance, and now you want to bid a project that is significantly larger than the biggest project your company has ever done.

Your past performance reflects your proven capacity. Despite what you've already done, that courageous, step-up bid can look risky to a federal buyer or prime. Your offer also needs to show *risk mitigation*: specifically, how you've lined up all the specific commitments and resources you will need to start performing that contract the day you win.

Successful first-time vendors in the federal market usually have a track record with customers outside government. Just like those who are growing their federal business, they leverage that experience to open doors to new opportunities.

You want to have relevant examples of your past performance close at hand for every call, conversation, presentation, and proposal.

Who can remember every single job or sale? *You* can. When you write 'em down.

If you don't have a chart like this, build one. Got tons of examples? Relax. Set a goal to write up a few each month, and you'll build a table that becomes your mini-database of stories that can get your prospects' attention. This will also help you in the next exercise, on Best Values!

When you begin, you might have a lot of un-summarized past performance, and many of your staff compiling that track record. Make it easy! Store the template on a shared drive or as a Google Doc / Google Sheet. Set permissions for who can view and who can edit.

This list is *just* for use inside your company. Keep it simple. Create a table or spreadsheet like this:

AGENCY or Customer Organization	Contract	Type	$	CO Info	PM Info	Description	Dates	Role: (Prime? Sub? Teaming Partner?)
AGENCY	#	GSA/ BPA/ IDIQ	$	Name Title Phone Email	Name Title Phone Email	Details of project	From-To	Prime? If Sub or Teaming Partner, Name, Title, Phone, Email
AGENCY	#	GSA/ BPA/ IDIQ	$	Name Title Phone Email	Name Title Phone Email	Details of project	From-To	Prime? If Sub or Teaming Partner, Name, Title, Phone, Email

Best Values

Your best values provide your clients with identifiable, quantifiable benefits that make it easy for them to choose you instead of another vendor, and be willing to pay your price when they do.

Whether you offer products, services, or both, your best values might be based on technical knowledge, unique production or business processes, or even the fanatical way you foster the best client loyalty in your industry.

Best values:

- Express what's unique about your company (not the same things everybody else does);

- Have value to your buyer (not just to you);
- Are specific to your team, approach, product or technology, and/or partners;
- Ideally, are quantifiable and objectively verifiable; and
- Are things that a buyer could specify if they wanted to justify choosing you...including at a higher price than your competitors.

Bigger competitors can nearly always lowball you on price. Unless you have huge volumes of business, tiny margins on government contracts will make you wish you had never won the project in the first place. So you may not want to make every contract a price shootout. Put positively, one of the best ways to get buyers to return your calls is to show those federal prospects exactly why you're *the low-risk, top-performing vendor*. Otherwise, you're likely to find that federal buyers and primes won't give you the time of day, never mind return your calls or invite you back for a second meeting.

Why do your existing customers choose you over their competition and pay top dollar when they work with you? Brainstorm the reasons.

Then verify/validate your brainstorm by getting back in touch with your best clients. They like you, so they'll talk to you. If at all possible, do this by phone rather than by email. These are easy conversations, starting with something like, "My company is growing and we're looking for new opportunities with clients we can serve as well as we've done for you. Would you answer a couple of questions for us?" You want to know answers to the following questions.

1. When you hired us / bought from us, what problem did you need to solve?

2. How would you describe what I (or my company) did or delivered for you?

Most importantly: *record the precise words* they use to answer the questions. Those words are your power tools and door openers. For a customer to see you as the answer to their problem, they must believe that you understand that problem precisely as they do. You convey that by using their words. Even if you're the expert and think they should use different words, it's *their* problem, so you use *their* words to talk about it.

Now, narrow those responses down to three or four at most: reasons why your best customers choose you, time and again. This doesn't have to be a long list. It *does* need to be compelling.

If you were that risk-averse federal buyer, faced with a vendor you might want to work with but who is new to you, what could help you justify choosing that vendor as a qualified, low-risk, choice?

Examples of Best Values
- Past performance with a specific type of project or situation
- Experience of specific project managers
- Average years' experience[27] and/or education level of team members
- Proprietary processes
- Location close to the customer
- Delivery time
- Speed to deploy
- Safety record
- Number of years in business

Only include terms like "quality," "commitment," or "integrity" if you can quantify them. A federal buyer can't say, "I chose the company with the most integrity" without being able to prove how they made that evaluation.

Your best values position you. They shape your company's image in buyers' minds. Once you choose these, be constantly talking about them, in every conversation, in all your marketing collateral.

Unique Value Proposition[28]

- Why do your customers love you?
- Why did they choose you over your competitors?
- What do they love about how you do what you do?
- How do you help them solve their problem?

The Unique Value Proposition (UVP) is

- a concise appeal
- in the audience's language
- that focuses on their needs, problems and issuesWho are the leaders in your niche? Who are they selling to, and how? How can you position your UVP against theirs?

If a client already thinks they need what a competitor has, your route to success is blocked. However, if you can demonstrate you understand their problems better than anyone else, that can get you past the obstacle of even an incumbent competitor.

---

27   Don't say, "Our team members have a total of over 150 years' experience..." A big prime will always beat you on that. Instead, try, "80% of our employees have master's degrees," or "95% of our placements stay longer than five years."

28   Thanks for insights on Unique Value Propositions to Scott Lewis, Principal of PSPartnerships (http://pspartnerships.com/)

A good UVP creates interest, to entice someone to meet with you, and communicates easily how and why you stand out – by the value you deliver, as distinct from your competition.

Download a detailed guide and steps to develop your own UVP from *www.GrowFedBiz.com*.

PROFILE IN SUCCESS: NGrain

NGrain is a 30-person company that ranks among the top 100 military-training suppliers to the United States.

How did they achieve that success? Great technology wasn't enough. "We also had to learn to talk in their language, not ours," explained Gabe Batstone, then Vice President, Business Development & Professional Services.

He recounts describing their solution to a senior US military officer as offering "improved comprehension."

"He said 'Son, what's that mean?' We put away our marketing brains, asked our clients what they wanted to hear, and shut up and listened. We had to turn our language and solutions into solving their problems with their metrics."

So how well do you walk your talk? I wondered. "Tell me in one sentence what NGrain does," I asked Gabe. His answer was immediate.

"Our interactive 3D maintenance training aids allow people who maintain and repair military equipment to accelerate learning in complex equipment and enable first-time-right repairs and optimize operational readiness at a lower cost."

If you found that UVP hard to parse, you're probably just not the target audience! UVPs rarely have universal appeal. But NGrain's clientele got it right away... which was the point.

UPDATE: One of their clients today sums it up well. "The fact that NGrain is the only supplier outside of the US that has ever worked on the F-22 is a testament to their tracking and repair solution's effectiveness."
~ Jeff A. Babione, [then] Executive Vice President and General Manager, F-35 Program, Lockheed Martin.

Capability Statement

Nowhere in the Federal Acquisition Regulations will you find a description of the capability statement. Yet nearly every serious prospect you meet will ask you for one. It's an evolving art form, and a critical tool in your government-marketing kitbag. It's a simple document that gives potential clients a clear picture of your company, its strengths, and how it is different from your competitors.

What you need to know

Your capability statement starts with core content that you'll keep updating. Then you'll create unique versions for specific recipients or audiences by focusing on their priorities and needs, showing them qualifications and past performance that match their mission, and emphasizing unique characteristics that set you apart from competitors who are less focused and prepared.

What You'll Create

- A Microsoft Word file that has all the content elements that you might want to include in your capability statement

- A standard template in Word that includes your branding, logo, and contact information. You'll use that to copy in the right content for specific recipientsA 1- to 2-page document in PDF that can be printed on a single sheet

- OPTION: after you get the content elements right, hire a graphic designer to put it all together for you. What you *don't* create is a thousand printed copies! Expect to custom-tailor the best values and past-performance examples, and sometimes the key words, each time for the person you're meeting with.

When You Use it

- In person, during an initial matchmaking or networking event or conference

- Mailed as follow up from an in-person meeting

- Attached to an email saying something like, "Attached is a capability statement. I would like to schedule a capability briefing with you, to discuss how we might provide services that your agency would value."

- On your website, available as a downloadable PDF. (Obviously, this version can't be custom-tailored, so make it as universally applicable as you can.)

Capability Statement Tips

- Remember that there is no single perfect template! Shop around by looking at a few of your competitors' capability statements. Which ones really stand out for you? Pick and choose examples from specific elements you think work well. Your basic one will be unique, as will the variations.

- Create a basic capability statement for public distribution at events/trade shows – this one won't include points of contact for your project references.

- Develop variants you'll deliver in person for specific prospects and partners that include project-specific references based on their needs.

- Include enough margins & white space for people to make notes.

- Make modest use of graphics – keep it to two pages, tops.

- Use fonts no smaller than 10 point; 12 is better.

- Use point form rather than prose paragraphs.

- Use a long, descriptive file name to make it easier for the buyer to find it: E.g. "Judy Bradt – Federal Sales Training Business Development Programs – WOSB – 703 627 1074.pdf"

- Include the specific technical terms, keywords, and terms that your prospect uses to describe problems and elements of their environment/domain – even if you think those terms are duplicative or improvable.

- Avoiding generic terms like "world class," "we pride ourselves," or "a family-owned company." Focus your language on exactly what you can do for the specific agency and their mission, and who you've done it for already.

Structure and Content

Core Competencies

Present a set of core competencies – probably no more than four – based on the specific services or products the agency is looking for. How would you complete the sentence "We specialize in…" using less than twelve more words? Remember, you can – and should expect to – edit this document based on the initial conversations you have with your prospects.

Past Performance

- Spotlight work you have done elsewhere that is most similar to what the agency needs. Choose examples that will make their eyes light up: clients or projects they are familiar with! Provide references and contact data. Expect decision makers to call those references immediately. If you can't show them experience with a project very similar to what they need, that's a clue that you're wasting their time and yours.

- Consider *all* government experience. State, county, and local experience all count, especially if you haven't been a federal contractor.

- Subcontracting counts! List key details of the project, the prime, your point of contact, and ideally the government agency end-user and contact there.

- If you've got NO government experience… you can still use commercial past performance, especially with big-name companies.if the contracting officer is willing to consider it. Find out whether they're willing: ask the point of contact listed in the solicitation. Better yet, have the conversation long before the requirement is published, so that the contracting officer can draft the solicitation in a way that your experience qualifies you for award.

Best Values

Include the ones you just developed above. You might group them by things like:

- **Technology:** Process? Exceptional or unique materials/components?

- **Results:** Performance metrics and reliability statistics? Operational improvements? Quantifiable value of on-site/on-call service response time? Percentage of jobs completed on time and on budget? Extraordinary service, guarantees, warranties?

- **Basics:** Sometimes simple things that raise buyers' comfort are everyday advantages you might easily forget to mention. How about your number of locations, or how close they are to the buyer? Delivery times that are faster than the industry average? If you've got more than ten – or 20, or 30 – years in business, be sure to say so! Bonding capacity? If your products meet the definition of "Made in USA," this can be a place to mention that.

- **Niche leadership:** Industry recognition awards? Elite technical certifications or qualifications in your field, like CMMI Level 4? Pick ones that buyers know correlate to superlative skills and results that few (or no) competitors can match.

Company Data

- Legal company name and legal status (LLC? Corporation? Partnership?), number of employees, annual revenue, locations

- Business Codes: DUNS number or its eventual successor, the Unique Identity ID; Commercial and Government Entity (CAGE) Code, NAICS codes. Include the ones your research shows your buyers use to buy what you do, as well as others you qualify for. You only need to list the numbers, not the words, if you are short of space.

- Socio-economic / Small business certifications

- Current, relevant contract vehicles: GSA Schedule(s)? GWACs? IDIQ's? List the contract number, whether you are the prime or the subcontractor.

- Mandatory or usual certifications in your niche (like ISO 9001 or 14001, or LEED), so buyers know you cover the basics.

Contact Information

On front and back!

- Name, Title, Address, Phone (main, direct, and/or mobile), Email[29]

---

29 Make sure your email address looks professional, by using your company's domain name, not "@ gmail.com" or "@yahoo.com" or "@MyISP.net." You'll avoid the disadvantage of someone assuming incorrectly that your company is a startup with no experience.

Sample Capability Statement[30]

Capability Statement

Signs by Saenz is a certified Woman-Owned provider of high-impact marketing solutions for the federal government and industry. Signs by Saenz has strong past performance on numerous federal projects, and has built a reputation on expert consultation, design, and consistently meeting deadlines.

Products:

Marketing Materials I Interior & Exterior Signage I Exhibits

Art & Framing I Trade Show Services including I&D and storage

NAICS Codes: 238390, 323115, 339950, 493110, 541430, 541611, 541810, 541850, 541890

How To Get To Us: Procurement Made Easy

- WOSB certification allows for sole-source procurement by any federal agency

- We accept Government Credit Cards

- GPO Blanket Purchase Agreement (#450-80345) allows for sole-sourced procurement for many federal agencies

- GSA Schedule GS-03F-0084X DBA Lighted Signs Direct

- Network of trusted partners, including 8(a), ensures all projects are completed on time and meet high quality standards.

Designations:

SDB, MBE, SWAM, Woman-Owned

DUNS# 78-7227599, Cage: 4L0L6

Past Performance:

Nationwide projects with Border Patrol, ICE, DISA, NGA, Marine Corps, Army, Navy, Smithsonian Institution, Department of Veterans Affairs

Contact Information: Martin Saenz, CEO

Phone: 877.777.5734

Email: martin@signsbysaenz.com

Website: *www.TheSaenzGroup.com*

Address: 13331 Woodbridge Street, Woodbridge, VA 22191

---

30 "Find out more: visit *GrowFedBiz.com* and search on keyword "Capability Statement".

Keyword Set

This is a set of keywords – and *just* keywords – that you can use in online data profiles and registrations. Some profiles limit the number of words or characters you can use. List the keywords in the order of priority that you think someone will use to find your company's profile, so that, if you have to cut the profile short, you'll know that the most important terms got included.

Selecting your keywords

• *Listen* to your prospects and customers! When you talk with them, make a list of what they call things.

• *Notice, and log, differences.* Be prepared to hear what you think are duplicate terms. Learn your buyers' unique language before the competition, with conversations in the field! Different agencies or departments use different words for what you might think are the same thing.

"Facilities" in the Public Building Service is "installation support" or "DPW" on a military base, or "engineering" at Veterans Affairs. What one agency calls "moving," another might call "restacking," if they're referring to a series of moves reshuffling groups to different floors of a building during a renovation.

• **If you don't understand a term or acronym you hear,** be straightforward, and ask, "Would you clarify that please? I don't want to assume what that is. I want to get it right." That builds trust because you're willing to ask for help, and you want to learn from them. If you write a proposal, you want to use the terms and acronyms unique to the buying agency. Don't assume that every agency uses the same terms, or that one group got it wrong when they use a different term from another.

• Look up your competitors – on their web site, but also their published capability statements in SBA's Dynamic Small Business Search and in SAM. gov. If you want prospects to find you when they start out looking for your competitors, then notice the key words your competitors use in their own profiles. Borrow the ones that also describe what you do.

• Look up contract awards for purchases of products or services similar to yours in FPDS/Contract Data. Review the data field "Description of Requirements" and pull out key words that show up frequently.

Here's a keyword list example from one of my clients:

Systems Engineering, Data Science & Management, Integration, Requirements Analysis, Governance & Policy, Big Data Analytics, Cyber Operations, Information Assurance, Information Security, Technical Leadership, Acquisition & Evaluation, Software Assurance, Identity & Access, Curriculum Development, Software Development, Attribute Based Access Controls (ABAC), Identity and Access Management (IDAM), Cross Domain Solutions (CDS), Operations and Maintenance (O&M), Defensive Cyber Operations (DCO), Computer Network Defense (CND), NetOPS (Network Operations), Attack, Sensing & Warning (AS&W), Information Systems Security Engineering, JCIDS, DoD Acquisition, Systems Architecture, Test & Evaluation (T&E), IV&V, Legal Policy Oversight & Compliance, STIX, TAXII, CVE, CPE, CWE, CAPEC, SCAP, OVAL, IAVA, IAVM, CNSS, IOC, RMF, ATT&CK, MAEC, Kill Chain, SCM, Auditing, STIG, Agile Development, Threat Intelligence, SIGINT analysis, HUNT, Security Operations, malware analysis, endpoint analysis, Trusted Computing Group, streaming analytics, ingest, JQR, enrichment, Cloud Hosting, POM, IPL, UX/UI, anomaly detection, and machine learning.

READY FOR THE NEXT STEP? COMPETITION CHECKLIST

Stand out! Know:

- ○ Where to get competitive data
- ○ Who your target agencies buy from today
- ○ What keywords your buyers use most often
- ○ Your Unique Value Proposition for government
- ○ Your Best Values
- ○ How to create a basic capability statement
- ○ How to summarize past performance

Find out more

Visit *www.GrowFedBiz.com* for more detailed lessons & tools on topics including:

- Discovering Your Best Values
- Defining Your Unique Value Proposition
- Four Easy Lessons in Free Federal Market Research
- Creating Your Capability Statement
- The Capability Briefing: Six Simple Slides
- Attract Your Buyer: The Past Performance Workshop

Complimentary Federal Insider Club Power Pack
Strategies and Templates For Success

Go To ➜ GrowFedBiz.com/insider

As a special thanks for trusting me to help you grow your federal business, here's how to get a special toolkit to make that...easier!

No catch. No cost.

Download:

- Hiring A Federal Sales Professional: What To Ask
- 3 Steps To Choose Your Perfect Contract Vehicle
- Template: Capability Presentation in Six Simple Slides
- Template and Guide: Capability Statements And Beyond

GO TO ➜ GrowFedBiz.com/insider

Chapter Five: Teaming and Subcontracting

M*any kinds of partnerships can get you on the fast track to new business – if you know what partners want. Teaming can create winning alliances with the partners who can open doors to new business.*

What You'll Learn

- What's Teaming?

- Why Team?

- Affiliation Rules: What They Are And Why You Care

- Large & Small Partners: Why You Need Both

- Top Teaming Tactics

- What Primes Really Want: Their A-list Criteria

- A Teaming Agreement Checklist

- Tools For Effective Teaming

Teaming, Partnering, Joint Venturing: What's The Difference?

Some people use the terms *teaming, subcontracting,* and *joint venture* interchangeably. They're not. You need to know the difference – right from the start.

Why? The legal contracting relationship defines the power and responsibilities that each party – prime, sub, and buyer – has with the others.

FAR Subpart 6.9 defines a Contractor Team Arrangement in one of two forms:

- A potential prime contractor agrees with one or more companies to have them act as its subcontractors for a specific federal contract or acquisition program; or

- Two or more parties form a new entity (e.g. partnership or joint venture), which in turn is a potential prime contractor for a specific federal procurement.

- A unique example is a Contracting Teaming Arrangement that the General Services Administration permits between companies that hold a GSA Schedule contract.[31] The teaming partners jointly offer a set of products and/or services from among the items each supplies through its GSA Schedule to meet a government buyer's specific needs. The government may approach various team members directly to request products or services under the terms of that contract. If something goes wrong, the government will turn to the specific team member primarily responsible for the problem.

Teaming Agreements: are generally executed before the proposal is submitted. These written, binding, agreements are the formal legal foundation for the Contractor Team Arrangement, and are specific to a unique project or opportunity. At a minimum, they define the members and responsibilities of the team that will perform on the government contract if the team wins that project.

Just because you're on the team doesn't guarantee you will get subcontracting work. That's especially true if, for instance, your teaming agreement also doesn't specify the share of the work the winning prime will send your way.

Subcontracts: are executed post-award. On large project, they are often based on a Teaming Agreement. The subcontract defines the roles, deliverables, terms, and conditions under which the subcontractors provide services and goods to the prime in performance of the contract that the federal agency has awarded to the prime.

You can be a subcontractor without being part of a teaming agreement.

31   See details at *www.gsa.gov/contractorteamarrangements.*

Joint Ventures: are partnerships created for the purpose of pursuing a defined set of opportunities, and might or might not take the form of a separate legal entity. A correctly structured and managed joint venture under certain circumstances can significantly increase the federal opportunities for the partners to grow.

Strategic Alliances: may be formed by companies to pursue a range of projects, and may result in many Teaming Agreements.

Why Team?

Simple: The majority of successful federal contractors win work as both prime and subcontractor. Over half of successful small businesses also team with other small companies.

Don't get obsessed with the idea that you need to be a prime contractor to do business with government. Remember, you can be both prime and sub at once, on different projects. Here are some of the top reasons that companies team on federal contracts.

Get Access to Opportunities

Many companies enter the market as subcontractors. The experience and record of past performance they build as subs make them stronger contenders when they begin to bid as primes. Some companies perform *only* as subcontractors, and *never* as primes (and with great success, too)! Some reasons why:

- When the federal government buys what you do, it's always as part of a larger project;
- The scale of some federal projects or programs grows beyond the financing, bonding, and performance capacity of small business, and cannot be easily or efficiently split into smaller chunks that one or more small businesses can perform well;
- The number of experienced contracting officials who can administer competitions and contracts just keeps getting smaller; and
- Government often finds it faster and less costly (at least in terms of administrative expenses) to run one big contract rather than a bunch of smaller ones.

Rack Up Past Performance

Before a government buyer (never mind a prime) is willing to trust you, you're going to have to prove you can do the job. Your track record is that proof. I'm not going to argue with you about whether you have the strength or experience or resources to become a prime contractor. The market will determine that.

Subcontracting on a government contract "counts" as demonstrating the kind of past performance that government buyers and prime contractors are looking for. Teaming is one of the best ways to demonstrate past performance – whether you're aspiring to your first prime contract or looking for more subcontract work.

Get Support For Bonding

Bonding – especially for contracts related to construction, renovation, environmental remediation, and engineering contracts – can pose a significant challenge to smaller companies that are ready to grow their government business. But if your unique expertise, experience, and relationships with the government buyer are attractive enough, a larger partner may be eager to provide you with the financial backing you need to get that bond.

Conversely, many small companies that don't have a close relationship with a prime find themselves with limited access to working capital, or find themselves already leveraged so heavily that they don't have the assets to guarantee the size of bond that a government contract can require.

In fact, when Neeld Wilson, our service-disabled veteran aquifer engineer in Orlando, was getting ready for his first government bid, that's exactly the position he found himself in. The project he was bidding – for removal of an underground storage tank – required bonding, and he'd been turned down by his bank. I put him in touch with SBA's regional office in Orlando, who connected him with a source of financing that could help. That bonding was a critical success factor to his win.

If you're in that position, remember that the Small Business Administration can help you, too. SBA's regional offices have strong contacts with national and community banks.

Address Licensing / Certification

Let's say your company has a key role in a major information technology contract, and has just received its CMMI Level 2 certification, but the government wants the prime contractor to have CMMI Level 3 certification. Or your company, based in New Jersey, wants to bid an environmental-engineering contract in Louisiana. The Army Corps of Engineers is keen to work with you, but requires at least one engineer to be licensed to practice in Louisiana.

If you don't meet ALL the requirements for a contract, but the buyer likes you and wants to do business with you, one option is to seek a partner – small or large. Ideally, the government buyers also know your partner well. Your partner company has complementary expertise, can also profit from the project, and will lend the overall project proposal more credibility as well as the necessary credentials. You create a teaming agreement in which the prime agrees to assist the subcontractor with gaining the necessary certifications or licenses as part of the contract.

In both these examples, you'd want to ensure that each partner is bringing something substantial to the contract. *Beware anyone's suggestion that you participate in a partnership as a "pass through,"* for example with (or as) a prime contractor whose job it is to simply hold the contract vehicle while the subcontractor does all the work. That's particularly true if the contract is being awarded in part on the basis of the prime contractor's status as one of the kinds of small business and the so-called "prime" contractor is doing very little of the work.

The legal term for this kind of relationship is "ostensible subcontractor." It can be grounds for protest, and loss of, your contract award if your small business wins work based on its small business status but performs an insufficient amount of the work.

Where do you find a prime if you don't know one? Well, if the government buyer wants to do business with you and needs a contract vehicle, she or he may very well suggest and introduce you to a prime they trust and like to do business with.

People do business with people they like.

People do business with people they trust.

When a small business approaches a large one bringing a combination of expertise, experience, and relationships with a government buyer keen to do business, they are definitely more likely to get their calls returned.

Be A Small Part Of A Bigger Contract

Big contracts are convenient for the government to administer. While smaller contracts can be easier for small business to win, they also diminish economies of scale for government and can require contract administration people and resources that simply aren't available.

If you don't see many solicitations for what your company does, could the government be buying what you do as part of a larger requirement? Let's say your company offers training services. Data shows that the federal government awards millions of dollars' worth of prime contracts for training services every year. But that represents only part of your market opportunity. Consider which government program or project might need training services like yours as part of its broader operation. You might discover even more opportunities as subcontractor. Just keep in mind that in order to win those embedded opportunities, you can expect to invest time and money to build relationships with both the government customer and the prime contractor.

The scale of giant contracts can have the effect of locking out small businesses that don't have the capacity and resources to perform as primes, or the complete range of expertise required for the job. Huge projects often need the innovation and experience of smaller companies with specialized expertise to be successful. And government also needs to give some of today's small companies the opportunity to thrive as vendors in order to create a strong industrial supply base.

The approximately $500 billion in federal contract spending has a huge economic impact. So do all small businesses together. American small business collectively employs more than the nation's largest 100 corporations. The federal government creates economic opportunities for small business to grow through government contracting, including by requiring[32] all prime contractors who win awards worth more than $700,000 to have a small business subcontracting plan.

What happens if a prime contractor doesn't fulfill the commitments it makes in its winning proposal for small business subcontracting? The prime is liable for liquidated damages for failure to achieve its subcontracting goals. In practice, I have yet to hear of one who ever got more than a scolding, assuming anyone noticed at all.

What size of contract would your company consider too big to handle? Too small to be worth the effort?

Federal contracting has a unique concept of "small" – and not just with respect to business-size standards.

For instance, military installations need a huge range of facility operations and maintenance services just as a large commercial campus does: landscaping, renovations, repairs, paving, fencing, signage, and janitorial services. A small businesses with experience performing work like that in the private sector could do the same kind of work for the government. The base has hundreds of such small jobs all year long. You could imagine getting to know the folks at the base near you and doing some road-patching or lawn-mowing for a few thousand dollars a pop, right? Awarding a contract to your small company would also help them meet their small business goals, right?

If the expected annual value of such requirements is high enough, the contracting officer needs to show they competed the requirement. A year's worth of any one of these services can total millions.

But contracting officers don't have time and resources to run a full-blown competition every time they need the grass cut. Vendors don't want that them to do that, either. Small businesses want to be cutting the grass all year long, not writing proposals on how much sharper their mower blades are, and how much quieter and more fuel-efficient their machinery is than their competition's.

If these are things that two or more small businesses can do, the buyer has to give preference to small business. Here's what often happens: the contracting officer at that military base will group together this set of related requirements under a Base Operations Support (BOS) contract. These omnibus contracts are a type of

---

32   Read the details in FARs Subpart 19.7.

IDIQ: the buyer knows from the start that they'll need these services throughout the year, but doesn't know exactly when, or how much they'll need. If the requirement is big enough, they might award several BOS contracts. Then every new requirement would be open for competition among the handful of companies.

In the federal contracting world, BOS contracts can be created at a particularly convenient threshold.

BOS contracts can be popular candidates for sole-source awards to 8(a) companies: the contracting officer can take care of a whole lot of requirements for contracts that can be worth up to $4.5 million (or, to an Alaskan Native 8(a), up to $20 million) with a single contract, minimal paperwork, and not even the need to run a competition! That award can be renewed up to four times with minimal effort, while also making a fast, significant contribution to the agency's total awards to small business. A contract that size is small enough to be manageable by a small business. And it's big enough that large or small companies might subcontract specialty services to the 8(a) on such contracts without having to invest resources and risk to win the work in a competition.

Access Large Contract Vehicles

Your research may show that your target agency buys a lot of what you do or make through a contract vehicle you don't hold and can't get on easily. If you want to increase your chance of winning business by making it easy for them to buy the way they usually do, you'll want to pursue a subcontract with one of the large or small primes that holds that contract.

Federal agencies recognize the advantage that IDIQs give contractors, and want to open such advantages to small companies as well as large ones. As a result, agencies establish multiple-award Government- or Department-Wide Acquisition Contracts – GWACs or DWACs. In some cases (for example, Alliant and Alliant Small Business, or DHS' EAGLE II), the government competed and made multiple awards for one version among large businesses and another among small businesses.

This is the government saying, "Our department needs a lot of *this* kind of technology. We want to have *some* choices, and show we've competed our requirements to get best value and price, but not spend all our time shopping. We'll run a competition and set up *this* contract to create a pool of the most qualified suppliers we want to work with. Then we can run a small, quick, task-order competition whenever we need that technology."

Access Otherwise-Off-Limits Small business Set-Asides

Even if your business is small, the contracting officer may have designated an opportunity with a contracting preference that excludes your company. What then?

Why, you do exactly what IBM and General Dynamics and Northrop Grumman do: find a partner that *does* qualify for that set-aside, and team with them.

For one thing, very few businesses are eligible for every type of small business set-aside, so the odds are good that you'll run across an opportunity that may fit your experience, but that either the government or a prime contractor plans as a set-aside for which you don't qualify.

Teaming is the obvious solution...but are you ready for action? You want to know your partner well, especially if you've run across an opportunity with little time to spare. Start now to cultivate relationships among people you'd really like to work with, whose companies are experienced, well-qualified, and can also help you access the full range of set-asides.

Remember, it's not enough to find a partner who can access the right kind of set-aside. They've also got to offer the products or services that the buyer is looking for.

Some federal agencies' Mentor-Protégé programs (see more below) are evolving to require primes to take on a set of protégé companies who represent each type of small business set-aside. Thus, if you have a well-rounded set of partners, you may be able to differentiate yourself by not only bringing an opportunity to the prime, but also coming with well-qualified friends who complement you *on that specific program.*

Ensure Local Roots

Local presence raises confidence and credibility. How close are you located to your customer? Government buyers, like all the rest of your clients, want to know that you're close by and readily available – during the project or procurement as well as afterward for service or warranty or repair work. Sure, an opportunity might be open to companies from all over the United States – and beyond. Look carefully at the evaluation criteria – Section M of the solicitation. Is there any mention of a requirement for local presence, or any weighting given in the evaluation for the contractor's geographical proximity to the location where the work will be done?

If so...finding a local partner can be that key success factor.

Teaming with Big Companies

Of over 1500 small businesses surveyed[33] who were pursuing government contracts:

- 76% of successful companies also pursued work as subcontractors to primes.

---

33   Strategies for Success from Federal Small Business Contractors – A Research Summary for the American Express OPEN for Government Contracts: Victory in Procurement[SM] (VIP) for Small Business Program

- They worked hard at it, with average participation in about 8 proposals over the past three years that led 54% of those companies to win actual subcontract business.

- They meet those primes most often through matchmaking events, researching agency purchases, and introductions that arose out of relationships with agency contracting officials.

- Only 65% of unsuccessful companies have pursued subcontracting; they put in much less effort (averaging only 1.7 proposals over three years) with less than half the success rate – only 25% end up with subcontract work.

Teaming with Small Companies

Don't just look to the big primes for productive partnerships!

- 62% of active small business contractors – that's companies who have won government business – have pursued teaming arrangements with other small firms, compared to only 36% of non-contractors.

- They find those small partners in much the same places where the large ones hang out: matchmaking events and small business conferences, as well as by online research of teaming web sites, though the companies surveyed didn't find as many small-to-small introductions through government contacts.

Teaming with Channel Partners & Resellers

If you don't have, and can't easily build, a relationship with your end user, you'll need to meet the people who do. Channel partners may resell, package, or bundle your product into a more complex solution. You may need relationships with integration teaming partners. That's often the case in information technology, professional services, and construction projects. You may need partners in complementary industries, if government buyers need what you do as a component of a larger project.

PROFILE IN SUCCESS: Martin Saenz, VP, The Saenz Group

"Before we got our GSA Schedule, if I had a prospect who wanted to do business via GSA Schedule, I'd go to the GSA Web site (_www.gsaadvantage.gov_) and look up an exhibit company, because most of what we do now is permanent exhibits. When I found a GSA schedule contract holder who does exhibits and out in, say, Oklahoma, I'd call them. Chances are, because they have a GSA schedule, they have some level of interest. If not, they're not fully engrossed with federal work. If so, they're the right kind of person for me to explore a relationship with."

Why would they take Martin's call? That's easy: "With my past performance, with our connections and relationships and our location close to DC, they're going to be extremely interested in talking to me about potential opportunities."

Other considerations: When Martin calls up a partner, he brings an opportunity. There's no faster way to get your calls returned! He'll look at geography and track record – does that company represent a partner he could team with in regions or agencies where he wants to expand? Or would he prefer a partner who's not competing in his territory at all? Now that Martin's company has graduated from the 8(a) program, he might also be looking for companies eligible for set-asides that complement his own.

Think about resellers the same way. Just because you have a reseller agreement, even with a reseller who has a strong record of government sales in your industry, does not mean that they're going to win the business for you. You're still going to have to market in order to drive business through that channel.

Don't assume that your channel partners will sell for you. A channel is a conduit. Your agreement with your channel partner specifies what each of you will do for the other, and the margin the partner gets, right? Read the agreement carefully, for both what's there and what's not.

Take care when you negotiate your pricing. Expect to pay them margin for the privilege of utilizing their access to the buyer.

Unless the agreement spells out specific marketing commitments, don't expect that they're going to make any effort to sell your product or to recommend that buyers include yours rather than a competitor's in a bundle of complementary products they also carry. Do consider how the reseller might carry out or collaborate with you on promotional efforts for which you compensate them.

While resellers are very common channels in the information technology industry, the same principle holds true for construction products, consumer products, and… well, here's an example that might surprise you:

PROFILE IN SUCCESS: Linda Lazarowich, President, ProWear Gear

Linda's tagline today clearly says what she offers: "Ultimate Soft Body Armor Solutions For Serious Spike Threats." She began her federal contracting making uniforms for working canines.

Why would dogs need uniforms? Linda explains.

"In many jurisdictions, police dogs are legally warranted officers of the law. It can cost over $30,000 to purchase and train a working canine for specialized duty, and up to $1,000 a month to keep his skills sharp, for ongoing training and re-certification. During a duty shift, if someone other than the dog's human partner approaches and pats a dog that has been trained to identify substances like drugs or food by their scent, the dog can go 'off scent' – which means that that human-canine team may be out of action for hours. If the dog wears a uniform, people stay back and don't try to touch the dog…and the law enforcement team is more productive."

Law enforcement agencies were especially keen on her company's add-on packs for cold- and hot-weather canine uniforms. However, rather than buying uniforms directly from Linda, the canine handlers preferred to buy a whole kit of gear for their canines, including but not limited to hot packs and cold packs.

Linda conferred with the contracting officer's technical representative to find out which companies were in the running to produce those kits. Then she considered which of the leading kitters she wanted to work with on a deal that would ensure she could reach her prospects the way they wanted to buy from her.

UPDATE: Law enforcement officers liked the protective qualities of Linda's fabric and her outstanding design skills so much that they wanted ProWear for themselves! Over the next ten years, she has expanded her product lines to include gear for federal, state, and local human officers as well as their canine colleagues.

Affiliation Rules: What They Are And Why You Care

Rules and laws about joint venturing and affiliation can offer your company significant advantages. You want to know those rules well, though: a small business can lose its certifications, and both large and small firms can lose contracts as well as contracting privileges, if you win a contract award through an inappropriate business relationship.

Key rules you'll want to review concern:

- The Formal Definition of Teaming: FAR Subpart 9.6 provides details on agreements that may include joint ventures as well as subcontracts. In either case, the team must be formed before the proposal is submitted, and recognized before contract execution if not as part of the proposal itself.

- Ostensible Subcontractors: 13 CFR 121.103 (h)(4) says that the small business has to be prime contractor on a procurement that's set aside for small business. While the small prime can subcontract to a large company, undue reliance on a large subcontractor is cause for protest.

In discussions about teaming, beware the term "pass-through." Don't structure your teaming arrangement so that the small prime who qualifies for the set aside "passes through" nearly all the work to subcontractors.

First, doing so is against the rules. Second, if you get caught and/or protested, you risk losing your contract, contracting privileges (and a whole lot of trust). Your SAM Entity record will show you as "Excluded," which means you're out of the government contracts business until you clean up your act.

Both partners must have a substantive role, as required by the type of contract, in performing the work, and must meet certain minimum requirements:

- In a contract for services (except construction), no more than 50% of the amount paid by the government may be subcontracted to firms that are not "similarly situated," (that is, in the same small business program – 8(a), SDVOSB, ED/WOSB, or HUBZone.)

- In a contract for supplies or products (other than from a non-manufacturer of such supplies), no more than 50% of the amount paid by the government to the prime may be subcontracted to firms that are not similarly situated.

- In a general construction contract, no more than 85% of the amount paid by the government to the prime may be paid to firms that are not similarly situated.

- On a specialty trade contract, no more than 75% of the amount paid by the government to the prime may be paid to firms that are not similarly situated.

Definitions of affiliation matter tremendously because they affect whether or not a team that's pursuing a small business set-aside complies with the definition of "small" that applies to that particular contract. Size standards and determinations for unaffiliated small businesses, or those covered by relaxed rules (about which more in a moment) are based on the company's number of employees or level of revenue as per the details in FAR Part 19.

The size of companies that are determined to be affiliated is the *combined* number of employees or level of revenue of the small business and its affiliates (unless there's an exception[34]). If an 8(a), SDVOB, WOSB, or HUBZone company finds itself in an affiliation that bumps it up over its size standard, it can lose that extremely valuable certification (as well as a potential win) altogether!

If a small business is pursuing a set-aside, but teams with other, especially larger, partners, the partners must be absolutely certain that nothing in their business relationship – whether in formal agreement or in practice or appearance – would trigger a definition of affiliation that would make the team ineligible to meet the size standard that applies to the opportunity.

Well-structured teaming agreements avoid creating an affiliation, as defined by FAR Subpart 19.1 as well as SBA's rules at 13 C.F.R. 121.103. Both definitions focus on the extent to which one entity has actual or potential

---

34   13 C.F.R. Part 121 lists those exceptions. Would you qualify? Look it up and find out...or save yourself the risk and uncertainty, and get experienced legal help.

power or control over the other, or a third party controls both partners. FAR Subpart 19.1 gives the details on what "control" means.

Your formal teaming agreement needs to be drafted to avoid overt affiliation, and define the way partners manage things like financing, licensing, or contracting obligations to avoid even the *appearance* of affiliation. Either can inspire your competitors to protest a contract award that you worked hard to win.

Lower your risk by engaging legal help from a firm that, or individual lawyer who, has significant experience with federal contracting issues up front to clarify these issues on your very first teaming or joint venture agreement. You'll minimize the chance of an expensive protest that will damage your relationship with your buyer and your partner, and/or cause you to lose your contract.

About Teaming with 8(a)'s

Good news: The FAR allows contracting officers to award work to 8(a) program participants as sole-source if the requirements are worth less than $4 million for services or $7 million for products. Companies owned by Alaskan Native Corporations may receive such sole-source awards with *no* upper-limit dollar value on such contracts. Proposed awards estimated to be worth over $20 million receive extra review prior to contract award.

With the right partnership arrangements with an 8(a) partner, your company could team on multi-million-dollar federal contracts and slash time, cost, and the risk of losing the bid to competition.

Sound attractive? Be sure to learn the rules about teaming with 8(a)'s, get legal guidance before making agreements, and follow those rules scrupulously. Small business teaming relationships using the 8(a) program to win big-dollar projects receive especially close scrutiny as a result of a few highly publicized cases of improper contracting and teaming practices.

Leave yourself lots of lead time, too! Although 8(a) companies may team on sole-source contracts awarded through the 8(a) program, SBA must review and approve all such partnerships, including joint ventures, before contract award.

Joint Ventures and Mentor-Protégé Programs

Federal contractors may form one or more joint ventures (JVs) to pursue government business together. Companies don't need to be in a mentor-protégé program in order to form a joint venture. But those who do both can have a major advantage.

Let's start with joint-venture basics.

A joint venture is formed by individuals and/or businesses who combine their efforts, property, money, skill, or knowledge for the purpose (in whole or in part) to engage in and carry out no more than three business ventures for joint profit within two years.

The JV must be formed prior to bidding. The JV makes the offer and, if it wins, becomes the prime contractor on the contract.

Joint Venturing At A Glance

- JV must be recorded in writing.

- JV must do business (like pursuing opportunities and signing contracts) under its own name.

- JV must have a unique Entity record and be identified as a JV in SAM (and, if applicable, VetBiz).

- JV may be in the form of a formal partnership, informal partnership, or separate legal entity.

- A formal separate legal entity JV may employ staff only to perform administrative functions. JV employees may not perform contracts awarded to the joint venture.

However, joint ventures that are formed outside of a mentor-protégé agreement can cause the partners to be considered affiliated. In federal contracting, affiliation means the combined size (measured by either number of employees or level of revenue) of the partners can make their joint venture ineligible for small business set-asides that one or both of the individual partners might otherwise be able to win.

Many joint ventures take place between companies that participate in federal mentor-protégé programs. Why? Such joint ventures may receive relaxed treatment of the affiliation rules!

About Mentor-Protégé Programs

A mentor-protégé relationship is an agency-approved relationship between a small business and a successful government contractor. The established firm provides a range of business-development assistance to the protégé that will improve the protégé's ability to compete successfully for federal contracts. The mentor-protégé relationship is not formed for a particular procurement, nor solely to bid federal projects.

The Department of Defense launched the first federal Mentor-Protégé program (MPP) in the early 1990s to expand the defense industrial base by encouraging large primes to nurture smaller businesses into becoming strong, new, innovative suppliers to government.

The program succeeded on many levels. In just the five years 2013 - 2017, DoD's protégés were awarded over $6.5 billion in prime and subcontracts. The participating protégé firms say that, on average, they added 13.4 new full-time employees to their payroll and grew their revenue $7.3 million *each year* they were in the program.

Four civilian agencies, including SBA itself, also run federal mentor-protégé contracting programs. Here's some detail about the newest one, and, below that, links where you can find details on the others.

The "All Small" Mentor-Protégé Program

The Small Business Administration's initial Mentor-Protégé program, created specifically for 8(a) companies, became so successful that in 2016 SBA launched a similar MPP that is open to all small businesses.

Any small business, including all recognized small business categories, may participate. Mentor and protégé must write up an agreement and SBA must approve the agreement. The protégé needs a business plan.

The mentor firm may be large or small. Generally, a mentor has only one protégé at a time; SBA may grant an exception to provide for up to three.

The protégé must initially qualify as small for the size standard corresponding to its primary, or a secondary, NAICS code for which it seeks assistance. A protégé may generally have only one mentor at a time. SBA may approve a second mentor relationship if that second relationship will not compete with the first one and pertains to an unrelated NAICS in which the first mentor cannot provide assistance.

Mentor-Protégé Agreements must include an assessment of the protégé's needs and describe the specific assistance the mentor will provide over a minimum of one year. The agreement needs to show how the relationship will help the protégé to achieve its business goals. Either firm may terminate the agreement with 30 days' notice. SBA must approve the initial agreement as well as any subsequent changes, reviews the agreement each year, and may terminate it if the protégé is not benefitting.

Major benefits:

- In order to raise capital, the protégé firm may agree to sell or otherwise convey to the mentor an equity interest of up to 40% in the protégé firm.

- A protégé firm and its mentor are not determined to be affiliated or inappropriately controlled based solely on the mentor-protégé agreement or related assistance provided under the MPP. However, affiliation may be found for other reasons set forth in § 121.103.

- A protégé and mentor's joint venture may be considered a small business for any government prime contract or subcontract if the protégé qualifies as small for the procurement.

- Such a joint venture may seek any type of small business contract for which the protégé firm qualifies.

For a JV under an MPP to pursue set-aside contracts:

- SBA must approve the mentor-protégé agreement before the two firms may submit an offer as a joint venture on a particular government prime contract or subcontract in order for the joint venture to be considered excluded from affiliation.

- In order to receive the exclusion from affiliation, the joint venture must meet the requirements of 13 C.F.R §125.8.

MPP's don't guarantee growth. About one-quarter of the protégés GAO surveyed[35] said being a protégé brought them no new contracts or revenue.

MPP's have multiple goals. Each program has unique rules, but in all cases those rules require MPP agreements to have multiple objectives, and are not intended primarily as vehicles to generate subcontracts.

Protégés usually aren't novice partners. MPP's can be helpful – but they're usually not the first step in a relationship with a prime. More often, primes tell me, they want their small business protégés to be established companies (not startups) that have federal contracting experience. Why? So that both mentor and protégé are confident in a high return and the specific results they each seek from the time and money they'll invest in the mentor-protégé relationship.

Each agency's MPP program is different – in terms of criteria for participation, features, and objectives. Which ones might fit you? Check out the specifics of the programs your target agency offers and whether your partners would be eligible and interested. Then start thinking about what you as a protégé might want to include in your MPP agreement with your mentor, and how each of you would benefit.

Find out more: The following federal agencies currently run MPPs.

- Department of Energy (*https://www.energy.gov/osdbu/osdbu-programs-home/mentor-protege-program*)

---

35   *https://www.gao.gov/new.items/d07151.pdf*

- Department of Homeland Security (DHS)
  (*https://www.dhs.gov/mentor-protege-program*)
- National Aeronautics and Space Administration
  (*https://osbp.nasa.gov/mentor.html*)
- Department of Defense (DoD)
  (*https://business.defense.gov/Programs/Mentor-Protege-Program/*)
- The Small Business Administration (SBA), which runs MPP's for:
- firms participating in the 8(a) program (*https://bit.ly/2Lzt02s*)
- and all small businesses (including but not limited to 8(a)).

Once you're in a Mentor-Protégé agreement, you may then decide to create one or more joint ventures between mentor and protégé.

Under such agreements, small companies may combine resources with large (or other small) companies to create a larger and possibly stronger entity that would otherwise be considered affiliated and thus ineligible to compete for a set-aside. A JV between a large business and a small business may be considered unaffiliated if both companies are participants in one of SBA's Mentor-Protégé Programs *and* SBA approves the JV before the companies submit an offer.

A joint venture between similarly situated small businesses – again, those in the same small business program – remains eligible to compete on work set aside for their mutual small business designation. The rules for each joint venture program are unique (see links to details below).

In such a situation, each partner in a qualified joint venture must individually meet the size standard for "small," but the size determination of the joint venture doesn't combine the partners' revenues or number of employees.

While the JV needs to be created through a formal agreement, the JV itself doesn't need to be a separate legal entity. Confer with your lawyer on how to set up a JV intended to leverage the advantages of Mentor-Protégé. The JV can win no more than three contracts in the two years after it wins its first contract award.

There's a lot to learn. Start by reading the rules. Maybe take a class or webinar to learn more. Be sure to engage a lawyer to help you create agreements that comply with those rules. If you read the rules first, you'll spend less on the lawyer. If you engage a lawyer who knows their way around this stuff, you'll spend a *lot* less on legal fees as well as avoid expensive protest litigation later.

Where to find all the details on joint ventures that are eligible to win set-asides for which the protégé is eligible:

- All-Small: 13 CFR 125.8

- WOSB/EDWOSB: 13 CFR 127.506

- HUBZone: 13 CFR 126.616

- SDVOSB: 13 CFR 125.18(b) and, for awards in the Department of Veterans Affairs, 38 CFR Part 74

- 8(a): 13 CFR 124.513(c)

What Does Teaming Success Take?

Lead With Opportunity and Capability. Close With Set-Asides.

The primes have to meet small business subcontracting goals. You're a small business. Or an 8(a). Or a service-disabled female veteran who owns a small business in a HUBZone. Natural fit, right? How hard can that be?

Um, harder than you might think it should be.

Being a small business, or even being qualified for a variety of small business preferences, is simply Not A Good Enough Reason for a prime to return your call.

The primes absolutely have a legal responsibility to make their best effort to award subcontracts to small business. Because they take that responsibility seriously, they work tirelessly to ensure they've always got more than enough trusted, experienced small business suppliers ready to meet those goals on current and prospective opportunities. While they know they need a certain inflow of new small business suppliers to replace those that outgrow their small business size standards, *most large primes usually have enough small business suppliers to meet their small business subcontracting obligations.*

A successful approach to the prime is going to show them which piece of business they are more likely to win with you on their team. Your set-aside designation(s) are secondary. That being said, all other things being equal, the prime is likely to choose a company that's eligible for and/or holds certifications in all four of the small business programs over one that holds fewer.

Always keep in mind the prime's number one goal in any conversation about teaming: to win the work, perform outstanding work, and build business based on that success.

Get Way Ahead Of The RFP

Have you ever won a place on a team by pitching a contending prime about a big RFP that's just a couple of weeks from the deadline, or a winning prime right after the contract award?

Those approaches usually succeed only in exasperating the prime contractor's personnel, pegging the supplicant vendor as naïve (at best), and making it hard to get a second chance from busy small business liaison officers who answer thousands of queries like this every year.

When you see the Olympic bobsled team barreling across the finish line in triumph, or the last runner of the relay team sprinting to victory, you know that that foursome didn't just meet in the bar for beers a couple of weeks before the race. They've been training and prepping and working on strategy and studying their competitors for months or even years.

Teaming on a government project is much the same! Start thinking about government contracting as the business Olympics.

How much time do you think large primes take when they're teaming – as an incumbent, and as a competitor?

When I talked to Small business Liaison Officers from companies like Hewlett-Packard, Boeing, BAE Systems, and then-General Dynamics IT, they cited surprisingly similar lead times for teaming:

- If they want to displace a competitor, they start putting together their teams six to twelve months before the RFP drops.

- If they're the *incumbent*, they take even *more* lead time! They're looking for partners twelve to eighteen months before the recompete.

Find Potential Teaming Opportunities Before Everybody Else

So, if those primes are putting together teams so long before the RFP comes out, how can *you* try out for the team?

Nothing beats leads that come from trusted relationships and personal marketing calls.

Don't know many people? Just getting started? You are not alone. The more tightly you focus your effort to build that network of relationships in your target agencies, the faster you'll put together the detailed intelligence about people and requirements you'll need to pinpoint good teaming opportunities. Relationship-building will start to feel energizing rather than hopelessly daunting.

Relationship building is most effective when you start with research!

The sources of public intelligence about federal buying can be overwhelming. Good news: Many of these sources are free. Well, your only cost is time. Make the most of your time: Start with a broad list. Evaluate which sources are genuinely useful. Then narrow down to those you need to follow regularly in detail.

For starters, consider:

- Agency Published Forecasts – These generally give you more lead time for opportunities than Contract Opportunities in SAM.gov. Forecasts most commonly publish information on opportunities estimated to be worth more than $150,000. Some agencies include opportunities below that threshold in their forecasts; others do not.

- Agency Listings – Did you know? If the agency's requirement is expected to be worth more than $10,000 but less than $25,000, the agency can post the requirement on its own web site, or someplace even less formal (and less accessible – including a hardcopy posting on a bulletin board near the buying office). You're probably only going to hear about those by word of mouth – including in conversation with the buyers themselves. So have those conversations.

- Twitter – Follow the federal agency accounts.

- Reports by the Government Accountability Office – Dozens of these reports are published each year, to present the results of investigations requested by Congress into many aspects of government operations and programs. They're especially useful because they frequently identify *problems* in federal agencies, and recommend solutions to Congress. Whether or not Congress *acts* on the recommendations, the research data itself is rich and valuable. Your tax dollars paid for that research; why not use it?

- The primes' web sites, particularly the press releases.

- General and industry-specific business news, both national and in your own region (for example, your local BizJournal.)

- Government-specific trade press and supplier news and social media. Depending on your industry, you might want to consider:

  - *GovExec.com*. Think of this as a government internal newsmagazine. It's a daily free publication, sort of a cross between CNN and TMZ for government employees. Content often includes who got hired, who got money, and who solved problems (and who didn't). You'll see lots of names and titles of key officials, and lots of pain (which translates into opportunity). When there is a disaster, particularly, agencies use this to communicate with one another about moves and projects. You can get this as a daily newsletter and/or a monthly magazine.

  - *NextGov.com* is the IT version of GovExec. Full of pain and names. Information about changes, office moves. It's a news network in near-real-time. If they are releasing pain, opportunities and names are there. Those stories can catapult you in to the CIO. They put things here because they don't think there's a solution out there. Grab the names and follow up. Pay extra attention to articles that you want to share with your customers. Use those as a conversation-starter.

- *GovCon.com* is a one-stop shop for government contractors! This site features government bid opportunities, teaming partners, products, services, educational resources, career services, industry news, and more.

- *GovLoop.com* is a social media platform for federal, state, and local employees. You as a vendor can also set up a profile. Again, it's free. Over 275,000 members include lots of IT people and middle managers, and features a Daily Awesome, usually an IT person. *Your future customers are here.*

- Presentations and events produced by your key industry associations.

- Searches in federal contract subscription databases. We talked about these in Step 4. While these subscriptions cost anywhere from hundreds to thousands of dollars a year, your Procurement Technical Assistance Center (or even one of your friends) may be able to share access or let you do some searches without you paying for your own subscription.

When you do focused research to identify specific opportunities and key players in both the primes and the government buying agency, you significantly improve your odds of getting on the team. Research combined with long lead time can give you an advantage over competitors who may be approaching the same partners.

Make sure that your research includes what the primes are already contracted on, and what they might be angling to win. Imagine being in a meeting like this one:

A senior official at a large prime told me about a meeting he had held with a small business that was seeking to team on a major program. Everything was going fine, right up until the small business owner's big finish to the pitch: "...and when we team up, together we'll defeat the incumbent."

Wait for it.

The senior official looked at him, deadpan.

"We *are* the incumbent."

Even a *little* research will help you avoid the humiliation of watching your credibility evaporate in front of someone you had hoped to impress.

Aim to be as well-informed as they are (or better) about emerging pre-RFP opportunities.

Dozens of public sources track broad trends and insight into a few big programs, key officials, and primes. Stay on top of those stories. Your prospective teaming partners are certainly following that public intelligence and other sources, too.

Go beyond the usual hunting and list-making. Apply your own good thinking and intuition to what you're reading and hearing. What do *you* think is going to happen next? Check out your hunches with your contacts.

For best success, approach a teaming partner with a small selection of well-researched opportunities in hand. *Don't* bring a long list of open solicitations from Contract Opportunities or a data service! The primes can tell right away when you've done that, because they're using the same data you are.

Instead, aim to winnow that list down to no more than three opportunities. Pick agencies where you have past performance, capacity, and established relationships with customers in the agency who are keen to work with you. Be prepared to show how the opportunity fits within the prime's lines of business and current federal contracts.

Looking in Contract Opportunities? Remember:

- Focus on pre-solicitation notices such as bidders' conferences, draft RFPs, broad agency announcements, requests for information, or Sources Sought rather than on final RFP notices, particularly for a large, complex opportunity. The more lead time you have when you approach a partner, the better your chance of getting on the team.

- If the government buyer needs something they haven't purchased before, agencies will often publish a Sources Sought notice to find out which small businesses might be able to meet a new requirement.

- Primes may be especially receptive to your teaming proposal on opportunities estimated to be worth more than $700,000, because that's the threshold above which they're required to have a small business subcontracting plan.

- Large primes are also interested in substantial programs that might be worth less than that and are set aside for small business. Why? Because they are quite willing to subcontract to *you* to get another piece of business they couldn't win on their own.

  While they want that business, they also want to mitigate risk. The large primes expect a *lot* from a small business proposing to act as a prime partner. Bring a well-developed opportunity and be ready to show all the reasons why, together, you can win the work. That includes details about how you'll manage the proposal effort as well as the contract if you win.

  Be ready to show strong relationships inside the agency as well as significant past performance, management and operations experience, and financing.

With that general background in hand, consider that many of the opportunities you're interested in aren't going to show up in even the agency-focused media. Perhaps the requirement is too small to show up in reporting, or maybe it hasn't been invented yet, but is something you're going to discover and perhaps help develop through one-on-one conversations.

Look Back In Hunger

Let's return to "backcasting," and the tools and techniques you learned in Chapter Four. You can also analyze past contract award data, particularly the contract end dates, to estimate when the follow-on competition might be shaping up and divine teaming opportunities that haven't been published anywhere.

Open either USASPENDING.GOV or Contract Data/FPDS, and Contract Opportunities, in your browser.

- Look up all the contract records for the type of work you want to win. Use the techniques we covered in Chapter Four; that might include keywords as well as NAICS or PSCs.
  Tip: When I work with clients, I prefer to use keywords and pull a dataset that might include things we're *not* looking for, and filter those out later, rather than search so narrowly that I miss something important.

- Export your search file to Excel.

- By filtering on criteria (data fields, which are named in the column headers), isolate the contracts for the agencies you want to do business with.

- Notice which vendors hold the current contracts for work you want to win. You will either have to team with those companies or displace them if you want to win similar work. Which will it be?

- Look at the detailed records for those contracts – specifically, the date the contract is set to expire.

Now work backwards. If the buyer were to recompete that contract, or award a follow-on contract, they'd ideally want the recompetition to be completed by the time the current contract expires.

What are your options to figure out when that might happen?

- *Ask.* Get in touch with the contracting officer or the point of contact listed in the database, and inquire about whether they plan a recompete, what kind of acquisition strategy they have in mind, and what timing and milestones to expect on the way.

- *Estimate.* If it's a big program, you'll want to be building relationships and gathering your competitive intelligence anywhere from 12 to 18 months before the current contract expires.

- *Market.* The strongest source of teaming opportunities is also the one that takes the most work on your part. Your meeting with a prime will move into high gear every time you describe specific programs and opportunities for both what you offer and what the prime can do, *and* describe the relationships you've developed inside the agency with those Five People You Need To Meet (most particularly the End User.)

If the government buyer doesn't know you, or doesn't yet know they need what you've got, you'll need to get to know them long before they put even the first pre-solicitation notices on the street. As you develop that trusted relationship, they'll see that you understand their problem in their terms, and let you show how your company is uniquely prepared and experienced to solve that problem.

A Note about Congressional Funding Bills and Clues for Teaming Opportunities

You can certainly look for opportunities in agency funding bills, when Congress decides the agency needs something (whether or not the agency agrees) and authorizes and appropriates funds to buy it. Sometimes those funding bills include what used to be called "earmarks" – that is, provisions that specify types of technologies, pilot programs, innovative approaches, or concept testing on which the funds must be spent.

If you've gotten to know your potential primes and the programs they want to win, those earmarks can give you another clue about opportunities that the prime may be pursuing. You're still going to need to develop contacts in the agency, and get them excited about what you can bring to the program, for this advance source of opportunities to be useful.

Earmarks don't specify a vendor. But you can bet that the company that invested time and effort to get the earmark in the bill worked closely with both the members of Congress who supported the earmark and the agency players, so that it could position itself to win that business the moment the funding is transferred to the buying agency.

By the way, if you do hunt for opportunities by reviewing funding bills, you might find something in a bill that looks like a perfect fit for you, even though you didn't lobby to put it in there. If it looks too good to be true, it probably *is* too good to be true. You might do well to find out what clever competitor got the provision into the bill, and how they did it.

Look To – But Also Beyond – Incumbents

Being the incumbent contractor can be an advantage – but not an insurmountable one. Don't assume that the company that holds the contract has a lock on its renewal. Sometimes the incumbent has done a poor job, and knows it, and won't try to recompete. Smart companies pick up intelligence on troubled government projects from news reports and web alerts as well as their personal networks.

Other times, the incumbent gets complacent and *doesn't* know it! The project you want to bid on might never hit the news, but you can bet that a poorly-served government buyer is quietly scouting out new suppliers. You definitely want to develop relationships with the program manager and contracting officer long before a new solicitation hits the street. Those key contacts are receptive to keeping up with new suppliers who have ideas of how to do a better job when the time comes.

Consider Exclusivity... Carefully

Smaller companies commonly pursue partnerships, and get on teams, with multiple leading primes who are vying for the same project. That's not rude, it's practical: you never know who's going to win. Primes aren't offended by that.

If you have something unique, and discussions go well, a potential partner may ask you for exclusivity on a project bid. In other words, if you are on their bid team, you won't also team with any other company pursuing that business.

There aren't very many good reasons to offer – or agree to – an exclusive partnership with a prime. The biggest reason a prime would want to do it is to get a jump on their competition. Be flattered, but don't lose sight of what's in it for you. Do you share their high confidence that they're going to win the work? If so, then exclusivity can lower your marketing costs. If you are only on one team, you'll spend less time and money to develop relationships with, and contribute to the proposals of, one prime than you will when you team with many.

You can try to negotiate to get the prime to pay you a premium for exclusivity... but, in this business, everybody shares the risk. Don't be surprised if they come back to you by saying, "Hey, to be on the winning team IS your premium. If you don't go exclusive, we know your competitor will, so take it or leave it."

Show Primes What They Really Want

I've interviewed well over a dozen senior executives from the top prime contractors to ask them what they look for in a potential small business partner. Your status as a small business, by itself, is of minimal interest. All that does is get you in the "small business" door.

Two big realities:

- Large primes, and experienced small ones, know the rules of the subcontracting game well, and have a diversity of small suppliers to choose from. They put thousands of dollars into small business liaison, and make it a point to reach their small business goals each year.

- Even if, for some reason, they were to fall short of reaching their goals, it wouldn't be for any documented lack of trying. So they are extremely unlikely to be penalized for such a shortfall in accordance with the provisions of the FAR.

Your status as a small business isn't what they need from you. It might make a marginal difference, all other things being equal, between you and another small supplier vying for the same subcontracting berth. And if the difference between you and your competitor comes down to which flavor of small business you are... better beef up your marketing, because that's just too close a call.

What *are* primes looking for, then? What should *you* be bringing to the party?

Here's a list that pretty much every prime would agree with.

- *Opportunities you've identified* where your company's products or solutions bring the team a winning edge over the competition.

- *Strong relationships with government buyers* who clearly prefer your solution or product and have told you that they would like to see you on the winning proposal. Better yet, a direct introduction from the government buyer to the prime, before the RFP comes out, that sounds something like, "Take a look at these guys. We really like their approach."

- *Well-defined core capabilities.* One prime after another has told me, "Don't tell us 'We do everything.' Nobody does everything well." When you say that, what the prime hears is "We're not really good at anything." That feeds right into...

- *Strong differentiation from your competitors.* What are the two or three most compelling, appealing reasons the prime would consider you instead of your competitors? How do you stand out? What three or four things do you do better than anyone else in your niche? When should you be top of mind for something the primes and their clients need?

- *Past performance & reputation.* The only client more risk-averse than the government buyer is a prime contractor. Raise their confidence by showing them a short list of programs or projects you've done, for the same or a similar client, that most closely resembles the project you want to be considered for. Look at your corporate résumé for things like project scope, problem solved, location, duration, staff requirements, innovation, technical certifications and qualifications, and project management.

- *Price.* Let's get right down to it: money talks, too. Remember to talk about the profit margin the prime has to gain if you're on the team. Part of "best value" comes from pricing.

- *Financial strength.* Come prepared to open your books. The prime wants to see that you're an established and profitable company with well-managed financial records, a clean audit, and plenty of working capital. Hundreds of small companies are surprised by how long big corporations take to pay them as subcontractors on government projects. Don't get caught. You have to have enough money to develop the business, win the business, perform, and then stay in business until you get paid. Yes, government pays… but if payments to the prime get delayed, then payments to the subcontractors might arrive even later.

- *Personnel experience.* Who on your roster is the shining star of talent in your industry niche, with experience in exactly the kind of project the prime is bidding? What kind of capability can your team contribute that will make the difference between success and failure on the project? Expect to submit résumés of key personnel on the proposal, and expect to have to make good on those commitments if the prime wins. That can pose a challenge for a small company that needs to somehow keep people on the payroll or available when the contract award is many months away from the proposal submission date.

- *Low turnover.* The prime wants to see you've got a stable workforce, because that lowers their risk. Be ready to show those stats, too.

- *Location, location, location.* Your geographic proximity to the government customer can raise your buyer's comfort, especially when that gives you an advantage in the quality or speed of your service or response to the customer Where will you perform your part of the work? Will your team telework, and, if so, how do you manage that? Where is your head office? How close are you to the end user, and to the location from which the prime will be serving the end user? If you demonstrate geographical diversity through partner relationships, be ready to explain how those partnerships work. What are your service-level agreements and your track record on response time?

- *Dependable, responsive team player.* Big projects and contracts can run into big problems. What examples can you show when you went all out to solve the problem or save the day? When did your personnel, responsiveness, or surge capacity make a critical difference to a project's success?

What Primes Won't Do For You

- *Find opportunities for your solution?* Not gonna happen. They want *you* to find opportunities for *their* solutions, and if yours happens to fit into the big picture, come and tell them all about how.

- *Introduce you to key contacts?* Why would they do that? Only if partnering with you brings them a capability that's a unique complement to what they do, and brings the government end user something they want badly.

- *Market you to their clients/prospects?* Nope. The prime is in business to market *their* stuff, not yours. They're only going to market you if yours is the game-changing element of the project and they can't win without you.

- *Call you up to include your firm in bids/projects?* Ah, no; they expect *you* to bring *them* the business, to invite *them* to business you find.

Great Expectations

What do primes expect of you? Big companies give this advice to any firm seeking a partnership in the federal market:

- "Know our clients, our markets, our key projects." The prime contractor's contract awards are public information. Primes expect you to have researched who their government clients are, and to know which ones your offering fits best.

- "Know how we do business." That includes easy-to-find information like which contract vehicles the prime holds. How does the government buy from them? And before you approach a prime you want to do business with, read (and register on) their Supplier Diversity Portal. Many big primes have a section of their websites for current and potential partners to post their basic corporate profiles, and sometimes also allow you to upload capability statement, links, or video. Take the time to make your profile complete. Pack your profile with the keywords your federal buyers and primes use to talk about problems and solutions in your niche.

- "Fit. Show us where what you do fits out business and our clients."

- "Grow our business." How is having you on the team going to bring profit to the prime?

- "Solve our problems." That may mean the prime's problem, or the government's problem, or both.

- "Show us your past performance." One of the most common questions people ask me is how much past performance you need. The secret? Think quality, not just quantity. Show the prime – and the government end users, too – a tight selection of examples to convince them that you've got the experience you need to be a totally reliable partner.

Get Procurement-Savvy Legal Advice

Mistakes with teaming rules can create expensive protests or other legal complications, damage your company's reputation, and temporarily or permanently bar you from federal contract awards. When you choose a lawyer to help you with your federal business, make sure you choose one who has extensive experience with federal contracting. Check their references. Beyond that, do give positive consideration to a firm or lawyer who does a lot of outreach to small business and is generous with their time by giving substantive educational seminar and presentations.

What Can You Bring?

New Task Orders on Incumbent Business: If you're calling on a government buyer who likes what you've got, they also need a way to get it. Using a task order (for services) or delivery order (for products) against an existing contract is not only faster and easier than running a totally new competition… but the FAR requires the contracting officer to give priority to current contract vehicles before awarding a new one. Now, think about what your government buyer could use from the prime as well as from you when they draft that task order. Finally, remember that the prime needs to mark up your price before it reaches the end user. You have to be comfortable with the idea that you're not going to circle back to the federal buyer later and cut an independent deal at a lower price.

Solutions to Known Problems, *and* Track Record on Relevant Past Projects: Instead of saying, "Tell me where you can use me," try a *tactful* approach based on a need (or problem) your research shows this prime has. For example, "I'm wondering whether you might need a few more cleared engineers on this project?" or "I understand from Federal News Network[36] that demand for this program in your client agency spiked again last month. I'm wondering if you'd like some surge capacity for some of the key hard-to-find call-center technical reps. That's *exactly* what we gave one of our clients in a related agency for a few of their peak days last month. If you've got 30 minutes, I can tell you how we did it."

Entirely New Business: Imagine a modestly-sized (e.g., between $250,000 and $1,000,000) requirement you've developed quietly with relationships in an agency. Maybe the prime already has business elsewhere in the agency, or wants to break in there. The requirement hasn't shown up in a forecast or other pre-solicitation notices. You and your prospective prime each have past performance in your prospective roles. And there is no previous incumbent. Think you'd get a meeting with the prime if you could bring that to the table? I bet you would.

Opportunity to Displace a Competitor: The competitive research you did in Chapter Four has already identified who the incumbent primes are in your target agencies. If you've picked a couple of other primes that your research shows would be stronger contenders in a recompetition than the incumbent, then decide whether you want to approach just one, or several. Start with your top-priority candidate partner, and make the case for why you think the two of you would be most likely to win. This is the kind of situation where you'd want to consider the value of a mutually exclusive teaming agreement.

Relationships: First, which of the players involved in the decision in the target agency know you, like you, and trust you? How do you know they do? Second, you

---

36   That's a real thing, an all-Fed-news radio station! If you're outside the DC broadcast area, you can hear it and read their stories at *www.FederalNewsNetwork.com*.

need to be able to make clear to the prime that you've got the ear of the key players involved in the opportunity. You can talk about the nature of the relationships you have, and your interactions with these contacts, without handing over your full contact list. If you and the prime decide you're going to work together, then you should feel comfortable sharing more details. Don't think that, just because your company is small, you have to give a big prime all the intelligence you've spent months gathering just to start a conversation.

Supplier Portal Registration

Most large primes (and many smaller ones, too!) require prospective and current suppliers to register and submit a profile on their supplier diversity portals. Things to remember when you start to do that:

- Don't expect anything to happen just because you complete a profile. (On the other hand, you can expect *nothing* to happen if you *don't* register.)

- Register selectively. Even if you are just cutting and pasting content from your own core reference document, it might take an hour or more to complete the original profile. It takes time to keep all these registrations current. You'll get the best return on your time if you create profiles only on the sites of the primes that are your current partners or serious prospects.

- Read before you write! Does the portal have a section called something like "How to do business with us"? That's where the primes tell you what they expect a well-written profile to include. The small business liaison officials (about whom there is more in the next chapter) put heart and soul and passion into this advice, based on hundreds of outstanding profiles (and thousands of awful ones) that they've reviewed. They expect you to pay attention. You can expect a blunt, brusque, brutal critique if you don't.

- Many primes will require you to register before you meet with them. Pre-meeting registration is a great idea, even if it's not required. Primes screen potential suppliers starting from their first contact with you. What kind of first impression does your profile make? They only want reliable, low-risk suppliers. The time and care you invest to create a comprehensive profile can get you past more gatekeepers on the path to a first, and subsequent, meeting(s). Take this opportunity to show, even in a small way, that you are responsible, anticipate requirements, and follow instructions.

- Once you register, keep track of your login information and update each profile at least once a year.

- Update the profile more often if you do something like move, add or drop employees, buy another company, are acquired by one, win a big new project, or launch a new product or capability.

- Designate one person as responsible for keeping these profiles up to date.

- Make it easy for that person: maintain a single online reference file that the appropriate members of your update constantly with the most current basic corporate data and info. Then that document can also be a "read-only" reference file for cut-and-paste for anyone who creates or updates any kind of marketing material or proposals for the primes.

- If you update all your profiles with the primes just after you update your Entity information on SAM.gov, you'll have the added benefits of having all your data complete, current, and consistent across all platforms. That kind of consistency builds trust, by showing others you're a reliable supplier who takes your responsibilities (even for small things like profile updates) seriously

---

Wouldn't it be easier if you could register in just one place where all the primes could find you?

Govmates is as close as it gets.

Since 2016, this free online service for federal contractors has made over 20,000 matches and over 2,500 introductions among large and small companies pursuing work across more than 59 federal agencies.

Once you complete your govmates profile, govmates matchmakers do the rest. When govmates receives requests from prime contractors or government agencies seeking partners, they use that profile to determine if you're a match, and facilitate email introductions. The key to success is that your company must intend to perform as a prime on a specified opportunity, and be seeking subcontractors.

Is that all you need to do? Of course not. But it's one of the best new places to be seen, it's growing, and it's free.

Govmates also holds matchmaking events for large primes and conferences in the federal market, and presents special high-value networking and educational events. Find out more at www. govmates.com.

The Best Capability Briefing Ever

How's this different from the Capability Statement?

The capability briefing is the basis of a follow-on presentation or discussion. You're most likely to present this briefing at a *second* meeting with people in a government agency, prime contractor, or prospective partner, after you've used your capability statement to introduce yourself (e.g., "You'll find my capability

statement attached. I would like to schedule a capability briefing with you, to discuss how we might provide services that your agency would value.")

Ideally, you'll be able to give your capability briefing in person. Alternatives might
be:

> Webinar, with or without online video conference (ideal for multiple persons/
  locations); these are better than...

> A phone call with the briefing emailed as a PDF or link; which is still better
  than...

> A plain phone call with no reference materials.

Use PowerPoint.

Include just highlights of your talking points, forming a visual backdrop. You don't
want to be reading your slides... and you want your audience to be focused on
what you're saying.

Whether you've been given a five-minute time slot or an hour, be ready to compete your presentation in about 20% of the allotted time, and have 80% of the time
left to exchange questions and answers.

Why? Because if you spend the whole meeting talking, you've missed the opportunity to *learn* more about your prospect by asking questions.

For a 30-minute meeting (a typical length of time), rehearse your presentation so
that you can limit your briefing to just six slides you can present in no more than
ten minutes. Sounds impossible? It's not.

Creating Your Capability Briefing: Six Simple Slides

*Review and edit these slides each time to address the specific needs of the per-
son, agency or company you're meeting with!*

Slide 1. Who You Are

• Legal company name

• Number of employees, Annual revenue

• Locations

• Business Codes: DUNS number / Unique Entity Identifier, CAGE Code,
  NAICS codes (just the numbers)

• Socio-economic certifications

• Current, relevant contract vehicles – GSA Schedule? GWACs? IDIQ's?

- Contact Info
- Name
- Address
- Phone (direct and mobile)
- Email

Slide 2. *Core Capabilities*

No more than four bullet points. These points are how you'd finish the sentence, "We specialize in..." Be ready to answer any question about how government contracting fits into your plans to grow your company overall. Focus on capabilities that your research has shown this prospect needs most.

Slide 3. *The Opportunity*

How does your solution fit the agency's or prime's specific business areas?

- Which government programs or specific contracts might use what you do? List the programs on the slide; add concise facts to explain where you fit and why.
- Presenting to a prime or partner? Speak in terms of opportunities you can help them win (including both forecast procurements and unpublished requirements that you know about from your relationships with the buyers.)
- Point to past performance to demonstrate why you're the low-risk supplier or partner to work with.
- Which relationships can you bring?

Slide 4. *Unique Value Proposition & Best Values*

- If you have a Unique Value Proposition, tailor that as need be for the person you're meeting with.
- Center on the products or solutions you provide (what it is, and how it works.)
- Emphasize your Best Values: provable, quantifiable, characteristics or qualifications that set you apart from your competitors (again) as the low-risk choice...

- and which a buyer might specify when defining their requirement, to make it easier to choose you.

Slide 5. Past Performance

Choose (from the past performance chart you completed in Chapter Four) a few key examples of clients and projects most similar to the kind of project that you want to work on with this prime or agency.

Even better: pick projects or clients you know your buyer or partner is familiar with, ones they've mentioned positively to you already.

Focus on ones that would rivet their attention, and leave them thinking, "Wow, I have got to have these guys on our team!"

Don't load up the slide with every project you ever did. If you are concerned that a short list of projects would give the buyer a mistaken impression that you've only completed a handful of projects, you can improve your own comfort level (and perhaps your own) by titling this slide "Selected Past Performance."

Slide 6. Meeting Objectives

Finally, ask for what you want *today*. Be up front about what you hope to get from *this* meeting.

They know you're in the room because you want their business. While that's the ultimate goal, you're probably not going to leave an initial meeting with a contract or teaming agreement from people who are just meeting you for the first time.

For each meeting (and there will probably be more of them than you would prefer), choose an easy, natural next step that might get you closer to that objective. A non-disclosure agreement? A follow-up meeting with additional contacts you've identified in the partner company's organization? Selection of a couple of priority opportunities to explore together? Plan for a joint marketing call on a federal agency? Co-hosting a marketing event or webinar? Agreement to explore a collaboration?

Producing Your Materials

- Look like a pro: If you haven't gotten professional graphical design help, now is a perfect time to invest in creating a template you can edit in subsequent versions.

- PowerPoint: Remember, just 6 slides! What to do with your chock-full-of-content 20-page PowerPoint you love so much? In the early stages, draw from it as source material. By all means, have it as a backup reference. Check out the client's security policies for the best way to share your file.

- Capability statement: You know what that is now. (If you skipped that part, and figured you'd get around to it later, "later" has just become "now." You need to have this for your meeting with a potential partner.)

- Corporate overview: Put the backup/detail info in a softcopy format and medium your prospect suggests, and/or print out supporting material in a professionally designed and produced folder or package.

- Bring more than one copy: You never know where this stuff is going to go, and it does get passed around. Your materials are also marketing for you even when you're not there.

The Teaming Agreement

People often ask me, "What needs to go into a teaming agreement? Just send me a sample, and I'll take it from there." Online "samples" differ wildly, depending on whether the agreement is to participate in a proposal or to perform on a project after contract award, or includes provisions that become part of your subcontract if your team wins.

Get professional help up front. Teaming agreements for contracting are not do-it-yourself territory. Most of us see the value of preventive dentistry. Why do we balk at getting legal advice in advance?

Check references and engage a lawyer who has experience in teaming and partnerships on government contracts in your industry. Partnering with a big prime? Don't assume the prime's standard agreement has your best interests at heart. Partnering with a friend? If you value that relationship, then legal support for your agreement protects your friendship as well as your business.

An experienced lawyer spots things you'd overlook – both what's there and what's not. They'll have your interests in mind as they identify and recommend ways to minimize risks. You'll get insight into issues that affect your profitability, liability, and performance on your government contract. Those issues can make or break your company.

The list below is a starting point you might use to prepare to meet your lawyer, and also to review the draft agreement they create for you. How would your agreement cover:

- Business development expenses

- Proposal costs: Who's doing what, and paying for what?

- Work share: if you are on the bid team, what guarantee is there that you'll get to do any work on the contract?

- Pricing: What will you charge, and what will the prime charge the client?

- Payment: When and how do you get paid, and what does a correct invoice have to include?

- Exclusivity: Can you be on more than one bid team for the same government RFP?

- Confidentiality & Non-Disclosure: Yours *and* theirs.

- Terminations: Who can end the agreement, under what terms, with what notice, and are there any financial penalties?

- Dispute Settlement: Which neutral third party will you use to resolve differences? Which process: mediation? arbitration? negotiation? litigation? Under which state's laws?

- Shared Expenses: These can include costs of bidding as well as costs of contract administration and performance.

- FAR flow-downs: Which clauses explicitly flow down from prime to sub?

- Performance work statement: Does it include the scope and location(s)?

- Changes to your statement of work and/or pricing: Make sure those can only be made with your consent.

- Proposed, negotiated subcontract: Make sure it's part of the original teaming agreement.

- What happens if proposed subcontract and related work share is not awarded? Consider including a clause that pays you liquidated damages.

- Proposed substitute subcontractor: do you have the right to meet a lower bid rather than get automatically swapped out?

- Non-compete: Are any proposed limits on future business activities mutually acceptable?

- End-user access: What limits, if any, are there on the subcontractor's ability to contact and/or market to the government end user – including on other projects?

- Intellectual property: Who has rights to things that get developed under the contract, including promotional or marketing materials?

- Key résumés: What flexibility do you have to change commitments of personnel to a project?

- Employee poaching: Does the prime agree to compensate you if they hire your employees?

- Liability: Who is legally responsible, and will bear the work and cost to fix things, if something goes wrong?

Remember The "No Free Lunch" Rule

Kathy Kastner, CEO of The Health Television System Inc., was "just a subcontractor," who caught a problem in time to avoid a heavy loss!

"One of our early US government opportunities was with the Department of Health and Human Services (HHS). We sold them a marketing and awareness strategy, plus services to evaluate the effectiveness of the strategy. We had leveraged our existing hospital relationships to go into these hospitals to raise awareness of an information product broadcast by the Food and Drug Administration (FDA, a part of HHS) called 'Patient Safety News,' an Internet product for safety officers in hospitals.

"My FDA contact said, 'We know we want to do it, we just have to find the money.' There were two or three phone calls and a couple of different routes he could use to contract. It turned out that the fastest and simplest one was as a subcontract, and he told me, 'We (FDA) have an existing contract with a company we frequently work with. You'll send them invoices, they will issue you the check and may call you to get details.'"

Kathy was excited. HTS had won the business, it was a done deal; the fine points of where the money was coming from and how the contracting worked were minor details that she didn't need to worry about. Right? Wrong.

"Just before I got the call about deliverables, my FDA contact called, saying, 'Listen, I'm really sorry about this, but in getting this contract off the ground, I forgot about a contractual arrangement I didn't take into account.' He made it sound like an oversight; no big deal.

"He said 'It's going to affect the overall price of the contract, but not by much.' In the end, it cost us over 27%, by value. We were completely taken by surprise."

Expect that it will cost you some margin (and be prepared to negotiate that) if the buyer directs a prime contractor with whom he or she is currently doing business to subcontract to you. There's nearly always a price to be paid if you don't have a contract vehicle.

The lesson: there's no free lunch. Vendors must understand the buyer's acquisition options, and, ideally, be able to suggest a contract vehicle that maximizes convenience for the buyer AND benefit for the contractor. HTS had a rude surprise because they were unaware that the details of the acquisition strategy can have a big effect on your bottom line, whether you're a prime contractor or a subcontractor.

Kathy knew HTS couldn't afford to offer the same package of services for less money, and began to negotiate.

"Of course, that percentage revenue change meant that we had to alter the terms of the contract. We gave them a choice of fewer sites to be surveyed, fewer questions, or a more limited report. They chose both fewer questions and a more limited report."

However, live and learn. "The project served us well. It was chosen for presentation at three different conferences. It was an entree into the FDA, which led to a co-marketing partnership, and connections into the pharmaceutical industry, the American Academy of Family Physicians, the Health Care Educators Association, and the Northwestern University Communication and Medicine Conference."

The Health Television System Inc. list of clients grew to include the Department of Veterans Affairs as well as the Department of Health and Human Services.

READY FOR THE NEXT STEP? QUICK TEAMING CHECKLIST

O Understand what partners want and need before you seek meetings.

O Research specific prospective partners' involvement in your target agencies.

O Focus on two or three partners, tops, and invest the time to research them thoroughly before the first meeting.

O Register in their supplier portal if they have one.

O Bring a few focused opportunities.

O Explain how your company and that opportunity fit the prime.

O Propose the resources and effort you are ready to commit to winning the business.

O Build your track record as a subcontractor and teaming partner on increasingly large projects.

O Explore how mentor-protégé relationships and joint ventures could help you and your partner grow.

Find Out More

Visit *GrowFedBiz.com*, for bonus materials like:

- *Teaming Toolkit* – includes checklists on how to prepare, deliver, and follow up on teaming meetings that mean business
- *Capability Statement Examples*
- *Capability Briefing Templates*
- *Mentor-Protégé Tips*

Other Resources:

- National Contract Management Association *www.ncmahq.org*
- Govmates *www.govmates.com*

Chapter Six: Relationships – The Ten People You Need To Meet

A surprising number of business owners say they most often find out about government business from their friends. How can you find, and make friends with, the people who really do open the doors to new business? Discover the unique network of new contacts your team will need to build – in government and in industry – as you begin your quest for more government contracts.

What you'll learn

- Who are they?

- How to find them

- Why and how they can help you

- What to do next

Selling to government? Here's an open secret: Nobody actually "sells to government." You're selling to *people.*

Individual buyers, program managers, and contracting officers consider what they need, listen to what vendors can do for them, and start drafting specifications for what – and often who – they want.

Successful selling – which you'll have to do in order to win a contract – requires you to find and get to know the buyers who are (or could be) keen for what *you* have to offer. Even – and especially – when they're already doing business with your competitors.

You're an experienced business owner. You've achieved your success through a network of trusted relationships. Now that you want more success in selling to government, think about this next step as weaving a new layer of contacts who are well and deeply wired in government business, starting with threads that rise from the most trusted contacts you already have.

The most effective marketers are masters at building trusted relationships. Is marketing and selling to government a totally different game from winning commercial business, or is there really no difference?

The good news is this: if you're already doing business successfully with customers outside government, there are more similarities than differences.

Government business absolutely runs on relationships. Want to open doors more easily? Start by giving.

Whether you're meeting buyers or vendors, chatting up someone new, cultivating a connection, or getting back in touch with longtime colleagues, keep this question front and center in your thoughts:

"How can I help you?"

Generosity is a magic ingredient, in both your perspective and your approach to others.

Sure, there is a finite number of federal contracting dollars that are spent in every fiscal year. Competition is tough, and every project is hard-won. Did you know? Even top vendors can't (and don't) win them all. A 2016 report[37] showed win rates for incumbents surveyed to be only 54%, and win rates on new projects (where there is no incumbent) to be only 26%.

Fact: you're going to lose some. So, consider helping others on the journey. It's an easy, powerful, way to stand out and be top of mind.

Want more leads – connections as well as opportunities? Start by bringing them leads. There is plenty of business to go around. You're a business owner. You have relationships and contacts. If you're serious about the federal market, you're constantly, deliberately, building relationships. Don't hoard those connections. Share them. When you meet another business owner for the first time, start by being curious about what they do. After you learn a bit about them, *even if they might be a rival,* ask, "Who are your ideal clients? Who might you like to meet at this event? *Who should I be sending your way?*"

---

37   Grant Thornton 2016 Government contractors survey, at *https://www.grantthornton.com/~/media/content-page-files/public-sector/pdfs/surveys/2017/government-cntractors-survey-view-online.ashx*

Listen to the answer, and jot a note on their business card. Take a moment to think about who *you* know who could help *them*. Add that note to their record in your contact database, too. Rare is the company who is *only* a rival. Experienced federal contractors often compete with fellow vendors on one project, and team with them on the next!

When you meet someone new in government, what introductions or industry reports or innovative ideas could you bring your government contacts to make their day easier?

Remember that all these people you're meeting are also human beings, with lives and pets and mortgages and hobbies. Maybe what the contracting officer most needs, she tells you one day in August with fiscal year-end bearing down on her relentlessly, is a decent dog walker, because of all the overtime she's working. Gosh, and you just happen to know one.

Government business absolutely builds from relationships. When I ask experienced business owners, "Where did you hear about the government business opportunities you've actually won?" ninety percent of the replies are something like:

- "A friend told me."
- "Referral from one of my current clients."
- "My accountant had another client who needed me on their contract."
- "I followed up with somebody I met at a community event."
- "I got to know this woman over a couple of years through an association, and once she knew me well enough, she told me about the opportunity and introduced me."

Just as relationships are how vendors hear about buyers... relationships are also one of the most important ways buyers hear about vendors!

You'll meet hundreds of government officials and industry contacts every year. Some of them are critical to your success – first in their own agencies, and then in opening doors as loyal advocates and champions for you in other agencies. Then there are the ones who seem so easygoing: you can always get a meeting with them, they say all kinds of positive things about opportunities, and yet for some reason no business ever comes your way.

Why?

Some of it may be you, some of it may be them. Do you know *who* you're dealing with? And do you know what *they're* dealing with? Here's a way to think about it that can help.

Who do you need to meet?

- In Government – The Five People You Need To Meet

- In Industry – The Five People You Need To Know

As you learn about these key contacts, start a list: who do you already know in each category? Where are you kind of thin on the ground? And what relationships are you missing that you realize you really need?

Consider setting some goals for the relationships you want to build in government and industry. This isn't just a numbers game. Think about not how many people you want to meet, but who.

When you think about someone you already know, ask yourself how strong that relationship is now, and how strong you would like it to be. How can you tell when a contact has become an ally? Do your allies become referral partners or clients or teaming partners? Even better: who has moved from being an ally to becoming an outspoken advocate?

In Government: The Five People You Need To Meet

What's Different About Government Buyers?

Government buyers often have a lot in common with industry buyers and partners. They're proud of what they do, and want to do it well and get credit for it; they have families who depend on them; they work a lot of unpaid overtime; they deal with bosses and politics and infighting; and sometimes their organizations don't act rationally.

But in other ways, government buyers are very different:

- They are extraordinarily publicly accountable – sometimes in very visible ways – for how their organization performs. Bad performance can generate negative media attention very fast. Public perception of a mistake – even if they did everything by the rules – can get them fired.

- Projects don't focus on "maximizing profits," and often are less about cost efficiency than about using up all the project funds... because if it seems they didn't need all the money in their budget, they might not get as much next year.

- They have rules – often many more than the private sector does – about how they can purchase. Sometimes they will go silent, sometimes for extended periods. At certain points in the federal buying process – typically, after the competition formally begins and an RFP is on the street – buyers can only communicate with vendors in very formal, structured ways, if at all. However, the entire buying process is largely transparent. If you can't get the details of the procurement while it's going on, you can request and receive many details after the contract award.

- Some keys to a government buyer's power or status are the number of people who report to them, the public prominence of their mission or agency, or how senior they are in the organization. It's *not* the money they make. The most senior purchasing officials in the government are paid less than an associate at a major law firm.

- Many of the most experienced federal officials who handle purchasing are retiring. There are not enough people available to replace them. Those who remain are seriously overburdened, and it takes a long time for new ones to come up to speed.

- Stakes are high. In military procurement, lives often depend on the performance of whichever contractors, products, and services the buyers choose. Even in civilian agencies, millions of Americans put our trust in federal government employees – and, whether they know it or not, the contractors who support them – to deliver services we and our families depend on.

Government contracting is like commercial contracting in one other important way: especially when competition is close, people do business with people they like and trust. These are the five people who need to like and trust *you*. Each can unlock your access to others…if they want to.

- The Small Business Specialist
- The Contracting Officer
- The Program Manager
- The Influencer
- The End User

The Program Managers and the End Users develop an idea of the products and services they're going to need to do their jobs. The Contracting Officer works with them and the Small Business Specialist to figure out potential sources of supply and the best way to do business with those vendors. The Influencer can make it easier for you to meet any or all of the others.

The Small Business Specialist

Because federal government departments have a goal to award 23% of their contract dollars to small businesses, each agency has an Office of Small and Disadvantaged Business Utilization (OSDBU) staffed by Small Business Specialists in locations across the country.

You can find the Small Business Specialists in your target agencies by searching the top level of the agency's websites using the terms "OSDBU" or, especially in military agencies, "SADBU" or "Small Business". Once you start getting individual names, start Googling them and looking them up on LinkedIn.

The Small Business Administration negotiates annually with federal agencies to set agency-specific goals for prime and subcontracting awards to small business. Some of those goals might be higher or lower than the government-wide goals. For instance, while the overall federal goal is to award 3% of prime contract dollars to SDVOB's, the Department of Veterans Affairs had a 2017 goal of 10%, and in 2016 reported achieving 21%.

The fact that they have those goals isn't a good enough reason to approach every Small Business Specialist with your capability statement. The only ones who are going to respond to you are those you take the time to follow up with and get to know. To be effective, be selective!

The Small Business Specialist has both outward- and inward-facing missions. They focus on:

- Guiding small companies to contacts and business within the agency, and
- Ensuring the agency meets its small business goals.

The more you:

- research the agency and opportunities in advance,
- tailor your capability statement,
- focus on business that fits, and
- keep in touch,

the better the Small Business Specialist might help you:

- find out details on agency plans and processes,
- gain introductions to the contracting officers, directors, and program managers within the agency who may need what you offer, and
- increase your credibility and stay top of mind with those key contacts.

Want To Find The Right Small Business Specialist?

No matter what agency you're marketing to, the Small Business Administration (SBA) Regional and District Offices can be a great starting point.

Counselors and advisors in SBA's offices in your community are ready to help you get started. Make an appointment to ask for assistance with things like:

- Identifying federal buyers and contacts, including Small Business Specialists, within your state or region.

- 8(a) and HUBZone certification – These are the people who review, and have the authority to approve, your application!

- Information about SBA-backed loans

- Finding potential sources of bonding

- Introductions to key contacts in other partner organizations – community economic development, Chambers of Commerce, industry associations, and other business groups

- Special events and programs

- Locate your nearest office at *www.sba.gov/localresources/index.html*

Did you know?

SBA's Procurement Center Representatives (PCRs) are often on staff within buying agencies. PCRs view many federal acquisition and procurement strategies before they're announced. They work with the contracting officers to point out small business' capabilities and encourage opportunities to be set aside when enough qualified small businesses can meet agency requirements. They also conduct market research, assist small businesses with payment issues, and advise on the contracting process. **When they know who you are and what you can do, they can be a source of leads, too.**

See the full list of who they are and how to contact them at *http://bit.ly/SI-PCRs*

Commercial Market Representatives (CMRs) are SBA's front-line staff who ensure prime contractors understand and comply with their obligations under the Subcontracting Program. CMRs can help match prime contractors and subcontractors, help small businesses market their services to prime contractors, and more. They review prime contractors' compliance with requirements of their subcontracting plans, including via on-site visits to contractors and review of subcontractor activity reports. CMRs are assigned to SBA Area Offices by state.

See the full list of who they are and how to contact them at *www.sba.gov/node/12984*.

PROFILE IN SUCCESS: Deborah Stallings

I asked Deborah Stallings, President of HR Anew, how important the Small Business Specialist was to her first win. "The Small Business Specialist was very important! The contract was with NASA. In fact, it was a Small Business Specialist who connected me with the contracting office and the procurement folks to pursue this opportunity. We started networking with one of the OSDBU directors, at a business fair, and met the small business folks at NASA. We were invited to lunch-and-learns – opportunities to learn something new as well as network with other contractors."

"And one day the Small Business Specialist approached me and shared that there was an opportunity available that they'd like HR Anew to take a look at. We received an opportunity to be one of five companies they were considering to conduct a workforce study for them. And the project was for about six or eight months, worth about $100,000. We developed that relationship with them as a result of going through NASA's *Training and Development for Small Business in Advanced Technology* program, which at the time was a program they were offering to teach contractors how to do business with NASA. And the rest is history."

Of course, not all Small Business Specialists are created equal. Some are extraordinarily helpful, like Deborah's contact at NASA. Others, less so. But you'll make the most of what each has to offer you if you show up prepared, as Deborah did, and demonstrate how well you've already researched the agency and its needs.

If a Small Business Specialist knows of an urgent requirement, they often introduce vendors to program managers and decision-makers in need. Similarly, if a program manager has a need, some money, and the authority to spend it, Contracting Officers help figure out the options for a way to meet that need.

The Contracting Officer

The Contracting Officer (CO , or in the military, KO) manages the competition and contracting process. They develop the requirements and evaluation criteria from the Program Manager and/or the COTR (see below), and take all the required steps to publish the solicitation. Depending on the complexity of the acquisition, the CO may coordinate the selection or even choose or recommend the winning vendor. Oh, yes, and the CO may also be the person who ensures that you get paid when the work is complete.

The Contracting Officer cares about:

- Legal, fair, and proper process
- Establishing adequate competition among qualified suppliers to get a supplier who can meet the requirements and provide fair value for the money
- Locating the right vendors for buyers' needs
- Your readiness to do business

The Contracting Officer can help you:

- understand how the agency buys what you offer;

- know the outlook for acquisition plans – how they're likely to be buying, and when; and

- make contact with end users and program managers.

Above all else, the Contracting Officer has a "warrant" – legal authority, up to a specified dollar value or sometimes even with no dollar limit at all – to bind the federal government and a vendor in a contract for goods and services. *Only the CO may authorize, sign, and administer the contract.*

COs want to know about your capabilities to perform the work and manage the contract. They're very interested in your track record in doing the kind of work you want to win. Even though the COs aren't usually end users of the product or service they're buying, they often have end-user experience. They certainly influence how the specification and evaluation criteria are written...two things that determine who wins!

If you contact them well in advance of when formal competition begins (and if they like you and want to talk to you), COs can tell you a *lot* about the type of contract and competition process they plan to use. Again, if your questions show that you know how this agency usually buys, and the programs they manage that might need the kinds of things you offer, COs are much more likely to open the door to someone you really need to meet, especially the Program Manager or End User.

COs may be supported by Contract Specialists (CS), who assist in the planning to acquire goods and services. The CS typically prepares the proposal package, and may negotiate and even recommend a contract award. CS does not have a warrant, and so does not have the authority to award a contract. They can negotiate, but that negotiation may not be binding. The CO may designate a CS as your day-to-day point of contact for that program within an agency. They can support and guide you, or make your life miserable, depending on your relationship with them.

The CS does most tasks the CO does, with the exception of signing contracts. They are usually the "right-hand "of person" of the CO.

The Program Manager

The Program Manager (PM) is the federal official with decision-making and budget authority – including authority over acquisition – of one or more initiatives related to a specific mandate. For example, in the military, each specific type of equipment (e.g., each type of plane or armored vehicle) has a program manager. In civilian agencies, an agency headquarters program manager might be in charge of one or more technology projects, or a set of clinical trials. (Or even the agency's outreach to small business: that's a program, too!)

The Program Manager cares about:

- Delivering the agency mission to the best of their ability

- Responsible management of people and resources, including vendors

- Finding solutions that are innovative but also reliable and cost effective

- Spending all the money wisely and on time

- Meeting vendors with experience who understand their needs

The Program Manager can help you obtain things like:

- deeper understanding of their team's challenges and preferred approaches;

- insight into current vendors, planned procurements, and constraints;

- support for requests from End Users to try your products or pilot your solutions; and

- referrals to End Users.

Outside agency headquarters and beyond the Washington DC Beltway, a program manager might be the person who runs the agency's operations or delivers its programs in a specific region of the country.

The Program Manager sets the priorities for the budget. They know how much money there is, and have to figure out exactly how far it's going to go. The PM cares about how best to deliver the agency mission, including how to define requirements to select the best vendors.

The Program Manager has a lot of power, and can be hard to reach... which is why strong meetings with the Small Business Specialist and the Contracting Officer pay off. If you've established your credibility with them as a reputable problem-solver, the Program Manager may be eager to hear about the details of your solution and your approach – the kind of technical meeting you might have been hoping to have from the start.

When you meet the PM, you want to find out as much as you can about what their priorities are, and how you can contribute to solving the most important problems at the top of their list. If you can demonstrate where you're a fit, you're much more likely to get a hearing, and possibly an introduction to the End User.

PROFILE IN SUCCESS: ProWear

We already met Linda Lazarowich, President of ProWearGear. Here's how her relationship with End Users helped her both develop her first product line, and discover a new need that helped her grow the company.

Her government clients' interest grew as she evolved her product lines from garb that simply identified the dog as a working agency officer to protective uniform systems. She developed a close relationship with Program Managers at Ft. Leonard Wood, Missouri, who specialized in meeting the needs of federal canine handling specialists, after meeting them at a trade show of law enforcement and military K-9 handlers in Las Vegas.

Linda spent a lot of time with End Users. She knew she needed grass-roots research and credibility that would only come from getting buy-in on the front lines. When she was calling on Customs and Border Protection units on the southern border, where she knew many canine units were deployed, the officers told her they needed canine uniforms made of unique fabric that would also protect the dogs from slash or puncture injuries when working in hazardous environments like disaster cleanup sites, or running alongside barbed wire and jagged metal encountered on patrol.

Over the next three years, the technical team there gave her lots of feedback on her designs – including special add-on uniform packs to cool dogs working in hot places, or warm those working in cold places (and thus enable teams to work shifts up to three times longer than they would without protective gear.) They liked her – not least because she was very generous with her time and samples and expertise – and those relationships put her in the running with the much more established suppliers. As a result, Linda discovered a totally unexpected opportunity. When the human End Users saw how well those fabrics protected their canine partners, they wanted to know whether Linda could use her special fabrics to make uniform accessories to protect *them* from gash, puncture, and slash hazards, too.

That led her to a major opportunity to grow her business!

The Influencer

The Influencer could be a colleague, friend, writer, reporter, or blogger whom the decision makers and players trust. They may be distinguished members of the technical community you're selling into, industry analysts, or market researchers who keep tabs on the market leaders. They may be the Program Managers in other parts of the agency you're marketing to, or top professionals in the major prime contractors.

The Influencer cares about:

- Knowing suppliers/experts on the leading edge
- Being the first one with the hot stories – good and bad
- Supporting friends with the inside scoop on both of the above
- Changing the game, moving the goalposts, or raising the standards
- Promoting a point of view

- Making sure people know all their options and choices, especially the little-known or unpopular ones, or just…

- Sparking dialogue and controversy

The Influencer can help you by:

- Raising your visibility and credibility with the Program Manager and End User, and

- Getting potential partners interested in your company and eager to meet you.

Influencers are valuable because it's important to have people talking about you who *aren't* you.

The Influencer can get people excited to meet you, and receptive to your first direct contact with them. The Influencer can help open doors not only to government buyers, but also to primes and channel partners you may need to work with to reach those buyers, and to others who may seek you out because they want to back a winner. The Influencer provides a kind of independent validation of your message, and can have even more power than paid advertising, because Influencers represent trusted advisors within their communities.

Why would they care about you? What can you bring them?

Keep an eye out for articles or inside tips on market trends and leading-edge suppliers. Influencers want to share hot stories – good and bad – about vendors, problems and solutions. Be sure they have yours!

The End User

The End User is the front-line employee, or the person in the battle space. They're the government employees who most directly use the goods or services provided by vendors. In the military, that may be the person who drives the tank or flies the plane, or the person wearing the night-vision goggles on patrol in Afghanistan. In the Park Service, that may be the Ranger who's looking through the binoculars atop a fire station in Montana. So they're also the people who look good when you perform well… and who look bad or can end up dead if you don't.

A Contracting Officer's Technical Representative (COTR, often pronounced "COH-tar"), Contracting Officer's Representative (COR), or Project Officer (PO) may represent the End User within the contracting process. They're normally government employees (rather than contractors themselves.) While they don't have the authority to sign a contract, they may have the power to define the requirement, and ask the contracting officer to set up a requisition, a task order, delivery order, or other action related to administering a contract after award. Many have strong technical background in the domain that the contract involves, and are "industrial translators" between the contractor and the Contracting Officer.

The End User cares about:

- Serving the citizen and delivering the mission to the best of their ability
- Getting the job done right, on time, the first time, with the Best Stuff
- Making their organization, their agency, and their government look good
- Knowing why you'd be any better than the supplier they already know and trust

The End User can help you with:

- insider info on what they like (and don't) about the incumbent;
- Candid views on how your capability, experience, product or service fit;
- "Will it work?" – confirming, validating, or debunking your ideas for new approaches; and
- What it would take to give you a try.

The End User cares about getting the job done with the resources available. Get the End User's attention with your best values and outstanding past performance. How will you make their job easier than your competitors could? What parts of your track record give them the most confidence that you, as their new vendor, would deliver the solution or products or service and support that you promise?

End Users can ask senior managers for support to try your solution. They can also be your best source of intelligence on the strengths and weaknesses of current suppliers, what the Best Stuff would be, and how close your ideas come to that.

In Industry: The Five People You Need To Meet

- The Supplier Diversity Professional
- The Wise Guide
- The Service Provider
- The Superconnector
- The Outlier

The Supplier Diversity Professional

If you need to team with a large prime contractor in order to win government business, where do you begin? Whether or not you think you have contacts in the right division of the prime, the supplier diversity professional is a key player you need to know.

Large primes' government divisions include business development and capture staff as well as program managers and contracting officers...is this structure starting to sound familiar? And, just as government agencies have Offices of Small and Disadvantaged Business Utilization, the major prime contractors have Supplier Diversity teams.

As you will remember from Chapter 5 – Teaming, these offices are the prime's front-line team who actively seek small and minority-owned business partners to meet their subcontracting obligations on federal contracts worth more than $700,000. If the prime manages its supplier diversity programs centrally, then its relatively few people get spread very thinly, and must crisscross the country constantly. They are cost centers, not revenue centers, to the primes. They are under pressure to deliver value to the organization.

You'll see them at many of the same places where federal agencies' Small Business Specialists show up: outreach sessions, matchmaking events, speaking at conferences, and spending the long, long, days at the big booths on the trade-show floors across the country. Their business cards have titles like "Small Business Liaison", "Supplier Diversity", "Small Business Office", or "VP Supplier Development." They are gatekeepers as well as facilitators for small companies who want to do business with their organization.

They get the same questions all day long: "Can I be on your team?" "Would you add me to your contract?" "How can I fill a couple of seats on that contract for you?" "Who are your government customers?" and "How can I be your protégé?"

And they give the same answers: "Have you registered on our Supplier Diversity Portal? What part of our company do you want to do business with? Which of our government customers, programs, and contract vehicles do you fit? Tell me about your past performance and relationships that make you a low-risk choice that will help us win."

Do your homework, and they can help with the same kind of introductions on the industry side as the Small Business Specialists can open up for you on the government side. Show up unprepared, and you'll have even less success with them than you do with the Small Business Specialists.

Like most federal agencies, the large primes generally have no difficulty meeting their small business subcontracting goals in any category. Sometimes they run a little short on HUBZone or occasionally SDVOSB suppliers. They're constantly approached by small companies who often carry three or even all four small business certification and are qualified and have past performance. They can afford to be picky.

Those who run the mentor-protégé programs may be harder to find. While some primes manage their mentor-protégé relationships from a central office, other primes manage them from within the individual programs. As one Supplier Diversity professional explained to me, "No matter how much the protégés say they want technical training, what everybody really wants is subcontract business, and the only place that comes from is the programs themselves. You want to be our protégé? Tell me who you've done business with inside our company so far."

The Wise Guide

Imagine having a trusted advisor who's done it all, seen it all, worked with companies like yours and helped them win millions in government contracts, and who is passionate about helping business professionals understand how government does business. Now, imagine being able to afford help like that.

Did you know? Your tax dollars and corporate sponsors have already paid for several networks of free or low-cost help that's ready and waiting for you across the country, whether you're in Washington State, Washington DC, or somewhere in between. One Wise Guide might be the presenter of an online webinar whom you never meet in person. Another Wise Guide could be someone you meet with regularly at a local office close to yours. Still others may be facilitators at a matchmaking or networking event.

Examples of great wise guides you'll want to explore include:

- Procurement Technical Assistance Centers (PTACs)

  The PTACs are jointly funded by the Department of Defense and local partners. Their mandate is not just military or even federal procurement! 98 PTACs staffed by a total of over 500 procurement professionals are dedicated to helping you win government business at every level – federal, state, and local –by offering one-on-one counseling, classroom instruction, and events. Many also provide resources in support of mentor-protégé programs.

  Find out more, and locate the one nearest you: _www.aptac-us.org_

- Small Business Development Centers (SBDCs)

  Hosted by leading universities, colleges, and state economic development agencies, and funded in part through a partnership with the U.S. Small Business Administration, approximately 1,000 service centers across the country are available to provide no-cost consulting and low-cost training. Some SBDC's have more expertise in federal contracting than others.

  Find out more, and locate the one nearest you: https://americassbdc.org/ and search by zip code

- Service Corps of Retired Executives (SCORE)

  SCORE's 12,400 volunteers – current and retired executives – deliver expertise that spans over 600 business industries to serve clients both online and through 364 locations across the United States. You can work with them to answer one-off questions or for ongoing support. Counselors offer mentorship in your community, online and onsite workshops, and referrals to other SCORE volunteer experts.

  Find out more, and locate the one nearest you: _www.score.org_

Not all free help is created equal. Furthermore, different groups are a good fit for different people at different stages of their government business. You're not going to need (or have time to draw on) all of them. Ask other people who's good, and then meet them and test the personal chemistry yourself.

The Wise Guide may have limits on the number of hours they can devote to you, or the types of issues on which they can advise you, or the professional liability they have for the advice they provide. Eventually, expect that you'll need more help, quite possibly from...

The Service Provider

At all kinds of events, you'll run into bankers, lawyers, and consultants who specialize in the government contract arena. Why do you need Service Providers? Isn't this just one more cost?

Engaging the right provider at the right time can be an excellent use of resources.

Look at it this way. Do you do your own taxes? Maybe you do. My hat is off to you. How about write your own will? Maybe not. Why not? You know how to do what _you_ do well. You don't do this stuff every day. You want to get it right. You want to get every advantage, and avoid costly errors.

Federal business specialists are no ordinary service providers. These professionals have technical expertise on government contracts that your current set of experts might not.

If your current lawyer doesn't have deep specialty in federal contract law, then you'll want to have a good relationship with another lawyer who does. You need a lawyer with expertise on the FAR and teaming and intellectual property, just for starters. Proposal preparation and production for government is a unique art form. Some graphical designers have proven track records in creating websites, marketing materials, and exhibits that appeal to government buyers and primes. If your current accountant can't spell DCAA, and you want to grow your government business, be on the lookout for an expert who can get your accounting system in compliance with the requirements of the Defense Contract Audit Agency.

Talk to the people offering business coaching and marketing communications for the government niche and find out how they can help you

The ideal federal-market service provider has a commitment to members of the twin communities of vendors and government buyers. The best ones are generous with their expertise. They'll chat with you informally at events. They share their handouts. They answer questions or suggest people or places you can get answers. And they're genuinely interested in building a relationship with you. Just as it takes you a long time to win government business, they know it may take *them* a long time to win *your* business... and that when the time comes, just like the government buyer, you're going to do business with someone you know, and like, and trust.

There are plenty of choices. How to choose? Start by listening to what they say, and listen to your gut. Who you genuinely like? Do some due diligence; follow them online, and ask people you trust about them. When you get ready to engage, ask for (and call) their client references, too.

The best service providers know people on both sides of the buy/sell line: they're well connected with large businesses, small companies, and government contacts at many levels and in many agencies. More than a few of them used to work for those agencies.

What can you bring them? Simple: remember the give and take. Referrals and relationships are vital to their businesses. In order to stay in business, they have to know a lot of people, and they hear a lot of things. So do you. You can help each other.

PROFILE IN SUCCESS: Lisa Dolan, President, Securit

Lisa Dolan, President of Securit, a professional services firm providing background investigations, shares this example: She retained Jack Coley and Associates to get her firm on the GSA Schedule – a choice that not only helped her win a contract with the Smithsonian Institution, but continued to benefit both companies. As Lisa notes, "That relationship turned into a friendship and we have been able to refer each other lots of business and contacts."

And while you may need a lot of help, it doesn't always have to cost the earth. Negotiate, and consider bartering services, too. Marissa Levin, CEO of Information Experts, agrees. "The amount of effort that has to go into government proposals is much more extensive than in the private sector. We hired help, including to prepare our GSA Schedule Contract proposal. As an entrepreneur, any time you can do a trade, you should. We do that quite a lot. We bartered GSA schedule proposal services for marketing activities: we did all their branding and marketing outreach. We outsourced our application for 8(a) certification, but negotiated a fixed price for that – with a money-back guarantee."

The Superconnector

Superconnectors come in two kinds: the obvious and the subtle.

The obvious Superconnectors are the ones that every third person tells you about: "You've got to meet so-and-so; they know *everybody*." Sometimes they're in leadership roles or on the executive committee of an organization. Sometimes they're the point of contact for an association's small business programs or industrial outreach. They also show up with no formal titles at all. The Superconnector seems constantly surrounded by a tide of people ebbing and flowing with introductions. When you do get to meet them, and tell them what you do, they get it right away. Within three minutes they've got half a dozen suggestions for people you need to meet, have introduced you to the ones who happen to be standing nearest to them at that moment, and tell you to keep in touch and let them know if there's any way they can help you.

In short, they're a walking example of the maxim that what goes around comes around. Before they head back across the room, be sure to stop them for long enough to find out what *they* do, and who's a good contact for *them*.

Then there's the subtle Superconnecter. You see them clearly representing their own companies. But they're also the ones who arrive early and help with the set-up. The event leaders obviously know them well. Even though they might have no official role or title with the host organization, they are constantly moving around, making people welcome. If you wander over their way, you'll hear them sharing government business development expertise and contacts that range well outside their own industries. Listen long enough and you may hear how they landed millions of dollars in federal contracts. They're motivated to help people who take the time to get to know them. They've been around government-contracting circles for so many years that they know, or can find, key senior officials in agencies all through government and industry.

The Outlier

While you're attending networking events, be curious as well as focused. If the person you've just met doesn't seem to have interests directly aligned with the nature of the event you're attending, then what? Instead of abandoning them as quickly as humanly possible, take another couple of minutes to find out about them and what brought them here. Jot a note on their card. You never know who you might need to know. And you can sure never know who else *they* know, and would be happy to introduce you to. Odds are good that today's outlier is tomorrow's shining-star contact, either for you or for someone you want to help.

In particular, remember that the person who arrives as "spouse of" could actually be someone who's an even more valuable contact for you than the primary guest. You'll only know that if you take the time to talk with them.

The Outlier might be especially happy to chat with you if everyone else has been ignoring them alongside their better-known mate!

Furthermore, if they're between jobs, spend some extra time to ask what kind of opportunity they're looking for and consider who you might know.

Have you *ever* forgotten the kindness of someone who helped you find a job? Of course not. What a lovely way to pay it forward.

Contact! Finding and Meeting Your Top Ten

For any opportunity you find (or, ideally, set out to create!), you need to become a detective.

Got a favorite detective or investigative journalist? Every investigator is trying to do one thing: put together a story. They use a combination of clues and conversations, figure out fact from fiction, and pinpoint the players at all the levels, until they know what really happened. The really good detectives and investigators are successful because they do so much research before they start conversations. No question or meeting is wasted...and a lot of work goes into testing theories or verifying what they've learned. The more research they do, the more successfully they put together the story. They're looking at what happened in the past...and trying to determine (and sometimes influence) what might happen next.

Your job in federal business development is much the same: to let the past give you clues to the future, and where your part might be.

So, how do you find these *actual* people, the ones *you* need to connect with? Why would they talk to you or meet you if you don't know them today?

You're going to spend time and you're going to spend money. All you get to choose is the mix. That mix is unique for each of us, and it changes over time, as successful business owners explain below. It's time to start making some choices.

First Person Singular

There is simply nothing as powerful as a personal relationship or, second best, a personal introduction. If only those weren't so hard to come by and didn't take so long. Remember the top advice from successful contractors? "Start Small" and "Be Persistent."

PROFILE IN SUCCESS: Carolyn Sawyer

Carolyn Sawyer, CEO and Chief Strategist of the Tom Sawyer Company, shared the story of her start in government business. Today, TSC supports governmental, NGO, non-profit, and private-sector entities in providing successful, high-quality customer care solutions worldwide. When she started the company, her focus was on communications services, including public relations, advertising, marketing, production, and training.

"Our very first government contract was a small contract, under $50,000. I can tell you exactly from point of contact to how it came to closure. I participated in a trade mission that was offered through the US Department of Commerce. It was a trade mission for 10 minority-women-owned small businesses. A collection of us from all across the country were invited to travel with one of the Deputy Secretaries from the Department to attend the International Women's Conference in Barcelona. And so, we took 10 days. We saw four cities in Europe. We started over in Italy and saw two cities there and visited small businesses. We got a chance to tour a manufacturing plant and hear about that family business and succession.

"On that trade mission was a woman who headed up the International Trade Administration inside the Department of Commerce. And she and I just started talking on the bus on one of our many stops. We were talking and I explained to her my background and what we did. And she said, you should call me when we get back.

"I called her when we got back. They had an HR video that they used for employees for orientation. And at that time, it was literally a video. And they wanted to update it so that people who were going to come to work for the International Trade Administration would be able to fill out as much of the paperwork as they could before they got there and to know a little bit more about the agency when they arrived.

"So, we took an old video and we turned that video into a tool that could be used on the Internet. And we also created a CD that gave people those forms electronically, and created information that could also be emailed out to people, so that they could fill out their forms in PDF format and then send them back. When they got to Commerce on their first day, they were ready to go to work. That sounds ordinary today, but back in the early 2000s when we were putting this together, sharing that information in advance made the client's whole HR intake process more efficient and cost effective."

Past and Current Clients

Short of meeting the buyer yourself, as Carolyn did, the next best thing can be a warm introduction from a client who's already had a good experience doing business with you. Whether you're new to government business or have already won a couple of prime or subcontracts, ask your best clients who they know who might appreciate the superlative products, service, and results you've already brought to them.

Deborah Stallings, award-winning President of Maryland-based human resources company HR Anew, couldn't agree more. "Ninety-four percent of our business comes from referral business, usually from existing clients and/or repeat business. And so, the opportunities that we win, for the most part we win because we have an established relationship with the client. We've already done a good job and we have great past performance. Our win rate at bidding on proposals that we just see published is not as great. I think the key is building relationships before you need them, being proactive, and working it from there."

Board of Advisors

Companies often convene a Board of Advisors when they want to grow, or enter a new market niche, or both. This is not the same as your Board of Directors if your company is a corporation!

When you choose candidates for your Board of Advisors, you seek people willing to share the knowledge, experience, track record, and connections you need to achieve your business goals. If you have, or are forming, a Board of Advisors, find out whether they have relationships in agencies and companies where you need access, and can open doors for you. Expect to compensate your Advisors, and have a plan to work with them in a regular, structured way.

One of my favorite experts on this topic is Marissa Levin, the CEO of Successful Culture International. She wrote her first book, SCALE, to share what she learned in creating a Board of Advisors that helped her grow her first company, Information Experts, into a multimillion-dollar federal-contracting enterprise. Here's her expert advice!

Recruiting The Best Advisors

The vast majority of business owners who implement an advisory board fail to see a strong return on investment because they haven't followed guidelines to pick the right advisors, and haven't set them up for success.

If you are considering implementing an advisory board, follow these first steps to attract and recruit your best advisors:

1: Complete your Values, Mission, Vision, and Strategic Plan first.

To create a comprehensive board search document, you must have your foundational elements constructed. What do you stand for, why do you exist, and where are you going? You must be able to articulate this to any prospective board member. In addition, you must be able to share your target customer profiles and your competitive landscape.

It is not the advisory board's job to complete this work.

2: Select Advisors that are ahead of you.

Choose advisors that have already achieved what you are trying to achieve so that you can learn from both their successes and their mistakes. You don't want to sit around a table with others that are exactly where you are.

3: Make sure your Advisors fit your needs.

Are you expecting your advisors to only work with your C-level execs? Or do you want them mentoring your other employees? Are you expecting them to be available during meetings? Or only show up quarterly? Are you expecting your advisors to make key introductions to customers or investors? These are just 3 of the many considerations you must think about when selecting advisors.

4: Start small.

An advisory board takes on a life of its own. In addition to running your company, you will have to manage the individual and collective contributions. Start with no more than 4 advisors. If you successfully identify your needs, you will be able to prioritize your top 4 seats.

5: Institute a one-year agreement with each Advisor.

An advisory board is an evolving, dynamic entity that will likely change as your business grows. You want the option of re-evaluating each advisor at the end of each year to determine if they are aligned with your goals for the coming year, and if they have met your expectations.

We advise our advisory board clients to institute a restricted stock agreement if they are giving equity to their advisors so that they can buy back the stock at the termination of their service.

Aligning Advisors to Your Holes and Goals

Selecting the right advisors is just as important as selecting the right employees. The wrong advisors will be a waste of time and money, and can potentially lead you down the wrong path.

Especially in today's rapidly changing environment, companies must constantly evaluate what types of expertise they need. For example, an expert in cybersecurity is now a critical addition to any board.

The more intentional you can be when selecting your advisors in aligning them to the "holes and goals" of your organization, the more successful they will be in helping you achieve your growth objectives.

Find out more!

Link to the book www.builttoscale.info
Enjoy a 5 minute intro video on the SCALE Model: *http://bit.ly/SCALE-Intro-Video*

Six Free Federal Lead Sources You Need To Know

It's time to go back to the data you've extracted from the competitive intelligence sources you've been using since Chapter Two – Focus to research opportunities, competitors, and market share. This isn't an exhaustive list, but it will give you plenty to get started.

1. ***Past Contract Data***

Data exported from FPDS/Contract Data includes some contact information for government buying officials and potential teaming partners. Now that you're focused on certain types of opportunities, specific projects, and selected agencies, you can go back into those databases.

Contact information for a contract that's already been awarded is definitely useful. Why? Because contracting officers handle many contracts within the same organization, often for similar things. If they've run one competition that fits what your company offers, they may very well be able to tell you about other similar opportunities.

Here's where a paid data service can be worthwhile: once you are focused on specific agencies and projects, you may be able to pull up even more complete information about key contacts involved in that agency and acquisition much more quickly.

Search for examples of past contract awards for the kind of work you'd like to win. Sort those by contract expiry date as well as by date of most recent activity. You'll want to meet the people who are actively awarding lots of work in your niche. You'll also want to track down who has most recently modified records related to a competitor's contract that is expiring sometime within the next year or two (for bigger projects, look for longer lead times) so you can get to know that person long before a notice is published for recompetition.

Then start tracking down the contacts most recently listed as creating, modifying, or approving contract award records. Sometimes the database will give you a full, working, email address for a point of contact. Other times, the published email address will have additional characters you'll need to remove before you can try emailing the person. Either way, identifying these points of contact gives you a starting point when you're planning your calls and your networking.

2. *Federal Agency Forecasts*

Many federal agency forecasts list a point of contact for each planned acquisition. Review your target agency's forecasts for items related to what you do. Sometimes that person is a Small Business Specialist; other times, a Contracting Officer or Contract Specialist. Some organizations make it a point to always list a program manager as the point of contact in the forecast. Regardless, the agency has pointed you to someone related to that opportunity. Pay attention, and put them on your list.

3. *Contract Opportunity Notices*

Solicitations and contract award notices usually end with a point of contact: name, title, and either or both of phone number and email address. Peel those out and put them in your plan. Again, you want to see who's most actively buying what you do from your target agencies in the regions where you want to win business. Make a note of what they were buying, and the type of solicitation or notice they published.

Don't get distracted during your search and start chasing RFPs! Stay on task: you're looking for people you can get to know who can help you open doors to future opportunities.

4. Federal Agency Contact Directories (Free)

Many federal agencies publish some (and in some cases wonderful!) online contact directories of their employees. Specific pages within agency websites include additional lists of contacts and often profiles of their executive leadership, particularly for officials with responsibility for serving the public directly. These sources can be helpful for both initial prospecting (for example, searching for all agency employees with particular keywords in their titles) and contact verification (when you have partial or older information from a contract record and want the more complete, current information about that person).

5. *LinkedIn*

Over 2.2 million current US federal employees are on LinkedIn. When I searched for *just* those with the title "Contracting Officer" I found over 155,000. Try doing that yourself.

When I narrowed that to just the Department of Veterans Affairs, I had 2,173. I have a first- or second-level connection with 484 of them. That's particularly helpful to do when your target agency doesn't have an especially comprehensive online employee directory.

Then do another search for federal employees whose titles have keywords similar to the decision makers who buy from you today.

You can narrow that list by office or geographic agency. Review individual contacts, learn more about their past assignments, see who else they are connected to, and perhaps tap an introduction through a mutual friend. If you reach out by making a connection request, be sure to do so with a personal note explaining the value to them of connecting with you.

As with federal agency directories, LinkedIn can help you develop initial lead lists as well as do deeper research that can let you craft a compelling, short, personal email or otherwise get in touch with them or meet them for the first time.

Can other social media platforms be helpful? Of course! Expect to see different agencies using different platforms for different purposes. See what works for you, and work it deeply and consistently.

6. *Google*

Yep, absolutely. Once I have a whole or partial name, from contract data, and I'm not finding anything on the agency directory or LinkedIn, sometimes I'll dive right into Google. Search engines (you might like another one better) scoop up con-

GOVERNMENT CONTRACTS MADE EASIER | **197**

tent that includes a ton of agency PowerPoints, PDFs, and reports as well as the agency's current and past web pages.

You can usually pick out the potential search results very quickly, based on the agency, geographic location, and job title.

Even when I'm only researching contacts, I almost always find stuff like agency strategic plans, long-term acquisition overviews, and deep dives on specific projects that remind me to go back and do this again by searching on the agency and acquisition.

Can other search engines be helpful? Certainly. You'll see in Chapter Seven, for instance, the extent to which YouTube is the planet's second-most-popular search engine. Again, see what works, and create a good process to help you work it consistently.

Contact Databases & Contract Research Services (Paid Commercial Subscriptions)

Before you shell out any money for a commercial contract research database, check to see what resources your nearest Procurement Technical Assistance Center can offer you. Over half of the PTACs in the country give their clients access to services like bid matching, contracting officer search, and databases of primes and partners.

You probably won't get the same level of day-to-day access that you would if you had your own subscription. Every PTAC will have its own policies for how they give clients access to those resources.

You can save a ton of money and often get a limited hands-on preview of whether or not these systems would be genuinely useful for your company for more than the occasional search.

Things to think about:

Do you need a couple of one-off searches, or do you need to be in the database every day? When you're getting started, remember that the big feature of many of these databases is a constant feed of opportunities in your inbox. Sorting out that feed can waste more time than it saves you. If you're getting ahead of the game, you're building relationships from the contact sources you've researched a long time before bid notices come out.

The companies that publish contract data dashboards and offer services and market intelligence often include agency profiles and/or contact directories as part of their service. If you're considering one of the data providers, ask for a demo of the agency contact intelligence they can provide, how comprehensive it is, and whether your subscription includes assistance from the company's research team to help you pinpoint the contacts you need.

Also consider how you want to work with contact information once you search. Can you export the data to your own systems, or must you use it within the vendor's platform/portal?

If you're creating a major marketing campaign and need a constantly-refreshed listings from a large number of federal agencies at once, the top two companies publishing federal contact directories are Leadership Connect (*www.LeadershipConnect.io*), and Carroll Publishing (www.carrollpublishing.com). Their information products, unlike many government online contact directories, are constantly updated – because that's what you're paying for. Different editions include Federal, Federal Regional, Congressional, State, and Local.

These directories contain the names, addresses, phone numbers, email, and often alumni information for agency officials from Cabinet Secretaries and appointees down deep into the middle ranks of the decision-makers. These directories also give you information on how the agency is organized – who reports to whom, who's in the chain of command, at least at the senior levels. That's critical information when you're marketing.

General Business Networks: A Fresh Look

You probably belong to a couple of business groups: your local chamber of commerce, maybe a Business Networks International (BNI) group, maybe a local chapter of a national organization. Do any of them have programs, committees, or events focused on government business that you'd never noticed before? If so, you may be able to tap new value from memberships you're already paying for.

Simply being a member of an association and attending its events *doesn't* open doors. Membership is an opportunity to build trusted relationships by contributing your leadership and talents to the community of members. Over time, that investment opens doors to new business. That takes true quality time, not just repeated showing up.

You might research and sample a few associations that have a significant commitment and programs to provide members with resources and connections for expertise on government contracting as well as advocacy on critical procurement issues. Attend a couple events as a guest and ask the members how or whether they find their membership contributes to their pursuit of government business. Some examples: National Contract Management Association; National Veterans Small Business Coalition; the 8(a) Association; Women Impacting Public Policy.

Associations

When I ask people who are growing their government business how many associations they belong to, most belong to at least one or two. Only a few people –

usually those who work for larger companies – belong to more than five. Why the law of diminishing returns at that point?

The value of the time and money you invest in association memberships comes not from paying your fees, but from paying your dues.

In Your Own Industry

Individual contacts change jobs, change companies, move, rotate from public to private sector. And so, probably, will you, for that matter! The right industry associations can be the foundation of your network of relationships in government-business development.

By "right," I mean "right for you, your company, and your focus in the government market."

Once you choose these associations, the relationships you build there are good for you personally as well as for your company. Your networking prowess and federal business contacts are big assets if your employer lets you go or your company shifts its focus to niches other than yours. The people with the most friends and the best networks are also the ones who find a great new job within a few weeks of needing one.

Remember: no matter what class of membership you buy in an association, your ROI comes from the sweat equity, time, and talent you put into building that community you want to belong to. You can pay your fees in a keystroke...but expect it to take a full year, possibly more, before people in the group really decide you're paying the kind of dues that lead to trusted relationships and the unwritten benefits of membership.

You don't have to join everything. You can supplement your regular rounds (and also keep tabs on which associations are growing and which are waning) by attending selected events as a non-member. Most groups are eager to attract new members and welcome the chance to show you their strengths.

I'm going to assume you already belong to one or two of the most influential associations of companies in your niche. A strong association offers personal connections and programs that help you stay informed about the leading edge of your industry and make it easier to meet the potential teaming partners you'll need.

Many local or regional chambers of commerce have subcommittees, occasional programs, or special-interest groups that are focused on government contracts. Does yours? Have you looked? If not, consider whether you'd like to launch such an initiative. Even if you don't feel like much of an expert on government contracts, you can certainly play the role of "expert seeker"... and, in so doing, gain visibility in your organization that you can use to open more doors and build more relationships.

Public/Private Crossover

Where do your customers network? Go there! Consider joining at least one association where government decision-makers and industry leaders in your niche or domain come together: for example, the Society of American Military Engineers (*www.same.org*); Armed Forces Communications and Electronics Association (*www.afcea.org*); Association for Federal Information Resource Managers (*www.actgov.org*). Members promote constructive discussion between buyers, partners, and vendors at these associations' meetings, events, conferences, and in volunteer committee work on specialized issues like industry standards and procurement policy.

PROFILE: Armed Forces Communications and Electronics Association (AFCEA) International

Charter: A non-profit membership association that serves the military, government, industry and academia as an ethical forum for advancing professional knowledge and relationships in the fields of communications, IT, intelligence and global security.

Structure: U.S. Headquarters, U.S. and international chapters. AFCEA members are simultaneously involved in international and national projects as well as local chapter activities. Members of local chapters in areas with many government contract opportunities, such as Northern Virginia and San Diego, participate heavily both at the chapter and international levels. In addition, all members are invited to participate at the headquarters level to broaden contacts in other geographical regions, facilitating more contracting and teaming opportunities.

Membership Structure: Companies and individuals join AFCEA in a number of ways. All corporations are invited to become Sustaining Members. Companies may also choose to join at a corporate membership level that corresponds to their firm's size. A Corporate Membership term can be either one or three years with discounts for renewing membership. In addition to discount and corporate member-only benefits, each Corporate Member is entitled to designate a specific number of individual associate members to its employees based on the its level of membership. AFCEA also offers lifetime, one- and three-year individual memberships. Special rates are available for junior enlisted service members and students. All members are entitled to the same benefits.

Membership Benefits: Corporate benefits include discounted rates for exhibition space at AFCEA conferences and visibility in the Corporate Online Directories. The searchable directories include all AFCEA corporate members and features contact information, government contract access, NAICS codes, small business status and veterans programs information. Individual members receive *SIGNAL* Magazine each month, discounts on higher education and certifications, and continuing education session attendance verification for documentation required to keep certifications current.

Focus on Small Business: Distinct headquarters and chapter programs help small businesses team with large primes and with each other as well as connect directly with government buyers. Small business rates are offered for sponsorships, exhibit space and *SIGNAL* Media advertising.

Responsiveness to Government Members: Government members attend AFCEA events not only because the educational content and involvement by government speakers is high but also because an exceptionally strong commitment from corporate sponsors enables event participation costs to remain low. Attendance at many of AFCEA events are offered free of charge to military and government employees.

Courses: AFCEA members benefit from discounted pricing on a range of technical courses taught by top subject matter experts and offered year round. These courses can be held at an organization's site, saving travel and lodging costs. Because AFCEA membership is not required to attend courses, participants gain both content and contacts. AFCEA members who are subject matter experts and thought leaders also may contact the AFCEA Professional Development Center as potential instructors.

Continuing Education: Events presentations are often approved as continuing education that supports specific certifications. AFCEA provides its members with attendance verification documentation they require to keep certifications current.

Scholarships: Companies seeking additional visibility can sponsor chapter or headquarters activities, including underwriting scholarships and charitable contributions. The many scholarships awarded to members of the military and civilians in government service also help build strong government-industry relationships.

Events and Conferences: Forums range from highly specialized to broadly based national and international events with diverse program tracks. Attendees develop rich contact networks among partners and buyers in their own niche at some events and nurture crossover connections at others. While members and nonmembers are welcome at all events and pricing is set to remain attractive to cash-strapped government employees, AFCEA members get the best rates for participation in the association's events.

Publications: At the national level, AFCEA's monthly *SIGNAL* Magazine is a well-reputed technical journal that also reports chapter news and welcomes advertisers. AFCEA members can leverage *SIGNAL* three ways: suggesting editorial content that features government buyers who have implemented their solution or use their gear; becoming involved in chapter activities that are covered in the regular roundup; and purchasing print and online advertising space. Chapters also manage their own communications channels that offer similar opportunities for visibility and building brand recognition.

Social Media: AFCEA's communications team strives to stay at the leading edge of social media tools, so you can find them actively blogging, Tweeting and forging relationships and exchanging information on Instagram, Twitter LinkedIn and Facebook. Joining AFCEA-related groups, participating in discussions and Q&A, seeking introductions, highlighting your member involvement on your own profiles, following selected contacts in AFCEA's Twitter account, commenting on AFCEA's blogs and retweeting news to your followers are all low-cost ways to enrich your network of key contacts.

How do you choose?

If you want to know the value of any association to your federal business growth, ask the members. They'll tell you the good and the bad.

Ask your government buyers and your industry colleagues which groups they find useful, and why. Attend some of the events and programs that are open to guests. Talk to both its leaders and its members. Set criteria for what you want to get out of your membership. Each year, evaluate whether or not that association is showing a return on your investment. Associations go through strong and weak phases, and your own needs change, too. Be fair: are your results more a factor of what the association is offering and who belongs, or the time and resources you're putting into membership?

Some associations open their LinkedIn groups to people who don't belong to the association itself, as a way to promote membership. If the association has a LinkedIn group, you can request to join. Now you can connect with some of their members, follow and contribute to the discussions, see the level of activity, and ask candid questions about the value of membership, or simply tap members' expertise. However, keep in mind that associations' most active participants in person aren't always the ones who show up online, and vice versa.

Not all networks are created equal.

Once again, whether you are building your contacts among government, industry, or both, focus or go broke. Martin Saenz, VP of The Saenz Group, recounts learning this more slowly than he'd have preferred.

"Initially, we kind of did a shotgun approach with relationship-building. We kind of just joined all the kind of networking groups and put ourselves out there and 'meeted and greeted.' That yielded some results with government work, but nowhere near the level that we got when we refined our relationship-building to people within our industries."

Here are some ways you can focus and find that kind of success.

Hiring A Business Development or Sales Professional

There are many reasons why you might want to hire someone specifically to do a lot of this work for you. For example, you might have an ideal solution to a government buyer's problem that is time-sensitive, and if you take a year to get yourself fully up to speed, the opportunity will be gone.

Yes, of course, the market will gladly supply you with the help you need – but keep in mind that now *you* are the buyer, and if ever there was a time for "buyer beware," this is it.

Hiring a contractor, or even a full-time employee, to support your business development? Keep in mind:

1. Don't rush. Invest the time to research and find the right person, not least because...

2. ...these services will cost you significant money. It's not unusual for consultants to charge a flat fee of between $5,000 and $20,000 a month, with a six- to twelve-month minimum commitment. That's a realistic term of

engagement. If a consultant's proposed deal sounds too good to be true, it probably is.

3. Clearly define what you want the consultant to do. For instance, do you want the consultant to just provide services, or to also help you and your team build skills? Beyond lead qualification and relationship development, do you also want them to make sales calls? Do you expect them to write proposals? To close sales? Discuss that clearly, both during interviews and when you're negotiating an engagement or offer.

   Business development and sales are two different tasks. Many people do one, but not the other.

   Find out who else they've done work like this for. Get their explicit agreement on things including what they would do for you, over what period of time, what your role will be in working with them, and how you will measure and ensure accountability for activity and results. Make sure those things are in the consulting agreement. Beware any prospective consultant who says, "Well, nothing is guaranteed. I'm just going to go out there and do my best."

4. Expect to remain regularly engaged with your consultant and make sure that the engagement ultimately helps *you* to build personal relationships with the federal buyers.

5. Ask for, and call, their client references. Ask things like what ROI they got from their investment in working with the consultant, how responsive and available the consultant was, what they hired the consultant to do, what results they got, how their outcome compared to their expectations, what they liked best, what they didn't like, whether they'd hire this person again, and why or why not.

6. Have your lawyer review the terms of the consultant's contract before you sign it.

Elite Programs

Special business-education programs can be a meeting ground for exceptional connections, in addition to sharpening your business edge.

Martin Saenz was sponsored by Freddie Mac to a ten-day business-education program at Dartmouth for Minority Business Enterprises, where he joined other MBEs from around the country. The program was extremely valuable, but relationships he forged during that program were even more important than actual classroom content. "It was an incredible experience. But we also won business through connections that we made there that led to federal contracts. For instance, at Fort Drum, NY, we did a project through Bay Electric, a Minority Business Enterprise we met through the Dartmouth program."

Relationship Mastery: Some Final Tips

Focus

The seductive allure of government business opportunities attracts hopeful business owners to hundreds of outreach conferences across the country. It's much too easy to run all over town – or even all over the nation – doing brute-force glad-handing and thinking you're getting somewhere because you're just piling up the ol' business cards. That's especially so in the Washington DC area, where you can do breakfast, lunch, dinner, and galas pretty much continuously, wearing out your budget, your time, your health, and your patience – and getting nowhere.

Creating your new network takes time. Aim to grow a diverse mix of contacts that is nonetheless focused on your objectives, near- and long-term. Relationships are not only a key success factor for government business: minority business owners say it's the number-one tool in their kit bag. Focus, and you'll get the best return on a resource even more scarce than your money: your time.

Be Generous

Always come bringing the gift that is so very rare these days (and perfectly permitted by FAR Part 3): first and foremost, the gift of your full attention to the person you're with. When you ask, "How's it going?" or "What's new with you?" or "Who's a good lead for you", listen to the answer. Then be generous with your expertise and your connections. Who or what do you know that would help the person you're with?

Be Patient, Persistent…and Consistent

Ninety percent of life is just showing up – whether you're Woody Allen (whose quote that is) or Cal Ripken, longtime shortstop for the Baltimore Orioles, who broke the all-time major-league record for playing 2,131 consecutive games.

Expect to invest a year or two of solid effort before expecting to notice much of a return on your activity. You're going to give for a while… so you want to choose associations where you genuinely enjoy the people and feel passionate about the organization's mission and what the members want to accomplish together.

PROFILE IN SUCCESS: Deborah Stallings

Deborah Stallings, President of HR Anew, has an extraordinary record of contributing her time and energy at national and regional levels within at least three communities: women business owners, minority business owners, and the human resources management industry.

She tells this story: "I met a woman in the National Association of Women Business Owners' D.C. Chapter. Because of our interactions, because of her seeing me visible in a leadership role through NAWBO at the local level and with the Baltimore Chapter, I think that forged the relationship and created and established a level of trust.

"An opportunity came about maybe a year and a half, two years after we met: she was a government contractor, and she was pivotal in HR Anew's winning a pretty major contract with the National Library of Medicine. She felt good about me and referred me on when she heard about this opportunity."

Once you choose the associations you're going to join, focus your involvement on one or two projects that are important to the group as well as to you. Then step up. Be the person others can count on. Under-promise. Over-deliver. The track record you demonstrate in your volunteer work builds the confidence others have in you.

Fine Tune

Assess your activities and your contacts regularly. What were your goals for making connections in government and industry? How did you do – not just how many people have you met, but how strong do you consider the relationships to be? Have contacts become friends? Have friends become clients or partners? Have clients become advocates?

What's working? What's just not turning out the way you hoped? Be ready to drop and add associations and networking activities. Sometimes you outgrow a group; new ones emerge; leadership changes; groups evolve in other ways that are more – and less – useful to you.

READY FOR THE NEXT STEP? RELATIONSHIP CHECKLIST

Research, Meet, and Nurture

- ○ The Five People In Government
- ○ The Five People In Industry
- ○ Cultivate diverse contacts
- ○ Nurture your circle of wise guides
- ○ Strengthen your contact relationship management systems
- ○ Tap the six free sources of federal leads
- ○ Select and evaluate industry associations that work for you

Find Out More

Visit *https://GrowFedBiz.com*, for bonus materials like:

- • *Five Federal Lead Sources You Need To Know*
- • *Hiring Help For Government Business Development: What To Ask First*
- • *Top Ten LinkedIn Tactics*

Chapter Seven: Sales and Marketing

*E*verything you've done up until now has led to this. To drive revenue, you have to sell and close the deal. You will know your strategy is strong when you have a growing network of relationships with people in the right roles in a few target agencies who buy what you do. You'll have deep, detailed understanding of what those specific buyers need. You'll discover how those needs develop into requirements from the very early stages, long before formal competition begins. At that point, you're on track to become the vendor they want, and win the work you want.

What you'll learn

- Essentials for federal sales success;

- Ideas to build your federal marketing strategy and toolkit; and

- Specific tactics, language, events, publications, media, themes, and images that may appeal particularly strongly to federal buyers

Where we've been, and why we're here

At this point in the book, you may be ready to take the next steps, if:

- You know why pursuing federal government business is aligned with your business growth strategy;

- You are committed to dedicating the time and resources, over about two years, that it may take to drive steady, solid wins;

- You know what problem you solve for a government buyer, and who your highest-potential prospects are;

- You've adapted your product or service and message as need be to appeal to federal buyers you can help;

- You know who your competitors are, what they offer, how they price, why they win, and where you're unique;

- You've identified your best values: provable, quantifiable, meaningful things a federal buyer can specify to make it easier to choose you, at your price;

- You've identified teaming partners, if needed, who you most want to work with to win specific opportunities, and why they are more likely to win when they team with you;

- You know what gets the attention of the people you want to reach.

You're ready to start selling.

What do you think might be the best way to reach your top government prospects? How might you expect that approach to be different from, and similar to, the ways you're already reaching your commercial client?

"Selling to government?" one executive asked. "Expect to spend three times the time, and ten times the money, that you do reaching your commercial buyers." That was their experience, and it's a sobering benchmark. Let's see how we can beat those odds.

As you saw in Chapter Six, people do business with people they like – even when they have to follow tons of rules. "Trusted colleagues" are federal buyers' top choice for intelligence on vendors. "Found out from a friend" is also where the successful vendors most often say *they* get their best leads.

Sure, the journey of marketing and selling to federal buyers follows some exclusive highways, and occasionally follows by-ways with unique twists. You'll see a disproportionate number of distractions promising shortcuts, too!

As you consider federal marketing and sales decisions, stay on course to your goals by constantly asking, "How does this help us build relationships with the people we need to meet?"

You're already a successful business owner, so you know how to do that most important thing. Now, let's build on the things you already do well.

So our last chapter, Sales & Marketing, flows naturally into this one.

Business Development, Marketing & Sales: How They Fit Together

Once a business gets past its early stages, the business owner is no longer personally and solely doing all three of these things. At that point, a clear definition of the distinctions between business development, marketing, and sales lets you define and delegate these tasks to new team members.

Business development expands your company's reach. That might include partnerships to win work in new markets or agencies, or new relationships with contacts who can open doors or make introductions or referrals for you. It also includes things like researching, prospecting, and qualifying leads prior to sales.

Marketing gives you a foundation for sales, by building awareness, liking, and enthusiasm for you, your company, and your products or services to the people you want to do business with. Traditional business texts talk about the "Five P's" of marketing. Your decisions on Product, Price, Place, Promotion, and Process (including marketing automation and email campaigns) transform your cold, unqualified, leads into a stream of warm, qualified, ones.

Once you've got warm leads, that's where sales begins. Sales is personal. When you're selling, someone on your team – whether that's the business owner, another employee, or a contractor – engages key contacts in the buying organization on a personal level. That contact might be one-on-one or in a small group of people; in person or by phone or videoconference.

Federal Sales Essentials

Selling is more than endless rounds of "Do you want to buy my stuff?" It's a ton of listening and asking questions based on your research. It's how you learn more about your qualified prospect and their organization, through both direct conversation and more research. You uncover things like pain, needs, shortcomings of incumbents, and their visions for the future. You collaborate with people in the buying organization on developing requirements and solutions. This is also when *they* learn more about *you* and your company, and why your experience and capability and past performance make you the uniquely low risk choice they'd want to consider.

Sales activities also include calls to set up a conversation, product demonstration, or solution presentation. You'll address objections, and may learn things that let you fine tune your offering and pricing. You'll decide whether or not to bid an opportunity based in part on how well you get to know the buyers while you're selling.

If your offering is more complex than an off-the-shelf product or turnkey service, you can expect to take part in a competition against other vendors and submit a proposal (as discussed in Chapter Three, Process). To prepare that proposal, you'll need to gather intelligence to build your *win theme* for the specific opportunity. The win theme emphasizes how your company delivers those things that your prospect has told you or shown you that they care about most. Typical win themes include low risk, low cost, past performance, key employees, technical expertise, reliability, or performance-based accountability.

Your success in federal business is built on your relationships with the players at all the layers: contracting officers, end users, small business specialists, influencers, stakeholders, prime contractors. You'll need those relationships in every agency, office, and program where you want to win business.

Relationships drive the momentum and ultimately the sales that represent return on your marketing investment. The stronger your relationships, the more effective your marketing will be.

- Happy clients and receptive prospects who tell their friends about you are the most effective, fastest-return, highest-credibility, and lowest-cost marketing of all.

- Your research and subsequent focus on a few high-potential agencies and opportunities increase your effectiveness at developing relationships with the people who make, and influence, buying decisions.

- Marketing that's focused on your target agencies and opportunities supports more, and faster, sales results by reaching the people who are most likely to buy from you with the right message at the right time.

You'll need to use a mix of tactics and tasks, events, and activities to meet and get to know federal agencies' small business specialists, contracting officers, end users, and stakeholders long before they issue a formal RFP or award a contract.

The multitude of players and layers, stages, locations, and events underscores why focus is essential for success.

Small Business Outreach and Matchmaking Events Featuring Federal Agencies

Are you overwhelmed by invitations to government-focused small business events? Not sure which ones to attend? Or have you already gone to lots of them and are starting to feel like you're not making much progress?

If so, you're not alone!

Remember Neeld Wilson's story? Veteran, owner of an engineering firm in Florida? After he had spent a whole year, and over $60,000, going to veteran-focused small business events all over the southeast and getting nowhere, we chatted. Once we assessed his situation, he realized that he needed to spend more time building fewer, deeper, relationships in federal agencies close to home. Only then did he win his first contract...and even that took a couple of tries (about which more in a moment).

Business owners attend these events most often when they're beginning to explore the federal market. You'll make the best use of your time if you choose your events based on the target agencies and regions where you're concentrating your efforts. Once you find your sweet spot in the market, you'll know which ones are right for you.

Did you know?

The top annual national event for small businesses seeking a broad introduction to federal agencies is the Government Procurement Conference. This one-day event is held in Washington DC, usually in April, and includes presentations, panels, and an exhibit hall featuring large and small vendors as well as government agency booths. Early registrants (usually starting in January) may request on-site business matchmaking services.

This is a popular event because its capital-area location makes it easy (and inexpensive) for many federal agencies to send representatives from headquarters. They get to meet with thousands of small business owners in one day. You, as a small business owner, can connect with dozens of federal agency officials and other vendors in one day.

Remember, the agency representatives who attend this event are almost never buyers. They are usually small business specialists.

Most of the conference presentations and panels feature agency officials and industry small business liaisons who provide general overview information that companies in the early stages of government business find most helpful.

Event producer Federal Business Council (_www.fbcinc.com_, a commercial company despite its name) also produces smaller in-agency tabletop events across the country all year long. Check out which ones might work well for you.

For these events to be a good return on your invested time and money, you _must_:

- Target your agencies: look closely at which ones have the most need for what you do.

- Be selective: the biggest events aren't always the best fit. Look into smaller regional events that can get you right in front of those key people you need to meet. Ask around among business owners, and ask the agencies' small business specialists, too, about what makes a particular event worthwhile before you choose. They'll tell you which ones they like and why.

- Review the event program: what are the must-do elements? Which ones, such as business matchmaking, require pre-registration? Remember that those slots frequently sell out early. Are there opportunities to make a presentation, moderate a session, or take a visible leadership role? Maybe you don't need to attend the whole conference. Also, do you need to exhibit, or will you get more out of roaming around?

- Review participating agencies' forecasts, programs and priorities before the event. Come ready to ask the agency representatives about

  - line items in published acquisition plans, and about challenges you've researched that specific agency programs are facing and with which you could help; and

212 | Chapter Seven: Sales and Marketing

- what they like and don't like about major competitors that the data shows they buy from now.

- Look up their primes: which companies besides yours are they buying from? Do some detailed research on one or two you'd like to get to know, and head to their booths if they'll be at the event.

- Be ready to collect competitive intelligence: come to events prepared to ask the buyers about pre-RFP Activities.

Building A Sales Plan

You've already chosen no more than 3 to 5 target agencies, based on how much they purchase of what you do.

Put them in priority order, starting with those where you have the strongest combination of similar past performance and customer knowledge.

Next, list contacts who know you and your work and would be willing to help you meet others you need to know in your target agencies.

Now that you know who you know, you've got to track down who you need to know! Dig back into the detailed past contract-award data, starting with your top priority agency. Who are the specific players at all the layers who you need to meet? You don't need a subscription service to give you a huge list of people to email. So much of this information is available from free public sources!

You're looking for the points of contact who, for instance:

- approved contracts for goods or services like yours; or

- are listed in the agency's procurement forecast; or

- are included at the bottom of contract opportunity notices; or

- have job titles similar to buyers and decision-makers who usually purchase from your company.

Once you've got a couple dozen names, that's usually plenty to get started. Many conversations will open doors to new people you need to know!

The Selling Part (aka Relationship-Building)

The overall objective of all your calls is to get inside the heads – and the offices – of people who've never heard of you and who are almost certainly buying from somebody else.

People who are the most successful with federal sales make a significant investment of time and money to build strong relationships with decision-makers well in advance of formal competitions, solicitations, or even procurement forecasts.

You own a successful company. You have clients or customers today. That means someone in your company already has experience building awareness and liking with new prospective buyers, and converting leads into sales.

Many companies are founded by technical experts and initially grow organically through referrals based on one successful project after another. Strong past performance plus a couple of conversations with the right people open the door to something new. If that's your situation, and you're growing as fast as you want to, terrific!

Even so, you still need to keep close track of who you know in the agency, and where they go. You don't need a fancy database or complex Contact Relationship Management system and email programming platform. You *do* need a structured, central system where everyone in your company who's involved with the federal market can enter and update and share information about who they know, when they talked to them, what they learned, and what they're doing next.

Some of my clients do that by setting up shared access to a simple Excel file where everyone enters their contacts. In a few days, you can see who you know, and also notice and start to research who's missing: the people you *don't* know but need to meet.

"Government people change jobs all the time," vendors often complain. That's an asset, not a problem, if you keep in touch regularly with your contacts! They'll give you a heads-up when they're moving. You can wish them well and offer connections or resources that might help them in their new position. If they like you, they can introduce you to the person who took over the job they used to have...as well as to their colleagues in the new office. In other words, *their* move can expand *your* network!

There is both everything magical and nothing special about this. It's absolutely ordinary because it's the same way sales happen everywhere. And it's perfectly magical because thousands of people think you can't call government buyers.

You know better. You remember our friend, FAR Part 15.201.

15.201 Exchanges with industry before receipt of proposals.

(a) Exchanges of information among all interested parties, from the earliest identification of a requirement through receipt of proposals, are encouraged. Any exchange of information must be consistent with procurement integrity requirements (see 3.104). Interested parties include potential offerors, end users, Government acquisition and supporting personnel, and others involved in the conduct or outcome of the acquisition.

(b) The purpose of exchanging information is to improve the understanding of Government requirements and industry capabilities, thereby allowing potential offerors to judge whether or how they can satisfy the Government's requirements, and enhancing the Government's ability to obtain quality supplies and services, including construction, at reasonable prices, and increase efficiency in proposal preparation, proposal evaluation, negotiation, and contract award.

Never, ever, ever, ever, brandish this regulation in your hand and go barging into a contracting office.

Do go back and read it on those days when it seems like you just can't get through. If someone doesn't want to talk to you, there may be any number of reasons why that's not happening. The only thing you can know for sure is that they're not returning your call *today.*

Keep in mind that:

- Polite persistence pays off. You would be surprised by how often a federal buyer you finally reach says, "I'm so glad you didn't give up on me."

- Federal employees almost always want to be helpful. Even if they're not the right person, they are often glad to point you to someone else.

- If someone sounds irritated or defensive or tells you they can't talk to you...that's gonna happen sometimes. You can't possibly know what's going on with them that day. Always think (and speak of them to others!) graciously and generously.

- They're people. Like you, they have good days and bad ones. If your conversations with them stray into topics like vacations and pets and hobbies...wonderful! Listen for the things that matter most to them. Little stuff counts. Take lots of notes. Make follow up personal. Get to know who they are, not just what they're buying.

- Finally, it's a big government. There is almost always someone else you can call on. Buck up and move on. Unless a contact says, "Never call me again," you can always try back later. You can research around them, build a relationship with a colleague in the same office, and find out who else you need to be talking to.

My clients who have done call programs to develop commercial business find it easy to adapt those programs to the federal market.

If you've never done lead-generation calls like this before, relax. This is a skill and process you can learn quickly. When I do a competitive analysis for my clients, I also teach them the federal sales game. Then, when I build their federal sales plan and train them on how to use it, they are making the new connections they never imagined possible within a matter of days. The research gives them confidence that they have lots of specific things to explore in conversations with each person they call.

Success takes more than pumping out proposals. Your proposals will only land firmly, and continually strengthen your competitive position, if you're also building relationships with the people who are reading them.

Companies in two situations benefit greatly from a concentrated lead-generation effort:

- You have commercial (and possibly state or local) past performance but have never performed on a paid prime or sub-contract with the federal government

- You have a strong base of past performance, especially in one or more federal agencies, and want to grow faster both in your current client agencies and beyond.

Those who succeed are willing to make good old-fashioned phone calls – a lot of them. They do a ton of follow-up, and a lot of detective work in between calls.

The good news is that you'll start with people you know! These people want to help you, because they already know how good you are. You make it easy for them to help you because you're asking them specific questions. You're asking them to confirm or elaborate on contacts and leads you've already researched. You're asking them to point you in the right direction. You're asking, "If you were me, who would you be talking to?"

Not sure what to do, what to say, what to ask, as you make those calls? That's going to be unique to you, your company, and the specific people in your target agencies.

If you've done your research and competitive analysis well, you'll have lots of ideas for what to do, and say, and ask. Some of my most successful clients create an outline or script to guide the initial calls and the follow-ups, to make sure they're covering the basic information and qualifying questions consistently. In the early weeks, they fine-tune those scripts based on what's most effective.

If you feel lost at the prospect of making calls, or no one in your company can do that, you're not alone.

At first, you might not need to hire an additional full-time employee to do this job. Some of my clients have gotten outstanding results by hiring a marketing intern or recent graduate from the business program of a local college or university! Expect to invest time up front to make sure they can speak knowledgeably about your company and product or service, and also train them on the players, layers, and language of federal agencies.

Make sure your call agent is working from solid research that you or they have done in your target agencies. Set goals and measurements for activity and results. Agree on accountability for both. Schedule regular reviews every week or two. Clearly communicate with your contractor the plan, goals, accountability, and, if need be, the exit plan you'll use if their efforts are not working out. A couple of months is usually enough time to tell if their efforts are headed in the right direction.

Signs of success include:

- Comprehensive notes on individual call records including the date of call, what was discussed, and/or message left, but also *what* the message was, and when the next call or follow-up activity will be.

- Contacts recommend and introduce you to additional leads.

- New contacts added and calls made to those contacts.

- Contacts ask questions about your company and want to know more.

- Contacts agree to review a capability statement or request more company information.

- Contacts agree to schedule a follow-up conversation.

- Phone appointments scheduled with the person in your company who's following up.

- Confirmation calls or messages are completed in advance of scheduled appointments.

- Phone appointments are completed as scheduled.

- Missed appointments are followed up and rescheduled. Missed appointments are absolutely normal. At the early stages, that can happen as often as 40% of the time. If you're a new vendor and not calling about your prospect's most urgent problem, it's easy for even the best-intentioned people's schedules to get overrun. Just get back in there. You'll be surprised by how grateful they are when you eventually reconnect.

Another option is to engage a lead-generation company to qualify prospects and set up phone appointments for you. There are companies that specialize in call programs for the federal market. If you go that route, ask for and call their references. Check out their clients' results. You can expect to invest time collaborating with them to develop marketing collateral and scripts and goals and milestones for your call program. Three months is a reasonable minimum time frame. Any less than that, especially for a first campaign, is unrealistic. You might expect to spend anywhere from $15,000 to $25,000 for a three-month effort.

As your success grows, you might consider hiring a full-time employee to do federal sales and business development.

Let's talk realistic budgets. A full-time professional with experience and a strong track record in federal sales will probably cost you a minimum of $180,000 a year in salary, plus benefits and performance incentives

It's extremely rare to find someone who promises – and delivers -- significant sales when paid on straight commission in the federal market. Don't try it. Your most likely outcome will be a year of lost opportunities and a lot of disappointment. .

Proposal Cycle Activities

Your sales activities continue with involvement in each of these formal opportunities to build awareness and knowledge of your company among the people who need to like you and trust you if you want to win.

- Requests for Information (RFIs): At the RFI stage, typically the government has no commitment to buy anything just yet. Government buyers issue RFIs when they want to know if industry has any ability to address their requirement. Responding to selected RFIs (within your target agency) that are a specific and strong fit with what you offer is a great way to build awareness and catch the interest of government program managers and end users. Your response to an RFI can also open doors to the contracting officer, and bring an opportunity to get feedback on how you can improve your submission and proposal skills for when the stakes are higher.

- Sources Sought: Similar kind of opportunity as an RFI, but with the added importance of potentially narrowing the competitive field. Respond not only to explain that you can meet some or all of the requirement, but also to encourage the contracting officer to set aside the procurement for the kind of small business that you own.

- Pre-bid conferences: Even if this event takes place after the RFP is published, and thus requires questions and answers to be published more formally, these conferences can be your best opportunity to meet potential teaming partners as well as to chat with program managers and end users.

Proposals and Debriefings

- Proposals

Every proposal is a marketing document – a very structured marketing document. Remember, you're being graded on how well you read instructions, how thorough your answers are, how well they're presented, how differentiated your offering is, how competitive your pricing and total value package are (including features, options, and service), and how well you really and truly understand the buyer. This is where winners blend in the themes and language they've absorbed from all those months of relationship-building – the subtle things that can tip the balance of favor in the evaluation.

- Debriefings

Take a moment to go back to Chapter Three – Process, or take a quick peek at FAR Part 15.5 to refresh your memory. Win or lose, this is your opportunity to be gracious if you lost, be humble if you won, be wise either way, and strengthen relationships in the agency for the next round.

The single best reason to submit a proposal when you don't know the buyer, you don't know the budget, you don't know the incumbent, and you don't know the project history is for this very moment: the chance to be face to face with principals in the contracting organization.

You spent a lot of time and money on your proposal. A formal debriefing (or, more often, an informal post-competition conversation) is an often-overlooked chance to get a return on that investment. Hundreds of smart companies take this hard-won opportunity to open doors for future contact with hard-to-reach agency officials. If you make a good first impression – both with a professional proposal and with poise and grace in the debriefing – your new contacts may be willing to meet with you again and answer your questions about possible future opportunities, as well as to introduce you to other contacts within the agency.

PROFILE IN SUCCESS: GEAR Engineering

A debriefing opened the door for Neeld Wilson, aquifer engineer and President of GEAR Engineering in Orlando, when he made his first proposal to replace an underground tank for the Department of Veterans Affairs.

He was disappointed when his proposal wasn't successful. After I urged him to go in and get a debriefing, he found out that the Contracting Officer and Program Manager really liked his proposal. They weren't able to resolve a couple of small technical deficiencies in the proposal, however, so they had to choose another vendor.

"But listen," the Contracting Officer said. "We've got another project coming up really soon that's a perfect fit for you. Come and bid that one!" He did. And, weeks later, that was the one he won, worth over $350,000.

Federal Business Development Means Relationship Marketing

Small business Industry Days, Networking Events, and Groups

Be selective! Your most scarce resource is your time. Just because someone is holding an event for small business does not mean you need to show up. When you're getting started, you may find your fear of missing out drives you to dozens of events. It's all too easy to mistake networking *activity* (going to lots of events) for networking *momentum* (building meaningful relationships with and for people you need to meet to build your business). Choose your events based on your objectives.

Who do you need to meet and build relationships with? What events do they attend regularly?

When you go, notice how naturally you gravitate toward the people you already know. Get and give more value from these events by moving beyond your comfort zone.

I've done a ton of networking over forty years. It's the job. We do it. After years of thinking I'm an extrovert, some days my introvert side quietly steps up and takes over. I find myself at an event and discover that I'm simply out of juice to have one more conversation or meet one more person.

Does that ever happen to you? You're not alone!

Sometimes, that feeling is a sign that it's time to go home. It's okay to do that. There will be other events. If you find networking truly hard, but you're the business owner and you know you have to do it, bring a wingman. Go with a friend. Not to spend all your time with that person, but to have a mutual home base, a friendly face you can circle back to, re-energize, and trade intelligence with, and then get back out there again. And someone who can rescue you if you find yourself unable to break away from a conversation.

Cultivate a "host mentality." One of the things a great host does is to make everyone feel welcome, right? Do that no matter where you are! Introduce yourself to people you haven't met before. In particular, look for people standing alone on the fringes. If you're both new to the event, say so, and then suddenly neither of you is quite so alone anymore. If you've been to the event at least once, then make them feel welcome, and look for other people they might need to connect with.

Do more than tell people who you are. Truly listen to who *they* are, and actively look for ways you can help them both now and in the future.

Conferences and Exhibitions

Some federal agencies host major conferences designed to promote exchanges between industry and government on broad program and policy issues. For instance, the Defense Health Agency produces such an annual event. Other times, an agency might have a close working relationship with an industry association, and might join forces to produce such an event.

These are distinct from small business outreach events or "Industry Days" that a federal agency, PTAC, or economic development organization might host. Large companies bring more than their small business liaison staff. Their CEO's are there to meet with the government stakeholders and develop business, too.

Research whether associations you belong to host major national or regional gatherings. These sometimes bring together key players in government and industry in your niche. Examples: The Society of American Military Engineers (_www.same.gov_), Armed Forces Communications and Electronics Association (_www.afcea.org_), the National Association of Corrosion Engineers (_www.nace.org_), the National Contract Management Association (_www.ncma-hq.org_).

Should you attend? Exhibit? Seek to be a presenter?

Read the website. Ask your federal buyers and prospects and potential teaming partners and competitors what events they always attend, and which ones are easy for them to get approvals and funding to attend.

Then check your budget. An event close to home might be more affordable. Even if you only attend as a delegate (not exhibiting or presenting), your resource commitment includes your travel time and cost, as well as arranging backup support for anything that might come up while you're away...and don't forget "mop-up" time to write follow-up notes and enter contact data once you get back. Sometimes it's possible to attend just for the one day that has the most valuable content or contacts, particularly when you're just checking out whether this is a good event for your company.

While your company is small, one or two of the right events *at most* is usually plenty for one year.

When you figure out which events are perfect for you, plan to attend year after year. That's doubly true if you decide to exhibit! Even if you don't seem to get much action or sales the first year, stick to it. A little like other kinds of advertising and marketing, repeat participation shows your commitment. The buyers notice.

More than once, I've heard federal buyers (and primes) say, "Yeah, we noticed you the first year! We've been watching to see if you were serious enough to keep showing up the next couple of years."

Lead Generation, Contact Relationship Management (CRM), and Follow Up

Just have a box of business cards? A random distribution of business cards not collected in a box? A bunch of stuff on your phone? That's still a start: it means you have contacts! But if you're serious about the federal market, you need something with a bit more structure.

- Good news #1: There's no government-marketing-specific contact database, just a government-market-specific reason to get around to it. That reason is...

- Good news #2: Just as with commercial clients, retention and referral are your two least-expensive sources of hot leads. If you keep in touch with them, and cultivate those relationships, they can help you continue to serve their agency and do business with their friends.

- Good news #3: If you've just got the pile of cards, or just random stuff on your phone, you're about to get your act together. Federal sales success requires you to get organized. Period. Make a commitment to starting.

Federal sales success is a relationship game. Over the 12 to 18 months you're developing any opportunity, you're going to meet thousands of people.

The value of any contact database is not how many contacts you can get *into* the database. It's how you can find, retrieve, and edit those records as you develop relationships.

You need to both keep up with the people you've met, *and* constantly meet new ones. Why? Because with no action on your part, nearly 25% of your contacts will be out of date a year from now. Maintain good "list hygiene" by at least periodically verifying contact data and following up on all bounced emails. You'll avoid wasting your money by marketing to people who literally aren't there. You'll also keep your open rates high, which can prevent you from getting your email service temporarily suspended for suspected spamming.

Follow-up – multiple "touches" or instances of contact -- is essential for marketing and sales. After you meet someone for the first time, you need to be able to find them again, and keep track of where they are, where they go, how and when you were in touch, what happened, and what's next.

If you don't have a fancy Contact Relationship Management system...relax. The most important thing is to get all your company team's federal-related contacts into a single secure electronic platform so that the appropriate people in your company can see, sort, add, query, edit, and update records according to their roles on your team.

A spreadsheet on a shared drive is a great place to start. Once you have all the info in a single spreadsheet, that can serve you well for months or even years. As your efforts grow, if you maintain your spreadsheet well, it will also be easily imported into a CRM system.

About those contacts on your phone: great for personal convenience, but make sure your data is synched in some way with your team's shared system.

Got a sales management system like SalesForce or Zoho or HubSpot? Be sure you tag your contacts with terms or key words that let you select and view contacts by agency and by role. You want to not only see who you know...but also to see who you *don't* know. In any agency where you want to do business, you need to see the "layers" where you don't have contacts, and start leveraging the contacts you have to meet the ones you're missing.

Not sure what to choose, or how it will work with the systems you have now, or how to migrate, or how scalable it will be as your business grows? Need to have users from multiple locations enter, update, and access the data? Get some professional advice to make a choice that will work decently for you. None of these systems is perfect. Each requires investment in setup and/or migration and training, and will have its own quirks.

Make sure that you also choose a system that provides the user support that serves you best. If you need 24/7 phone support from someone who can access your computer remotely, then don't pick the system that only offers customer support by email within 24 hours, or responds only via online chat.

Admin Support

There are certain time-intensive things that *only* the business owner or business-development professional can do. That's particularly true in the early stages of business growth. Yet, if you run, own, or have a leadership role in a business, you have to make sure that all the business functions get done.

Whether your company is very small or not, whether you're a technical genius or not, there are only so many hours in the day. Just because you *could* do everything doesn't mean you *should*. You can't do it all.

You and your company deserve professional support for your business development, sales, and marketing operations for things like data entry, tech support, accounting, choices of hardware, software, networks.

Just about everyone needs admin support. There are a lot of things that someone has to do if you want your company to grow. Some of those are things *only* you can do – like develop relationships. Many of the rest, which also have to be done, you can delegate. Like data entry of business cards. Creating email newsletters. Programming email marketing campaigns. Managing your social-media presence.

Realizing how much back-office support you actually need to convert your business development and marketing efforts into sales can leave you feeling stuck, overwhelmed, and paralyzed. I've been there (and still feel that way more often than I'd like.)

Good help gets you moving again.

You have plenty of options besides full-time, on-site help. Even if your company is very small, consider a virtual assistant or offsite contractor. If your company is larger, a full-service back-office support company could be the key to your success. You can concentrate on ensuring that your client gets the superlative service that keeps them coming back for more. Your support contractor can provide services like cost and price analysis, accounting, HR, and even hiring and recruiting.

Marketing Ideas To Support Your Sales

Studies show that closing a commercial sale, which often doesn't require a formal competition process, takes anywhere from eight to twelve instances of contact, or touchpoints. Federal selling can take even longer, depending on the complexity of the competitive process. Efficient, targeted marketing with the right messages can bring more of the right contacts to the sales starting line.

If your company is just getting started, you don't need a huge, expensive, elaborate marketing campaign! You'll need a website, a capability statement, a little social media, and a structured way to record and build out your calls on your contacts.

Successful marketing positions you as a leading contender for an opportunity, whether there is a lot of competition, a little, or (ideally) none at all. Sales has ultimate responsibility to close the deal and get the contract signed.

If you've been doing the homework in each chapter of this book, you've already decided what you'll offer, to which agencies, in which geographic locations, and at what prices. In this chapter, we'll focus on options for promotional activities in your chosen federal niche. That mix can include networking, conferences, telemarketing, social media, content marketing, webinars, video education, brand marketing, email campaigns, and direct mail.

You'll see large companies that are pursuing multi-million- or multi-billion-dollar projects invest in complex marketing campaigns that are opportunity-specific. Most small companies can get a lot of value from choosing two or three activities that help them generate qualified leads that they can follow up with in their own sales calls. The important thing is to ensure that you get a return on the time and money you put into any marketing activity, by measuring how well and how frequently those activities identify qualified prospects who ultimately buy from you.

Effective federal marketing doesn't need to take buckets of cash, but it does take some.

A small marketing budget supporting a sales effort based on solid research and focused on building the right relationships can be really effective! Let's tap some lessons from what the big firms are doing these days.

SURVEY RESULTS

2018 Marketing Budget Changes

■ Decreased spend in 2018   ■ Increased spend in 2018

	Decreased spend in 2018	Increased spend in 2018
Digital Advertising	11%	53%
Market Intelligence/Research	10%	48%
Podcasts	9%	47%
Video Marketing	9%	47%
Radio/TV Advertising	16%	47%
Written Marketing Content (eBooks/white papers)	11%	40%
Social Media Advertising	18%	38%
Print Advertising	12%	36%
Webinars	18%	36%
Event Sponsorships	18%	35%
Public Relations	17%	32%

Market Connections surveyed 200 federal contractors in May 2018. 80% were large businesses. 76% of those surveyed provide professional services. 59% of respondents were from companies that attribute more than half their revenue to federal business.

Source: Federal Government Contractor Study 2018 © Market Connections

Not exactly awash in cash for marketing? Cheer up: even the largest companies have to choose how to allocate money, time, and people. Consider that limitation a gift. What's the best choice for the resources you do have? Do a little research: check the track record of any marketing tool that has the potential to achieve the results you want. Then trust your intuition, set some goals, and try it your way.

I have tried *plenty* of things and spent *thousands* of dollars on stuff that worked for other people but didn't work for me. Those expensive lessons helped me make better choices. Yours will, too.

You can tap social media and other publications, events, radio, podcasts, and webinars as both sources of market intelligence on buyers, competitors, trends, and market drivers and potential tools in your own marketing mix.

How might you sort out what else would work for you? For starters:

- Notice how your most successful competitors are marketing. Where are they present on social media? Can you sign up for their mailing lists to see what they're putting out there?

- Find out how buyers are responding to your competitors' tactics. Ask them! Don't let competitors' campaigns limit your imagination, and don't think that you have to spend as much as they do or spend your money in the same places. Just because somebody else is doing it doesn't mean it will work for you (or even that it's actually working for them).

- Research, ask around, experiment, and have the courage to try something nobody else is doing. Decide how you'll evaluate it and how much time you'll give it, and be prepared to refine it or just try something else if it's not working.

- Your customer's response is ultimately the only thing that matters.

Once you have assessed your initial results and are ready to invest more and step up your game with a more sophisticated marketing campaign, consider getting professional advice. Look for a firm that has a track record in creating and executing federal marketing campaigns that show a strong correlation with sales for products or services like yours.

Who Moved My Fiscal Year End? A Word About Timing

As you're planning your sales and marketing, remember to factor in your government buyer's fiscal year. At the federal level, the fiscal year ends September 30th. In 46 of 50 states, fiscal year-end is June 30th (exceptions: New York, March 31st; Texas, August 31st; Michigan and Alabama, September 30th – like the federal).

Why does that matter? Purchasing does take place all year round. But in many governments, especially the federal one, each particular part of the year has its own rhythms and its own priorities:

- First Quarter of the Fiscal Year ("Q1") (October to December at the federal level): Funding authorizations may not be complete. Legislatures – certainly at the federal level – often don't pass the budget for a particular fiscal year before that fiscal year begins. If so, your customers may have limited spending authority and may be unable to take on any new projects. Many government buyers are tying up contract administration from the end of the previous fiscal year. Some agency officials may be working on submitting their final proposals for the fiscal year that starts a year from now.

  This is a good time to plan and research individual calls, and focus on low-key relationship-building – renewing contact with people you know, and asking them about who else may be coming or going, and who they suggest you might want to get to know in the fiscal year that's just starting.

- Q2 (January to March at the federal level): Funding flows begin. Agencies should have their budgets by now and be able to move ahead. Buying activity for the highest-priority programs will be underway, and priorities set for the rest. You'll also typically see conferences or briefings offering spending outlooks. Some of the largest associations also hold major conferences; AFCEA West in San Diego is one of the largest. You might want to take in a couple of those, depending on your industry, to get a sense of major buying trends and priorities.

- Q3 (April to June at the federal level): Marketing and purchasing accelerate. Really, fourth quarter starts in third quarter. Conferences and events really heat up in the second half of the fiscal year, and marketing gets much more intense now. You should have your A-list prospects well defined, and your marketing focused on very specific people, programs, and activities. Be sure to follow up with your current and past clients as well as your new prospects.

- Q4 (July to September at the federal level): Big use-or-lose buying surge. Time to get ruthless: take an honest look at where you ought to concentrate your efforts. What business do you have the best odds of winning? And did you check in with your current and recent clients? What last-minute needs might they have?

  Product companies are even more likely than services companies to see this surge. It takes time to perform services, but it's possible to buy a year's supply of something at the end of the year. If you've been developing your prospects all year long, the buyers you've been so patiently courting may be ready to order.

Big-bucks, broad-brush marketing can get people talking about you for a while. But companies who get their money's worth from the kind of big marketing push you might see at fiscal year-end have been building relationships with their clients and target prospects all year long.

Next: Fiscal year-end may be closer than you think – and different in every agency.

Did you know? Federal buyers' year-end spending authority can be limited by agency-specific acquisition deadlines.

I discovered this first hand in 2010 when I was working on the first edition of this book. Partway through the year, a federal buyer I had spent 18 months getting to know wanted to place an order for a bunch of the books. "What's the publication date?" she asked. When I told her October, she replied, "We won't have any money then. Our buying cutoff for commitments is in early July! What can you do for me by then?"

It turned out that her office could pay an invoice for a small purchase order in July for items to be delivered at a discount later in the year. That was how I won my first federal contract!

Here's an example of one agency's recent memo:

1. Simplified and FAR Part 13 Commercial Acquisitions

Action Value	Cut-Off Date
≤ $15K	FRI 07/27/18
> $15K - $150K	FRI 07/06/18
> $150K - $1M	FRI 05/18/18
> $1M - $7M	FRI 04/13/18

2. Orders under an Existing Contract

Order Value	Under Multiple Award Contract	Under Single Award Contract
≤ $15K	FRI 07/27/18	FRI 07/27/18
> $15K - $150K	FRI 06/22/18	FRI 07/06/18
> $150K - $1M	FRI 05/18/18	FRI 07/06/18
> $1M - $10M	FRI 04/13/18	FRI 06/01/18
> $10M - $50M	FRI 12/15/17	FRI 04/20/18
> $50M	FRI 11/17/17	FRI 04/20/18

As September 30th approaches, make sure your marketing stays ahead of buyers' deadlines! Federal buyers must often heed other agency-specific ordering cutoffs. You show your prospects that you appreciate their constraints when you first research, and then confirm their cutoff dates for making the purchase you've been talking with them about.

Each agency's internal procedures are different. Even buyers who like you and want to do business may get busy and distracted, and may assume you know their deadlines. Best case, ouch: your win (and your cashflow) get pushed back for months. Worst case, your competition knew about the deadline, and takes the business away from you.

Get comfortable routinely asking questions like:

• What requirements have been defined?

- What's your deadline to submit purchase requests to contracting?
- Which contracting officer would handle the purchase if we do business?
- When will the Fund Certifying Official authorize the buy?
- How can I help you draft some language to describe requirements to get you what you want?

While one form of marketing can seem less expensive than another, you also want your prospects to see or hear your message when it arrives, welcome it, and share it with others. More than anything, ask your prospects: how do they want to hear from you? Some actually *want* information from you by email. Can you send details via an attachment, a link, or neither? Many organizations' IT departments block both, which is another reason why many federal vendors still distribute hardcopy collateral in the mail and at events.

A Basic Marketing Toolkit

This is not the definitive list of every marketing option you'd ever want to consider, or of all the tools that companies use to market to government. It *does* offer some ideas to think about as you begin.

Just because I've listed a tactic doesn't mean it's the right way to reach your prospects. Conversely, if I didn't include an idea that you already know works for you and your prospects...bravo!

- Your Website
- Digital Advertising
- Content Marketing
- Organic Social Media
- Marketing Automation
- Direct Marketing
- Other Media Marketing
- Conferences and Trade Shows

Your Website

The next generation of federal buyers is even more likely to find your company through a plain ordinary Google search than through a government buying portal or even from a friend. If you make a positive impression, they'll visit the site multiple times before you ever hear from them.

Get your website right, and invest constantly to stay current. Make it easy to find you and alluring to visit.

- Optimize for Mobile! The fastest-growing group of federal buyers is more and more likely to access your website on a phone or tablet or other mobile device.

- "Government" section: When federal buyers land on your home page, lead them right where you want them to go, by creating federal-specific content that's instantly visible. You might consider:

  › A navigation element called "Government" that links to federal-specific content. At a minimum, have your basic data like DUNS, CAGE, NAICS codes and PSCs, contract vehicles, best values, list of marquee-name clients (whether government, primes, or commercial customers), socioeconomic / small business eligibilities (saves the contracting officer the time to hunt for that), and point of contact.

  or

  › A full "Government" tab that includes, in addition to the above, Past Performance, case studies, and a link to your Capability Statement.

- Downloadable Capability Statement: You want this to be downloadable in PDF, especially to make it easy for clients to share info about you with their friends!

- Make sure your contract vehicles are linked to their respective ordering pages, and to a list of marquee-name clients (whether government, primes, or commercial customers).

- Site layout: Government buyers are pressed for time. If they can't find what they want in about seven seconds, they're gone and they won't be back.

- Search-engine optimization: Invest in improving your SEO so they find you in the first place.

- Key words: Check your competitors' metadata on their sites, and their online profiles, for keywords that can help buyers find you.

- NAICS Codes: If you haven't finished researching what NAICS codes buyers use most often to purchase from your competitors, get that done and add those codes to your capability statement as well as to your SAM profile and your website.

- Past Performance: Government buyers love to see who else you've already done business with. As you build your past performance, as either a subcontractor, a prime contractor, or both, ask your clients whether you can:

› List their agency name and/or logo on your website

› Highlight the key project metrics: what you did, for whom, and the result

› Write up the project in a case study or white paper

- Product/Service Facts: Describe your offering to government – with special attention to the pricing for government and to features that you know appeal to your government buyers.

- Teaming Partners: Relationships with well-known vendors enhance your credibility. If you're teamed with prime contractors, or are part of reseller or supplier agreements with well-known vendors in your niche, list (and link back to) your partners.

- Contact information: Make it easy to find. Put your principal location:

  • at the bottom of your home page, and on

  • a "Contact Us" page/section, where you can also list any additional office locations and points of contact.

Tip from a former contracting officer:

"When I was a CO, I would Google the address. If it were a residence, depending on the size of the contract, I would be hesitant to do business... were they really capable of handling this particular government contract from their home?"

That's just one person's perspective! There are two lessons here: first, remember that every person who sees your web page will see you differently. And, second, consider this perception factor when it comes time to consider the investment and cost of moving your world headquarters out of your home and into some kind of business incubator or shared space.

- Basic corporate data: Government buyers – and especially contracting officers – appreciate seeing your corporate identification information all in one place, particularly your:

  › DUNS Number or Unique Entity Identifier

  › CAGE Code

  › NAICS Codes

  › Product Service Codes

  › Tax ID

  › Set-Aside categories

- Contract Vehicles: Government buyers want to know how they can get to you. List the specific numbers, and link to the ordering pages, for contracts they can use right now to do business with you, whether as a prime or a sub, such as:

  - SmartPay Card

  - GSA Schedule Contract(s)

  - Government-Wide Acquisition Contracts (e.g. 8(a) STARS II, VETS2, SEWP, CIOSP-3)

  - Agency Multiple-Award Contracts (e.g. Navy's Seaport NEXGEN, DHS EAGLEII)

  - Single-Agency, Single-Award Contract

- Animation and/or Video
  People visit more often, and stay longer, on sites with engaging video. Make it short! The majority of the most-watched informational videos are less than two minutes. You can host on your own site, or send visitors to your own YouTube channel.

Organic Social Media

"The new generation entering (or growing within) the federal workforce has a very blurry line separating work life from personal life, especially online. It is not unusual for this group to jump back and forth between work-related social media and personal social media within minutes (or seconds) of each other."
~ Aaron Heffron, President, Market Connections

Federal contractors need to consider the most effective ways to create social media presence and digital media visibility – whether via simple organic reach, paid digital advertising, or both -- where their buyers live and work.

In the early stages, organic social media on a small scale – that is, sharing and posting content and connecting and participating in groups – may fit your budget well. It will take you time, but most early-stage companies can tap time more easily than money. The key is to pick one or two social-media channels and participate with consistent frequency, high quality, and sophisticated engagement.

Human beings, including your federal buyers, are social creatures. Whether we're introverts, extroverts, or somewhere in between, we are built to thrive on some kind of connection with each other.

Whether you like it or loathe it, your federal buyers use social media. You need to know the most appropriate and effective ways to become part of the conversations and communities that matter to them.

Your company almost certainly has some social-media presence already. Are you using it to push, or to engage?

Expect the best results when you use social media in the federal market as:

1. An extension of techniques you use today to build all your business networks.

2. A tool to follow what government is doing.

3. A way to open relationships with government people who want to hear from you.

4. A channel to connect with key industry players and influencers who may be harder to reach in other media.

5. An element to consider using in proposals to government buyers for projects that involve collaboration or communication – within or among agencies, and/or with the public.

6. A tactic to engage vendors with government players to build community and share ideas and best practices.

Some Social-Media Listening Posts For Federal Market Intelligence

Whether you're just entering the federal market or fine-tuning your presence, start by listening more. What do you see and hear? Who are the key players? Who's talking? Who's sharing?

Then focus on engagement.

The federal government has negotiated unique-to-government terms of service with dozens of social-media services. Government's social media is largely focused on "citizen engagement," a continuum from marketing to public participation and brainstorming through collaboration and co-creation. Does your target agency host a social-media forum on their own website(s) for programs you want to support? Check in or sign up to learn more.

• U.S. Digital Registry is a public resource that agencies, citizens, and developers can use to confirm the official status of social media and public-facing collaboration accounts, mobile apps, and mobile websites. There are over 4,000 accounts that represent official U.S. government agencies, organizations, or programs — more every day. You can search for accounts and download the ones you want at *https://digital.gov/services/u-s-digital-registry/GovLoop (www.govloop.com)* and @govloop) – This site connects over 18,000 active users including innovators from federal, state, and local government. Over 25,000 followers on Twitter.

- The Federal Contractor Network (*www.tfcn.us* and @tfcn) – Arguably the largest online network of government contractors, its 30,000+ members also connect via its LinkedIn Group, to focus on teaming, promoting products and services, sharing expertise, and posting events and job openings.

What Social Media Do Federal Employees Visit Most?

Top Social Media Sites Visited

Trends Up in 2017

Feds accessing social media at least once a week

2016	SITES	2017
62%	Facebook	71% ↑
62%	YouTube	67% ↑
45%	LinkedIn	48% ↑
26%	Twitter	30% ↑

©2017 Market Connections, Inc.

Based on this infographic, it's no surprise that 38% of federal contractors surveyed by Market Connections in 2018 said they planned to increase their spending in this area over the next 12 months. Here are some thoughts about each of the major four social-media platforms federal employees say they visit.

- Facebook (*www.facebook.com*): Where Work And Personal Come Together. Think "Community."

While some researchers characterize Facebook as more for "older people," 2018 data showed Facebook's biggest group of U.S. users – 58 million of them -- to be aged 25-24, followed by those 35-44 (42 million), 45-54 (35 million) and 55-64 (26 million). And visits by govvies are growing.

Facebook is unique because many people keep it open all day in background, whether on their mobile or desktop, and toggle in and out to check their feed of both personal and broader news. It offers a way to involve your clients and contacts in a closer relationship with you and with each other. Research your competitors' use of Company Pages and Groups. Consider how this platform might build buzz and loyalty among your influencers, if you use it to:

> Share the inside view of ideas or projects developing in your company (something publicly held companies need to manage with special care to avoid difficulties with insider information)

> Focus-test ideas, give you feedback on products or services, or tell you their views on critical issues

> Show prototypes or demonstrations of products and services

> Post video to support differentiation: client stories, instructional video, tour your production line

> Post action photos of conferences, guest speakers, events, plant tours, prominent visitors, or endorsements, and use tagging and captions to leverage search engines

- YouTube (_www.youtube.com_): Think "SEO."
  With a billion hours of video consumed every day, over 3 billion searches a month, and 100 hours of video uploaded every minute, YouTube is the planet's second-largest search engine. When you think of the power of story-telling, and the value of short instructional videos, that ranking shouldn't be that much of a surprise.

  Before you talk, _listen_. What can you learn about your target agencies and your primes from their YouTube channels?

  Now that you see what others are doing in your niche, how could your company use video to build awareness and liking for your brand, your team? How could you use video to share tips?

  > How is your target agency using video in its communications to citizens, and for internal communications and training?

  > What tips or technical advice could you deliver by video?

  > Could you post webinars or training on your YouTube channel?

  > What's unique about your team members and the expertise they bring to your clients, and how could you profile that?

  > Got some footage of community philanthropy that your company delivered? An event for veterans or first responders?

- LinkedIn (_www.linkedin.com_): Think "Connections."
  Mark Amtower's 2019 census of federal LinkedIn users topped 2.2 million. That's the strongest presence yet, and it's growing faster than ever.[38]

  Government employees are on LinkedIn in part because their agencies now officially encourage them to connect with industry through this platform. Even if they don't reply to you, they may very well accept a connection re-

---

38   Get the detailed breakdown of how many in which agency on Mark's blog, _www.federaldirect.net_.

quest, and they will certainly read what you post.

LinkedIn is also an outstanding way to seek background on federal contacts and prospects who show up in your contract data research...and to connect with them and their network.

Your Profile: Establish credibility by publishing a full profile. Showcase your track record in the SUMMARY part of your profile. Update your status at least a couple times a week.

Your Content: You don't have to write a ton of content. You can share links to content your community will value, and add short, thoughtful commentary on why you think the info is useful. Share links to industry news of specific interest to relevant groups. Build your reputation by answering questions on your key topics. Research your market and clients with polling questions or Q&A.

Your Connections: Research people you'd like to meet. Have a plan for how you'd like to develop the relationship. Then ask to connect. Send a customized note when you ask to connect, explaining how you know each other, and what's the benefit for this person to connect with you. Once you're connected, start a conversation. You can also download their contact information into your own database at that point. Have something to offer that would interest this person enough to get to know you better.

Your Groups: Research which groups your key agency prospects and contacts are part of. Join groups and start listening to those groups' discussions. Notice who is posting things that are thoughtful and substantive. Like and share those posts.

Oh, and realize that all these features can change!

- Twitter (*www.twitter.com*): Think "Contact."
  While, in general, Twitter users are more likely to follow brands online and recommend them to their followers, 2017 data showed a major decrease in how much federal buyers trusted opinions posted online by peers or colleagues (down from 25% in 2016 to just 17% in 2017).

  › Join and set up a basic profile. Include a logo or photo and describe what you or your company does.

  › Once you've set up your Twitter presence, stay on top of it. If any of your customers, federal or commercial, are unhappy with you or has a problem getting through to you, they may very well contact you through Twitter to get your attention.

> Listen: Follow a few key contacts (including Influencers and Small business Specialists but also official accounts) on social media. Federal agencies manage over 4,000 official accounts on Twitter alone!

> Follow what your competitors and primes are posting.

> Twitter can be a fast way to share information with journalists and influencers. Initiate contact with journalists, reporters, and bloggers who cover your niche, by first following them, forwarding links to their stories via Twitter and other social media, and offering comments on their articles.

> Foster reciprocal promotion and credibility with key contacts by retweeting their news and cheering for them.

> Build your reputation as someone who shares valuable content, by including useful links in your tweets.

> Use Twitter to share video, too!

In short, social media for government is one more playground with perfectly obvious rules:

• Make friends.

• Be a good listener.

• Think before you speak.

• Play nicely.

• Share the good stuff.

• Get your facts straight.

• Tell the truth.

• Help the other kids.

Digital Advertising

Digital advertising includes electronic promotional ads, email campaigns, social media, online advertising on search engines, banner ads on mobile or websites, and affiliate programs.

Search-engine marketing, online banner ads, and social media ads were the top choices for federal contractors in 2017.

The point of digital advertising is lead generation and engagement. You need to keep your lead pipeline, as well as your opportunity pipeline, filled.

"Companies implementing an inbound marketing strategy typically double their website visitor traffic and double their conversion rates from website visitors. In 2014, more than twice as many marketers cited inbound (45%) as their primary source of leads versus outbound (22%).

"Couple this with the fact that inbound tactics like blogging and social media cost 62% less than other lead generation methods, and you can see why generating a consistent flow of inbound leads is the best way to overcome database decay and a pre-requisite to running successful marketing automation campaigns."

~ Research reported by HubSpot *https://www.hubspot.com/database-decay*

Content Marketing

Content marketing creates and consistently distributes valuable, relevant content that attracts, engages, and retains your target audience and drives profitable customer action.

You build reputation two ways when you commission or pass along such content to your prospects. First, your prospects appreciate your effort to share objective, substantive information. Second, you help them by giving them something of value that they can share with colleagues.

An effective content-marketing strategy covers the five W's: who you want to reach; what they care about and why; when, how, and how often they will hear from you; and what action you want them to take after any individual piece and/or the whole campaign. What are your objectives, and how will you measure them?

Federal buyers respond more positively to content developed and published by third parties like industry associations or market analysts than to content published by a vendor itself. That's why larger firms might decide to sponsor the efforts of such organizations to research and create unique content that aligns with their marketing. If your company doesn't have the resources to sponsor research, you might belong to an industry association that could.

There's a lot more to know. For more in depth, check out Market Connections' 2017 Marketing Strategy for the Federal Buying Process at *http://bit.ly/MC-FedMktg*.

White-Paper Marketing

White-paper marketing takes many forms. You might tell a case story, profile an innovative technique and its results, highlight pros and cons of a controversial issue, review competitive products in your niche, forecast leading edge technologies, or offer commentary on a recent development in your field.

A Few Tips:

• Don't pitch: Make your paper educational and informative.

• Include contact data on an "About the Author" page. If you did a good job, people will want to get in touch.

• Watch the length: More than five pages; but probably less than 25.

• Be careful with agency case studies: Check out feasibility and understand the approval process from your government client and/or the prime you teamed with before you get too far down the road of creating the story you want to tell. Many agencies are eager to have success stories told…but the timing and permissions have to be done correctly.

• Be realistic about production time: Anticipate that the whole process will take longer than you think. If you're spotlighting a federal project, most agencies need approval from Legal and Public Affairs as well as from the program manager.

• Know your audience: What are their demographics? What technical language do they use? What problems get their attention?

• Go pro: once you've got the gist drafted, consider hiring a professional copywriter who specializes in kickass white papers that will really resonate with your audience. You're going to all this effort; make it count.

• Make it easy to get: Your white paper(s) invite your website visitors to take action: to take the first step in a relationship with you. Put the link where your target audience will see it easily, and take a few words to explain why the paper is useful.

• Build your list: It's absolutely reasonable to ask your visitors for at least their first name, last name, and email address, but don't require more unless you have a compelling reason to. The more information you ask for, the less likely people are to download.

• Assure and respect privacy: Do you share your list, or keep all your visitors' contact information confidential? Tell your visitors your list policy, offer options if appropriate, and then keep your promises.

Direct Marketing

Direct Mail

Why would government decision makers open and/or forward direct mail? Government recipients will open the direct-mail piece that:

• Is from a vendor they know

- Is something they asked to receive from you

- Meets needs they have right now

- Is for something that could help their staff or team

If you're considering direct mail, these tips will help get your mail to your prospect's desk:

- **Good list selection:** All lists are not created equal! Lots of companies will tell you their lists include "thousands of government buyers" or "everyone with a GSA SmartPay card." But how many of them are prospects you want to reach? How current is the list? Ask for references from other list users in your industry, and call them. Ask about their return rates and their response rates. Do consider list rental from a publication that you know reaches your target audience.

- **Go pro (design):** Engage a professional graphic designer who can show you their track record for effectively reaching government buyers in your niche.

- **Go pro (execution):** Consider engaging an expert to conduct a direct-mail critique and audit, both before and after your first (or your next) federal direct-mail campaign. *The* best in the business you can get is Mark Amtower. He brings over 30 years' B2G marketing expertise that has driven billions of dollars in federal contract wins for his clients, large and small. Run, do not walk, to contact him. You get what you pay for. He has plenty of affordable self-serve resources even if you aren't able to hire him for a solo consultation. Find him on LinkedIn or directly at *markamtower@gmail.com.*

- **Research agency mail-delivery limits:** How many pieces per day will your target agency or office accept? Violate that limit and you've wasted your money!

- **Focus your biggest spend in Fourth Quarter:** ... and remember the Fourth-Quarter push starts in Third Quarter! At the federal level, that means you're focusing from April through September.

- **Avoid cover "teaser" copy:** Don't get coy. Show the reader you know what's on their mind.

- **List contract vehicles:** Tell readers where and how easily they can buy from you. Got a GSA Schedule? Is your product on a GWAC? Are you subcontracted to someone else? List those contract numbers.

- **Emphasize differentiators:** How is your offering special? How are you the answer to their big problem? Use your best values to create compelling reasons for someone to contact you.

- **Include a Call to Action:** Be specific. Tell the reader what one thing you want them to do. Use short words. Make your "ask" clearly stand out from the body copy.

- **Make contact information obvious:** Drive readers to your website and 800-number.

Telemarketing

Could you be dialing for government dollars? Telemarketers who work from a good-quality list can reach hundreds of government buyers who are authorized to buy those products. A well-briefed call agent can introduce your company and qualify prospects. Your call agent can follow up with a capability statement, product information, or a "line card," and even book appointments for you!

Telemarketing might be a useful part of your mix if, for example:

- You hold a GSA Schedule Contract;

- You offer relatively low-priced commodities that are widely used by government buyers;

- You want to winnow down a prospect list to the highest-potential buyers for your sales team to call on;

- You hold a longer-term Indefinite Delivery Vehicle (Task Order/Delivery Order) contract and want to build awareness of your past performance and unique value proposition; and/or

- You want to introduce a new technology or product, and qualify interested buyers to follow up with.

What kinds of companies are using telemarketing to reach government? The companies who most often find value in telemarketing to government buyers offer:

- Information-technology products and services (far and away the largest group)

- Management and business-improvement services

- Health care (services and solutions)

- Staging and event-management services

The most effective telemarketing requires competitive analysis and research, including using tools like the ones you read about in Chapter Four, to build a targeted list of federal buyers that the data shows buy what you offer.

Thinking of a telemarketing campaign? Expect to spend $7,000 to $12,000 for a four- to eight-week campaign. When you interview your candidate telemarketing consultants, ask specifically about their experience and results with campaigns focused on offerings like yours.

Email Marketing / Marketing Automation

Making it to the Inbox

- Use a service. PC Magazine ranked Zoho Campaigns, MailChimp, Constant Contact, HubSpot, and Infusionsoft among the top ten email marketing services for 2018. If you're not already using a service, or don't like the one you're using, see which one would work for you.

- Get your money's worth from your tools. Email marketing services include powerful and sophisticated utilities. You can "set and forget" entire campaigns, once they're designed and written. Not only will the emails drop automatically, but you can determine what version or email someone gets based on whether they opened or clicked previous ones.

- Go Pro/Get Help. As the business owner, there are things *only* you can do. And there are things you could do yourself in a world of infinite time. Once you've made your decisions about who you want to market to, and what your key messages and calls to action will be in each quarter of the fiscal year, get professional help for copywriting, graphics, and programming for segmentation and timing.

- Practice anti-spam techniques:

  › Avoid CAPS and extra punctuation

  › Avoid trigger words, like "Click here"

  › Avoid red text or highlighting

  › Monitor/contact bounces

  › Ask recipients to "whitelist" your domain and/or add to address book

  › Confirmation/Opt-in

- Increase Your Open Rate:

  › Choose a recognizable "from"

  › Use short, relevant subject lines

  › Keep email short

  › Segment your list and design your content and delivery to send people the kind of content that your data shows they open.

- Provide high-value content specifically useful to your target agencies

- Look for ways to increase followers/shares inside your target agencies

- Interview and feature key agency officials

- Get support from the program manager to get the agency's IT shop to whitelist you

Time Spent with Media

Feds Spending More Time on Media Throughout the Workday ≥15 Minutes

ACTIVITY		2016	2017
NEWS	Accessing online news	54%	61%
	Watching news/ news programs	51%	57%
	Listening to AM/FM radio	48%	56%
	Accessing social media	31%	38%
	Accessing print news	28%	34%

©2017 Market Connections, Inc.

Media Marketing

How are government agencies using media?

One of my favorite – and most generous – experts on the government marketing mix is Lisa Dez-zutti, CEO of Market Connections.

The Market Connections team knows which trade shows and seminars government buyers attend and trust – and is often asked to speak at them or participate in panels. They not only read the publications your target audiences do, they also contribute articles to them.

Heartfelt thanks to Lisa, and company President Aaron Heffron, for sharing highlights of Market Connections' research on government users of social media. Visit and find out more from them at *www.marketconnectionsinc.com*.

Federal officials are spending more time than ever in online media, including social media, throughout the workday. Rather than hovering on a couple of social-media sites, the up-and-coming generation of federal buyers tends to hop among various news sites as well as social media and google throughout the day. They're also heavy users of mobile devices.

When you choose media marketing, make sure you have the resources – money and people – to participate and follow up regularly and consistently. A single ad is rarely effective. Plan your communications calendar with a longer view: repetition, repetition, repetition.

How can you find out, and choose among, your options?

- Observation: Open your eyes.
  When you visit government people, look at what magazines are on their coffee tables and desks or in their waiting areas.

- Anecdotal: Ask.
  When you meet with prospects, make it one of your call objectives to ask them what they read, click on, follow, and listen to.

- Research: Again, Go pro.
  Consider engaging a consultant who specializes in researching, creating, and executing marketing and media campaigns that reach government buyers. Check their credentials, call their references among companies like yours, and ask for summaries of their public research reports.

That credibility gives them access to thousands of government decision makers with billions of dollars of buying authority – which is why many of the top firms selling to the government engage Market Connections to provide qualitative and quantitative market research.

Consider print and electronic media in your marketing mix if you're selling:

- Computer systems or hardware

- Software

- Office equipment and supplies

- Training

- Information technology services

- Telecommunications

- Consulting services

- Information-technology security

- Facilities/Real estate

...because government employees who buy these things read specialty publications and websites, and attend trade shows and conferences targeted at government buyers.

Print: Advertising and Editorial

What *do* government buyers read? And what's special about print media and government (besides what publications decision-makers are reading)? Think about:

- Themes:
  Take care if you're adapting a commercial campaign for government buyers. Certain themes and language don't resonate with government buyers, such as "bottom line" or "increasing sales" or "improving profits."

- Language:
  Choose terms that relate to what your target agency does. Look at the language in the ads that are running now in the publications your clients are reading. You'll see themes like "delivering the mission," "serving citizens," "caring for our families," "keeping America strong," "protecting the public," "safeguarding privacy."

- Images:
  Look for images that appeal to your buyers – action images that show them delivering their agencies' mission, doing the things for which their agency is best known, or depicting the communities they serve.

- Buying Cycle:
  Is there a deadline (particularly a fiscal year-end or an indefinite-delivery-contract expiry date) for action? Mention that, and make sure you've timed your campaign for maximum impact before the decision-making deadlines.

- Appeal to the Contracting Officer;
  Emphasize how easy it is to do business with you by making other key information prominent: small business certifications (like 8(a), SDVOSB, HUB-Zone, Woman-Owned), GSA Schedule Contract number, and other relevant contract vehicles.

Then there's the regular stuff that people need to remember in any ad, including those for government:

- Call to Action:
  Tell readers what you want them to do. Get comparative...good use of their time? Get comparative product information from your website? Download a paper? Come to an event? Take an online quiz? What creative options might catch their attention and be a genuinely good use of their time?

- Contact!
  Tell readers where to find you: First, basic contact info like 800-number, website, email, contact person. Then add info about upcoming events where they can find you. List other ways they can connect with you, including your blog and social media.

Make sure that the person you choose to create your materials and campaign has a strong track record achieving marketing results like what you're looking for, and doing so for clients in your industry.

Ready to move toward decisions on what you can do with the budget you have?

If you're adapting a commercial campaign, or want to test the prospective effectiveness of your print ad to reach a government audience, arguably the foremost (okay, and most ruthless, but also most perceptive) critical advisor on marketing to government is Mark Amtower (_markamtower@gmail.com_).

Online Coverage: Seeking Coverage In Mainstream Media

Editorial content has more impact than press releases. Who are the reporters who cover government, and who report on business in your industry niche? Check out their stories, make contact, follow their work, comment on their stories, and build a relationship to become a trusted source – not just to feed them stories about yourself.

To establish credibility with any news organization, find out what kinds of stories most interest its reporters and editors: listen to the station, read its website.

What are the "most read" items on those sites right now? What kind of story could you bring a reporter that would appeal to their visitors/viewers? Some ideas:

- Trends you see in your niche: what emerging players should they be talking to?

- A big problem your government buyer or prime had, and what you did about it.

- How a successful implementation closed a security risk, improved service to under-served citizens, helped a community, healed a wounded warrior, reunited a family, protected a soldier.

- A pending crisis, what's at risk, and sources or quotes from government leaders who wish they had solutions like yours.

Federal News Network

You hadn't thought about radio to reach government buyers? Think again.

The web and live-streaming mean that radio reaches your prospects right across America and beyond. Podcasting keeps your content available 24/7 after the original broadcast. Thousands of people download educational and technical content to listen to on their daily commute.

How do companies use radio to reach government buyers, and why would you care about that, if both you and your government buyers are outside the Washington DC area?

To answer the question, look at the leader: Federal News Network (WFED, 1500 AM). Its 50,000-watt transmitter is the most powerful AM radio station in the Washington DC area. Its non-stop stream of news, information, and interviews is targeted towards U.S. government employees. But get this: Federal News Network was not only the first Internet-only all-news station, but also the first Internet station that made the jump to terrestrial radio. In other words, because Federal News Network was online first, it has a national following, not just a Washington DC audience.

Being based in the Washington DC area gives the organization now known as Federal NewsNetwork the opportunity to meet and reach a vast number of decision makers across the country in many ways.

You'll hear branding messages that align a company with a core capability, as well as feature a company's expertise for an upcoming rebid or a contract they're trying to go after. Other campaigns can target key decision makers within an agency or key teaming partners you want to connect with.

They are constantly looking for content. Their producers are listed on *wtop.com* and *federalnewsnetwork.com*, and you can find people whose daily job is to find topical content and air it to be useful for their listeners.

With 24 hours a day to fill, the station is always interested in content – editorial as well as advertising.

Both can be opportunities for you at the right time. If you've got a lead on a hot story, a key technology, or a decision maker who's willing and able to go on the air about an issue that affects buying decisions in your niche, your idea might appeal to the editorial team. Maybe you or your star client would be a great candidate for an interview.

Points of contact: follow Tom Temin (@TTemin_wfed) and editor Chris Dorobek (@cdorobek) on Twitter.

Public Relations / Promotion

There are no government-specific tactics; only government-specific channels, publications, reporters, and editors. Just as in the private sector, you want to get people talking about you who aren't you. Same drill, same kinds of media.

You need to know:

- How to engage the media on their timetable;
- What the media is saying about you right now;

- Ways to tap the crowd for quick action and make real-time customer connections;

- How to engage in instant web communication;

- What publications and writers your government prospects follow.

Ways to cultivate relationships with those key reporters/bloggers:

- Read what they publish.

- Comment on/promote their stories: cite them in your publications, link to them in your blog, follow them on twitter, tweet links to their stories to your followers.

- After you've done that for a while and established yourself as a fan, think about what kind of news and stories they would value if you could bring them leads.

- Contact them, including with praise for their work. Introduce yourself and explain how your expertise is relevant to them and their community. Find out what they know about you or your company. Ask them how you could help: what kind of news or stories or introductions to key contacts would they welcome from you?

- Offer commentary on current events or technology developments.

- Offer to be a guest columnist.

- Ask how they'd like you to stay in touch.

- Keep in contact: send them appropriate story ideas, intro's, and leads regularly so you'll be top of mind when they need a source.

A Word About Engaging Your Members of Congress

Your Members of Congress welcome your calls. For starters, that's part of their job. Your taxes pay them to represent your interests and help you solve problems. They have every reason to want to hear about you and your business, and to help you. Like anyone else, they can be even more eager to help when you show them how what's good for you is also good for them: in other words, when you show them your world from their point of view.

Who should you meet first? Members of the House of Representatives are generally more acutely focused on constituent interests than Senators. If the opportunity arises, or your company is a larger employer, call on your Senators as well.

Members of Congress (and the appropriate staffer(s) in their offices) are much more helpful when problems arise if they already know who you are. That's why you want to introduce yourself and your company when you *don't* have a crisis, and tell them what your interests are and why they should care.

Your Capability Statement is a great summary to share at such a meeting. You'll want to cover:

- What your company does

- How many people you employ and in which districts

- Your current involvement and planned growth in government contracting, including which agencies and programs fund those contracts

Beyond that initial briefing, you want to meet with your Member of Congress in situations such as:

- When your solution concerns an agency or issue in which the Member is particularly active;

- When current or proposed laws and regulations might expand or limit your access to federal business opportunities; or

- When program funding (and jobs) are threatened by budget cuts

Feeling a little shy? You don't have to go it alone. In fact, sometimes you can get more engagement and even action on an issue when you're part of a group! Did you know? Many industry associations organize group visits by their members to call on Capitol Hill or constituency offices, both for routine relationship-building and when specific issues arise.

READY FOR THE NEXT STEP? SALES & MARKETING CHECKLIST

O Consider your options

O List and prioritize targeted calls

O Prioritize marketing activities according to budget and expected ROI

O Set – and use – measurement criteria

O Evaluate and adjust the plan and marketing mix accordingly.

O Get Out There!

Find Out More

Visit *www.GrowFedBiz.com* for bonus materials like:

- *Federal Networking Master Class*
- *Five Federal Lead Sources You Need To Know*

Connect with Judy Bradt on social media

- LinkedIn
  - › Judy Bradt *https://www.linkedin.com/in/judybradt/*
  - › Government Contracts Made Easier Group: *http://linkd.in/JudyBradtBook*
- Twitter
  - › Handle: @judybradt
  - › Book Hashtag: #GCME
- *Facebook*
  - › www.facebook.com/SummitInsight
- Blog: *www.sell2usgov.com*
- Web: *www.GrowFedBiz.com*

Other Resources

- Direct mail
  - › White Paper marketing guru Bob Bly, renowned copywriter and author, offers dozens of books and resources. Start with the White Paper Marketing Handbook. *www.bly.com*
  - › Also see *www.whitepapersource.com*.
- Telemarketing

› E-mail marketing Constant Contact Tips and Hints at
www.constantcontact.com

• Media and Event Marketing

› Lisa Dezzutti, CEO of Market Connections
(*www.marketconnectionsinc.com*)

• Print advertising and editorial

› Edward O'Keeffe, President of Professional Advertising,
(*www.myprofessionaladvertising.com*), has published 1,056 free ideas for
effective print advertising, at *http://twurl.nl/4uq1w8*

› Phillip W. Sawyer, Vice President, Roper Starch Worldwide
Ten Principles for Effective Print Advertising
www.positiveresponse.com/Starch10Principles.pdf

Conclusion

The Party

So imagine you just rediscovered an invitation to another small business federal-contracting event. You've been to so many before, and nothing ever comes of them. When the invitation arrived, you were pretty sure you didn't have time to come, but you couldn't make up your mind.

As it turns out, things have been slow, you don't have much going on right now, and who knows – you might meet some people. You look at the invitation, and realize that nothing happens by staying home. You really didn't want to give up another evening for networking, but you take a deep breath and hope this time will be different.

Good thing there's valet parking, you think. People are lined up out the door, but somehow everything keeps moving and that leaves you surprisingly upbeat. You follow the signs (and the crowd) to the gigantic ballroom... and are there ever a lot of people here!

Once you get inside the ballroom, it's clear this is a first-class event. The food smells incredible and the prime contractors' booths are dazzling. The band is just getting ready for a new set on a stage with a backdrop that reads, "US Government Contracts: Billions and Billions Served. World's Largest Buyer. WELCOME Small business PARTNERS!" Guests who can hardly hear themselves think are eagerly scooping up handouts and tchotchkes while trying to look casual.

Suddenly you notice a friend who waves you over to join her. "I never knew you were interested in the federal market! Come with me," she says, and you stroll together into a smaller, quieter room next door.

Who knew? Here, lively conversations buzz. You're surprised by how many people you know! Funny, they never mentioned this event to you before... but now they smile, just a little weary, energetic but circulating with determination from one intense huddle to another.

"I've got drink tickets," says your friend. "Now, tell me what's new with you! And I'll tell you a little about who's here. Who are you trying to connect with?"

Half an hour later, you're seeing the room through new eyes.

"Just tell me one thing: How come I've never seen this part of the event before?" you ask her.

"You never asked me," she smiled. "Come this way. I think I know who you need to meet first."

Moral of the story? Talk to your friends. Your clients. Your contacts. Tell them what you're doing in the federal market. Ask them who they know who might help. The people who most need to meet you are probably a lot closer than you think.

What's next?

I hope you've got some new ideas, tools, and connections to work with... and are starting to discover new friends and resources who can help.

Want some company and help along the way? Let's talk.

- I'm always going to start by asking you whether you've tapped your local Procurement Technical Assistance Center (*www.aptac-us.org*). Their help is free or low cost.

- Check out the on-demand webinars, courses, and small-group programs at *www.GrowFedBiz.com*.

- You might be ready to step up to one of the programs I do one-on-one with company teams. Let's figure it out! Call or write, and we can set up a time for a quick chat. If I can't help you, I can probably suggest some options for someone who can.

- Let me know what's happening for you along the way! I love to hear your stories, and I'm always interested in business owners who want to share lessons learned on my webinars and podcasts.

I wish you all the best!

Warmly,

Judy

Judy Bradt, CEO
Summit Insight
(703) 627 1074 *Judy.Bradt@GrowFedBiz.com*

To Recap:

- Strategy: Be in this market for winning reasons
  - › Commit to realistic goals – a minimum of two years
  - › Draft a quarter-by-quarter work plan tied to those goals
  - › Get management support for the resources you need for the job
  - › Set interim goals & milestones for regular reviews
- Focus: Keep it tight
  - › Pick your sweet-spot offering and client characteristics
  - › Know what problem you solve & who has that problem
  - › Target no more than three agencies
  - › Research their missions & buying history
- Process: Know the rules of the game
  - › Where to find the rules that govern how you can sell
  - › How your target agencies buy
  - › Which contract types and/or GSA Schedules they use
  - › Which rules have just changed, and which are about to
  - › Which set-asides and preferences you can access
  - › When (and how) to submit proposals
  - › How to leverage the debrief

- Competition: Stand out
  - › Where to get competitive data
  - › Who your target agencies buy from today
  - › What's your Unique Value Proposition for government
  - › How to use capability statements, briefings, and past performance
- Teaming: Make Courtship Your Business
  - › Realize what partners want
  - › Research and court selectively
  - › Bring business

- Relationships: Research, Meet, and Nurture
  - › The Five People In Government
  - › The Five People In Industry
  - › Cultivate diverse contacts
  - › Nurture your inner circle of wise guides
  - › Strengthen your Contact Relationship Management systems
  - › Select / evaluate industry associations that work for you
  - › Build Community
  - › Play Nice and Help The Other Kids
- Marketing
  - › Consider your options
  - › List and prioritize targeted calls
  - › Prioritize marketing activities according to budget and expected ROI
  - › Set – and use – measurement criteria
  - › Evaluate and adjust the plan and marketing mix accordingly.
  - › Get Out There!

About the Author

Judy Bradt brings you the secrets to winning US government contracts – whether you're taking your first steps or expanding your footprint in pursuit of the world's largest buyer. A strategic advisor for government business, she helps clients and audiences explore their unique path to win the best opportunities that US government can offer.

One of America's top champions for savvy business owners who want to grow their federal business, **Judy Bradt is CEO and founder of Summit Insight** (*www.GrowFedBiz.com*). For over 30 years, she has advised more than 5,000 business owners who credit her advice for their wins of over $300 million in government business. Judy brings practical, powerful tools and no-nonsense advice to people who want to grow their federal business.

Judy Bradt began her career as a business strategist with IBM Canada in Toronto. Between 1988 and 2003, she was the top expert on U.S. government contracts at the Canadian Embassy in Washington DC.

In 2003, Judy founded Summit Insight to work in greater scope, depth, and creativity with inspiring and energetic women and minority business leaders as well as the growing community of veteran entrepreneurs all seeking federal business.

Her own U.S. federal clients include the Small Business Administration, Office of the Comptroller of the Currency, Office of Personnel Management, and the Smithsonian Institution.

Judy has taught for many Procurement Technical Assistance Centers across the country as well as for the Armed Forces Communications and Electronics Association's Professional Development Center. She's delivered national and regional programs for associations including the Women's Business Enterprise National Council, Women Impacting Public Policy, the 8(a) Association, and the National Veterans Small Business Coalition.

She first published *Government Contracts Made Easier* in 2010. She has hosted over 200 public webinars, and has just launched a new online learning center, *www.GrowFedBiz.com*, to offer small-group programs in addition to one-on-one private business strategy consultation.

Judy has been featured in media including Business Week, Fortune Small Business, Washington Business Journal, Smart CEO Magazine, Financial Post, Enterprising Woman, and Entrepreneur Magazine. She holds a BA from the University of Toronto and an MBA from McMaster University. She is also an instrument-rated private pilot and a rock-climbing instructor.

Summit Insight is an independently owned, global consultancy based in Alexandria, Virginia. The company serves established firms that want to win more federal business. Our mission is to assist business professionals to achieve their federal sales goals, by offering them effective training, proven tools, and high-integrity resources. We use a unique, three-step approach built around competitive intelligence. Our clients get the targeted research they need to create relationships with federal buyers and partners, and drive the wins they've always wanted.

Index

Made in the USA
Middletown, DE
14 June 2021